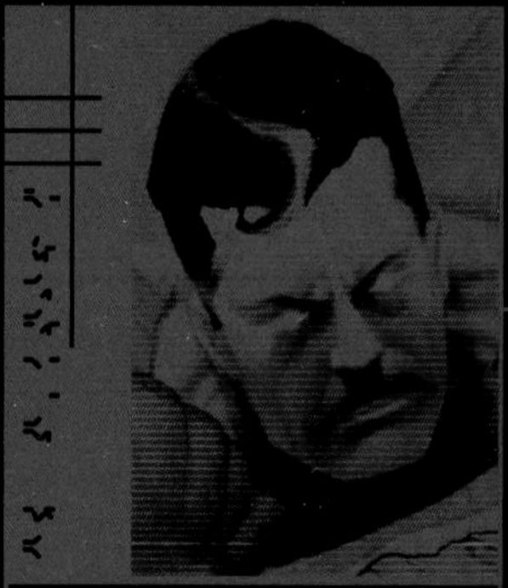

SUPERMAN AND BATMAN VERSUS ALIENS AND PREDATOR

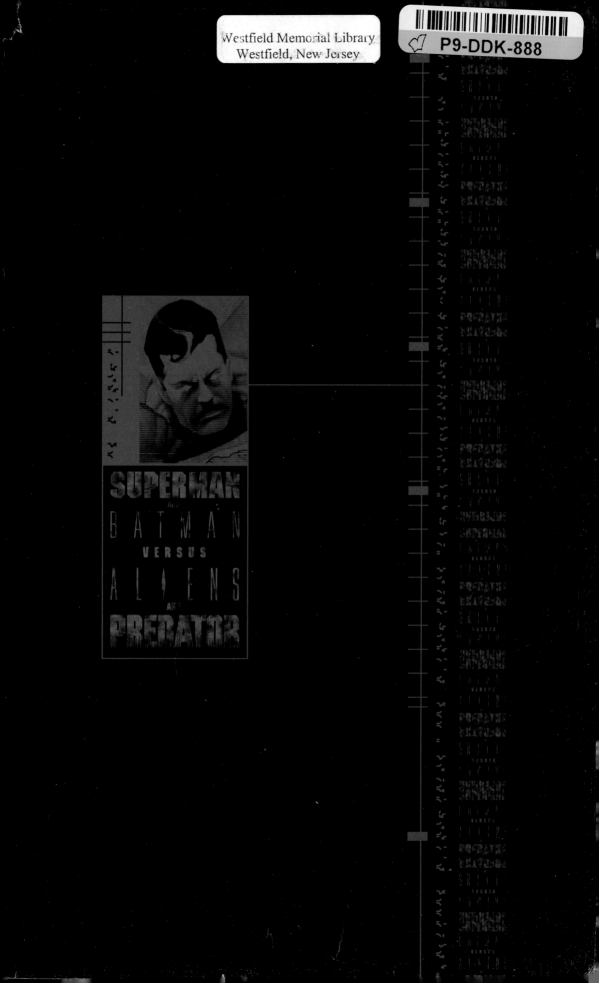

SUPERMAN AND BATMAN VERSUS ALIENS AND PREDATOR

WRITER: **Mark Schultz**   ARTIST: **Ariel Olivetti**   LETTERER: **Todd Klein**

SUPERMAN CREATED BY **Jerry Siegel** AND **Joe Shuster**   BATMAN CREATED BY **Bob Kane**

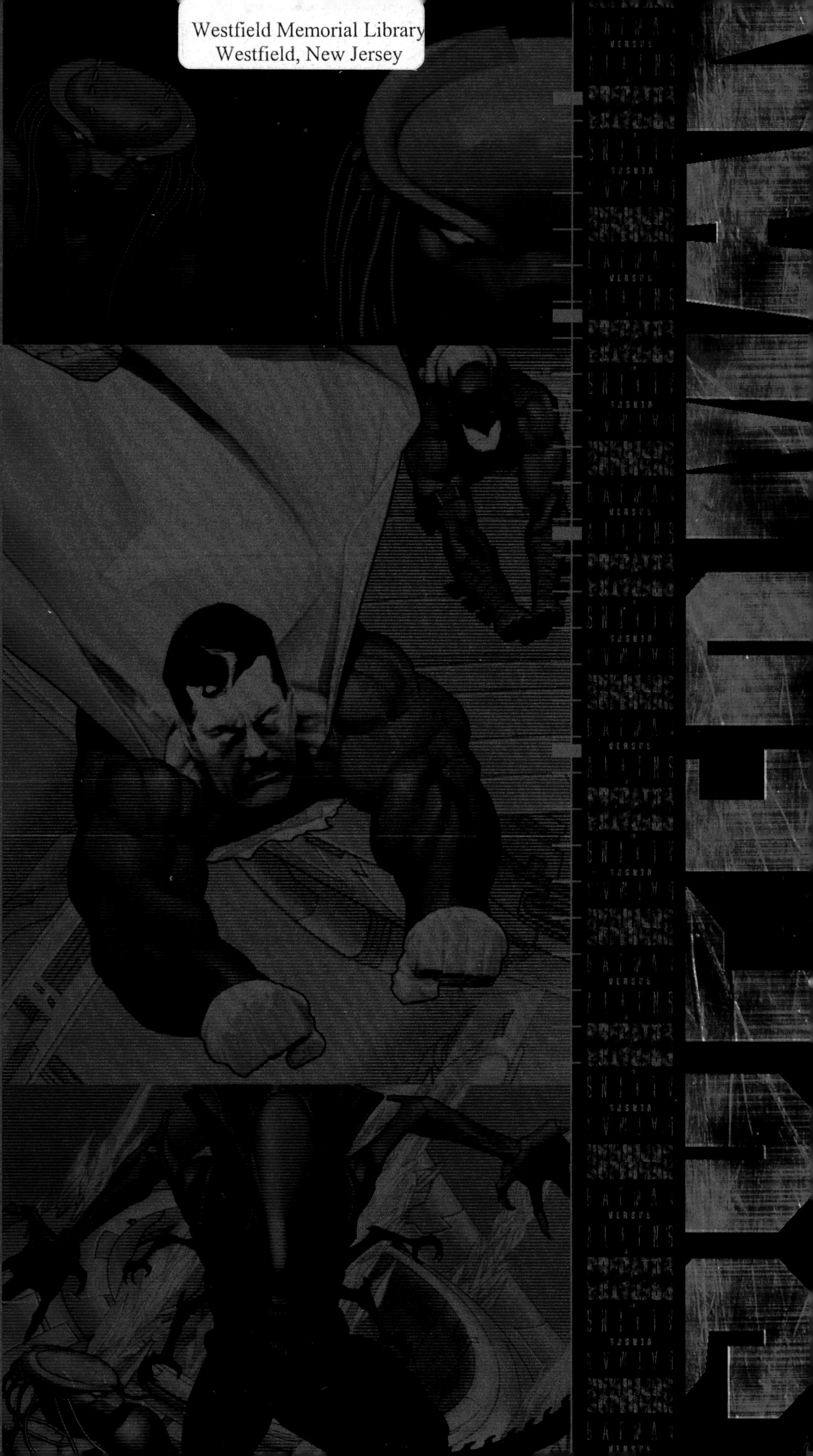

DC COMICS
Dan DiDio — Senior VP-Executive Editor
Joey Cavalieri — Editor-original series
Michael Wright — Associate Editor-original series
Bob Joy — Editor-collected edition
Robbin Brosterman — Senior Art Director
Louis Prandi — Art Director
Paul Levitz — President & Publisher
Georg Brewer — VP-Design & DC Direct Creative
Richard Bruning — Senior VP-Creative Director
Patrick Caldon — Executive VP-Finance & Operations
Chris Caramalis — VP-Finance
John Cunningham — VP-Marketing
Terri Cunningham — VP-Managing Editor
Alison Gill — VP-Manufacturing
Hank Kanalz — VP-General Manager, WildStorm
Jim Lee — Editorial Director-WildStorm
Paula Lowitt — Senior VP-Business & Legal Affairs
MaryEllen McLaughlin — VP-Advertising & Custom Publishing
John Nee — VP-Business Development
Gregory Noveck — Senior VP-Creative Affairs
Sue Pohja — VP-Book Trade Sales
Cheryl Rubin — Senior VP-Brand Management
Jeff Trojan — VP-Business Development, DC Direct
Bob Wayne — VP-Sales

DARK HORSE COMICS
Mike Richardson — Publisher
Neil Hankerson — Executive Vice President
Tom Weddle — Chief Financial Officer
Randy Stradley — Vice President of Publishing
Chris Warner — Senior Books Editor, Dark Horse Books
Rob Simpson — Senior Books Editor, M Press / DH Press
Michael Martens — Vice President of Business Development
Anita Nelson — Vice President of Marketing, Sales & Licensing
David Scroggy — Vice President of Product Development
Dale LaFountain — Vice President of Information Technology
Darlene Vogel — Director of Purchasing
Ken Lizzi — General Counsel
Lia Ribacchi — Art Director

DC Comics, 1700 Broadway, New York, NY 10019. A Warner Bros. Entertainment Company. Printed in Canada. First Printing.
ISBN:1-4012-1328-6, ISBN 13:978-1-4012-1328-2
Cover art by Ariel Olivetti

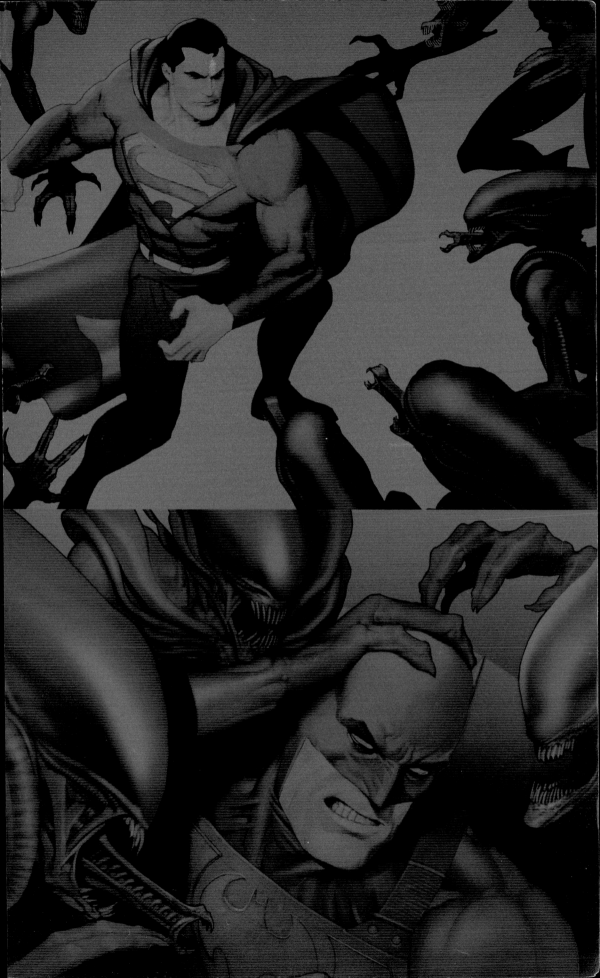

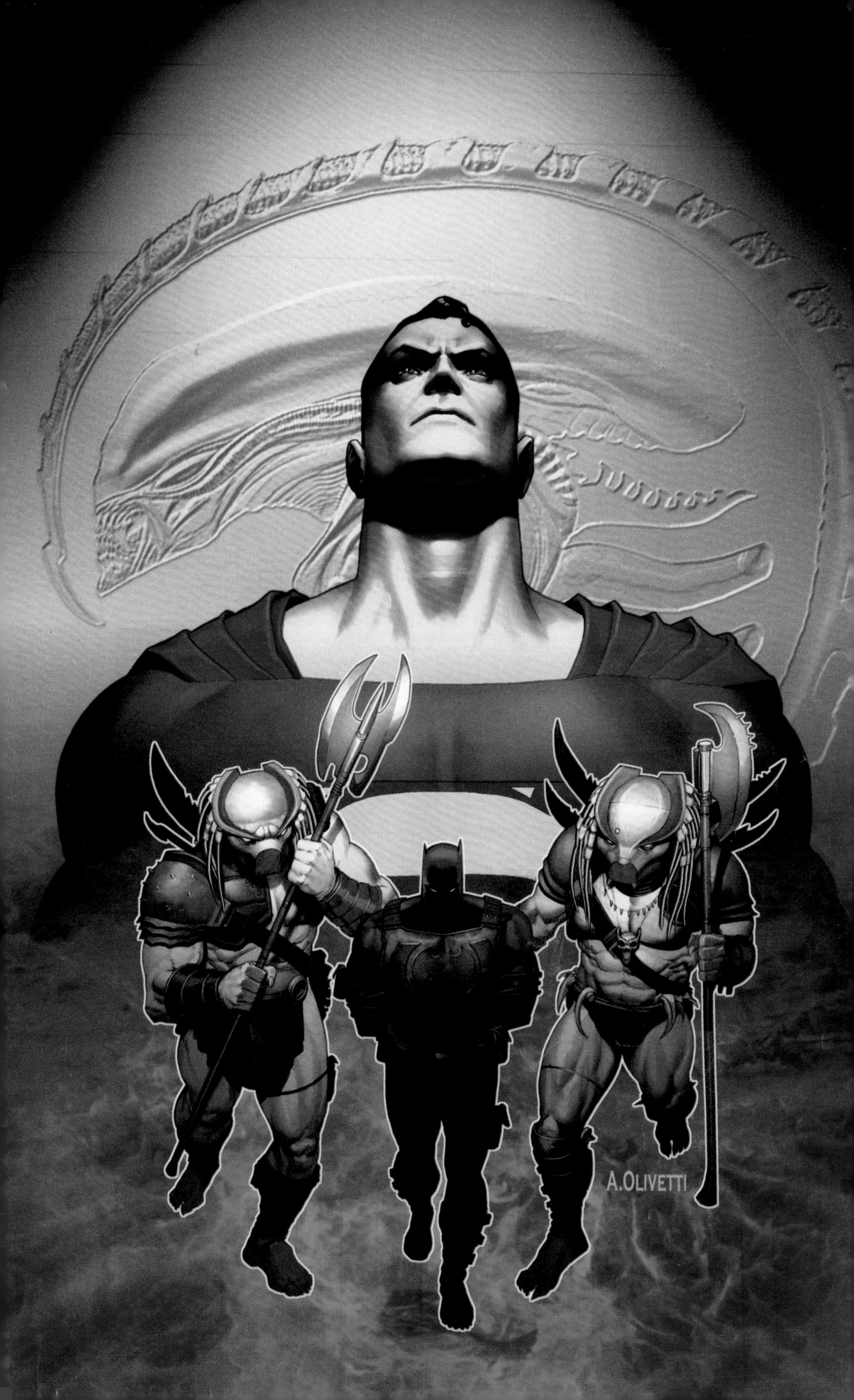
A.OLIVETTI

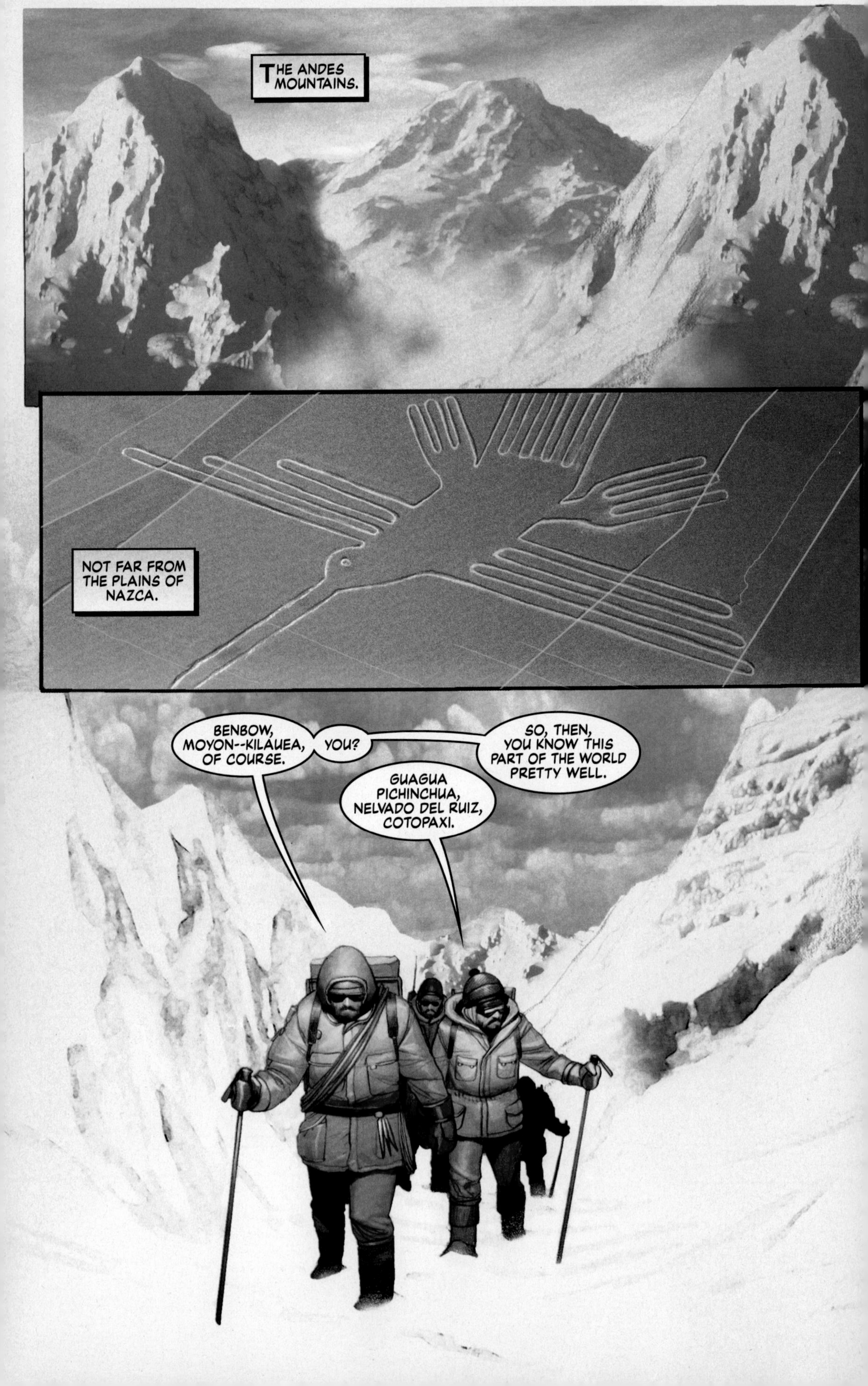
THE ANDES MOUNTAINS.
NOT FAR FROM THE PLAINS OF NAZCA.
BENBOW, MOYON--KILAUEA, OF COURSE.
YOU?
SO, THEN, YOU KNOW THIS PART OF THE WORLD PRETTY WELL.
GUAGUA PICHINCHUA, NELVADO DEL RUIZ, COTOPAXI.

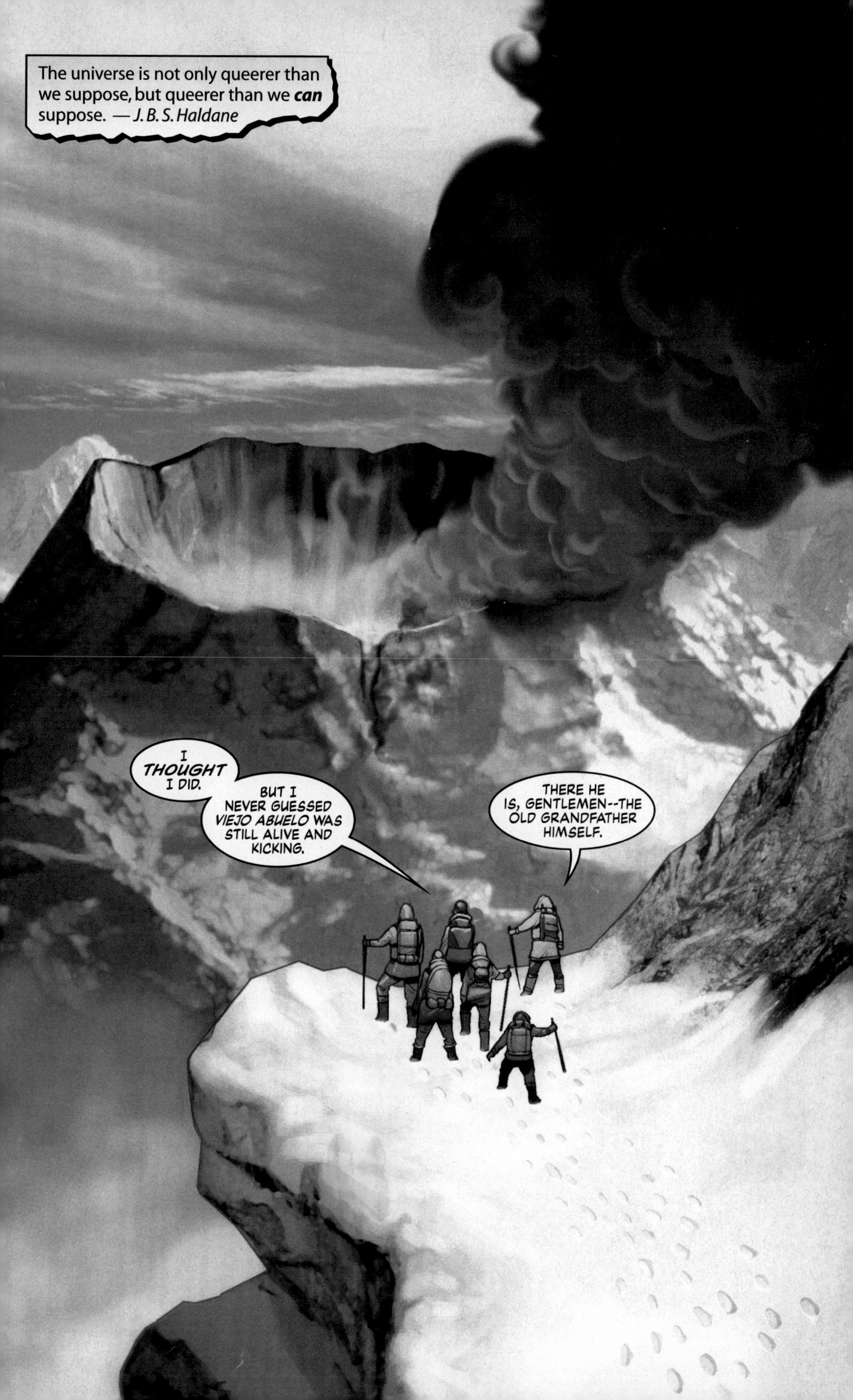
The universe is not only queerer than we suppose, but queerer than we ***can*** suppose. — *J. B. S. Haldane*
I *THOUGHT* I DID.
BUT I NEVER GUESSED *VIEJO ABUELO* WAS STILL ALIVE AND KICKING.
THERE HE IS, GENTLEMEN--THE OLD GRANDFATHER HIMSELF.

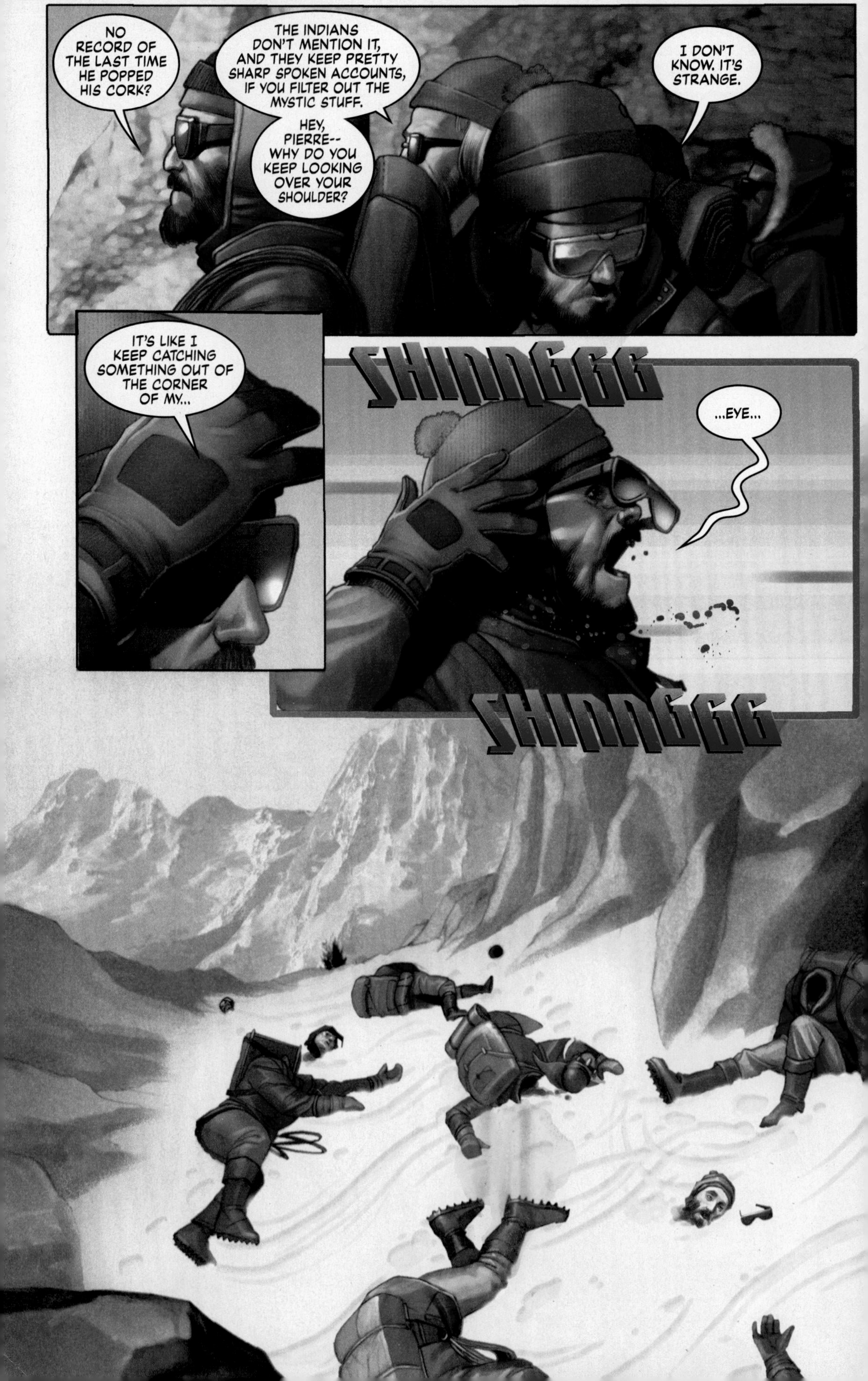
NO RECORD OF THE LAST TIME HE POPPED HIS CORK?
THE INDIANS DON'T MENTION IT, AND THEY KEEP PRETTY SHARP SPOKEN ACCOUNTS, IF YOU FILTER OUT THE MYSTIC STUFF.
HEY, PIERRE-- WHY DO YOU KEEP LOOKING OVER YOUR SHOULDER?
I DON'T KNOW. IT'S STRANGE.
IT'S LIKE I KEEP CATCHING SOMETHING OUT OF THE CORNER OF MY...
SHINNGGG
...EYE...
SHINNGGG

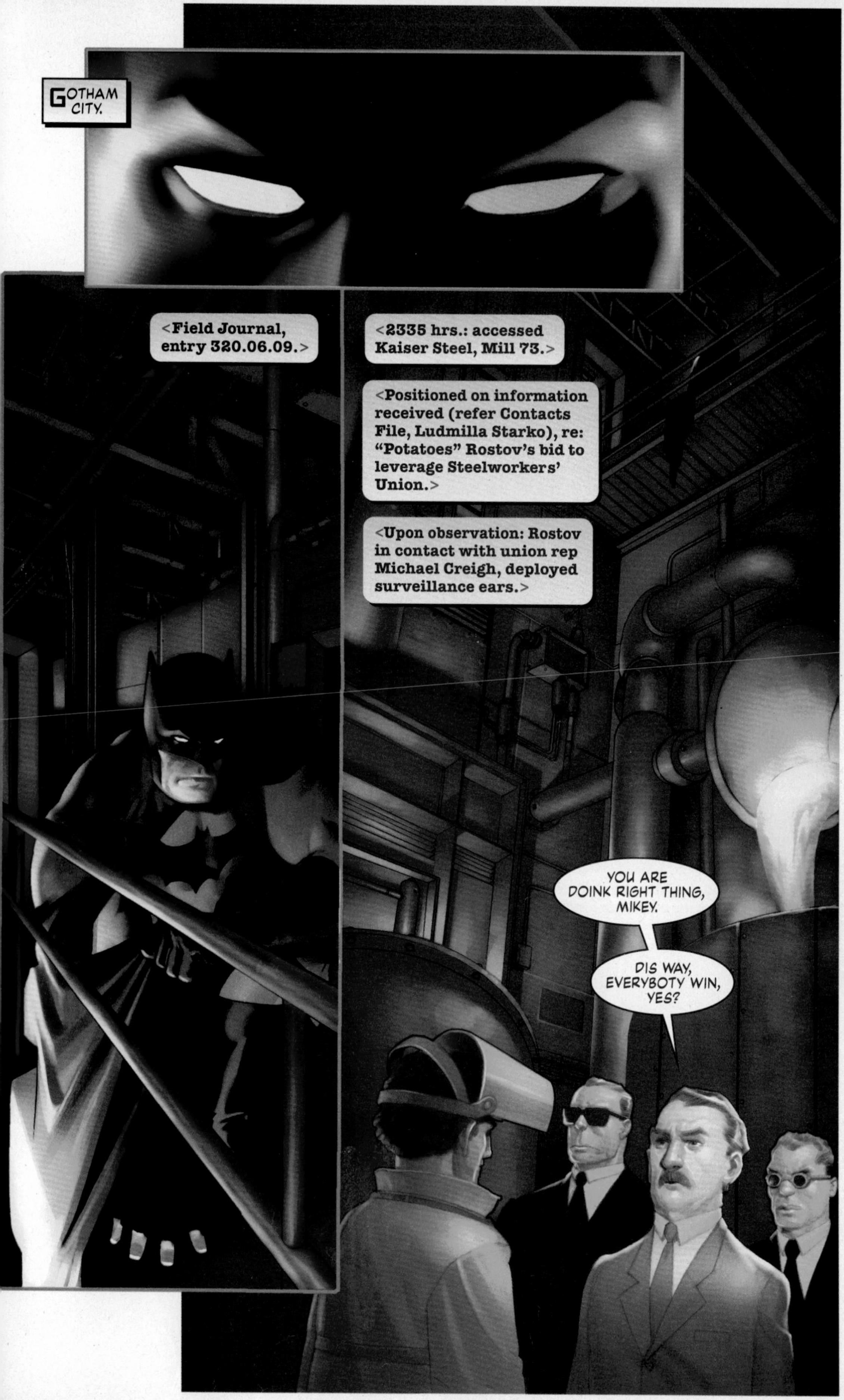
GOTHAM CITY.
<Field Journal, entry 320.06.09.>
<2335 hrs.: accessed Kaiser Steel, Mill 73.>
<Positioned on information received (refer Contacts File, Ludmilla Starko), re: "Potatoes" Rostov's bid to leverage Steelworkers' Union.>
<Upon observation: Rostov in contact with union rep Michael Creigh, deployed surveillance ears.>
YOU ARE DOINK RIGHT THING, MIKEY.
DIS WAY, EVERYBOTY WIN, YES?

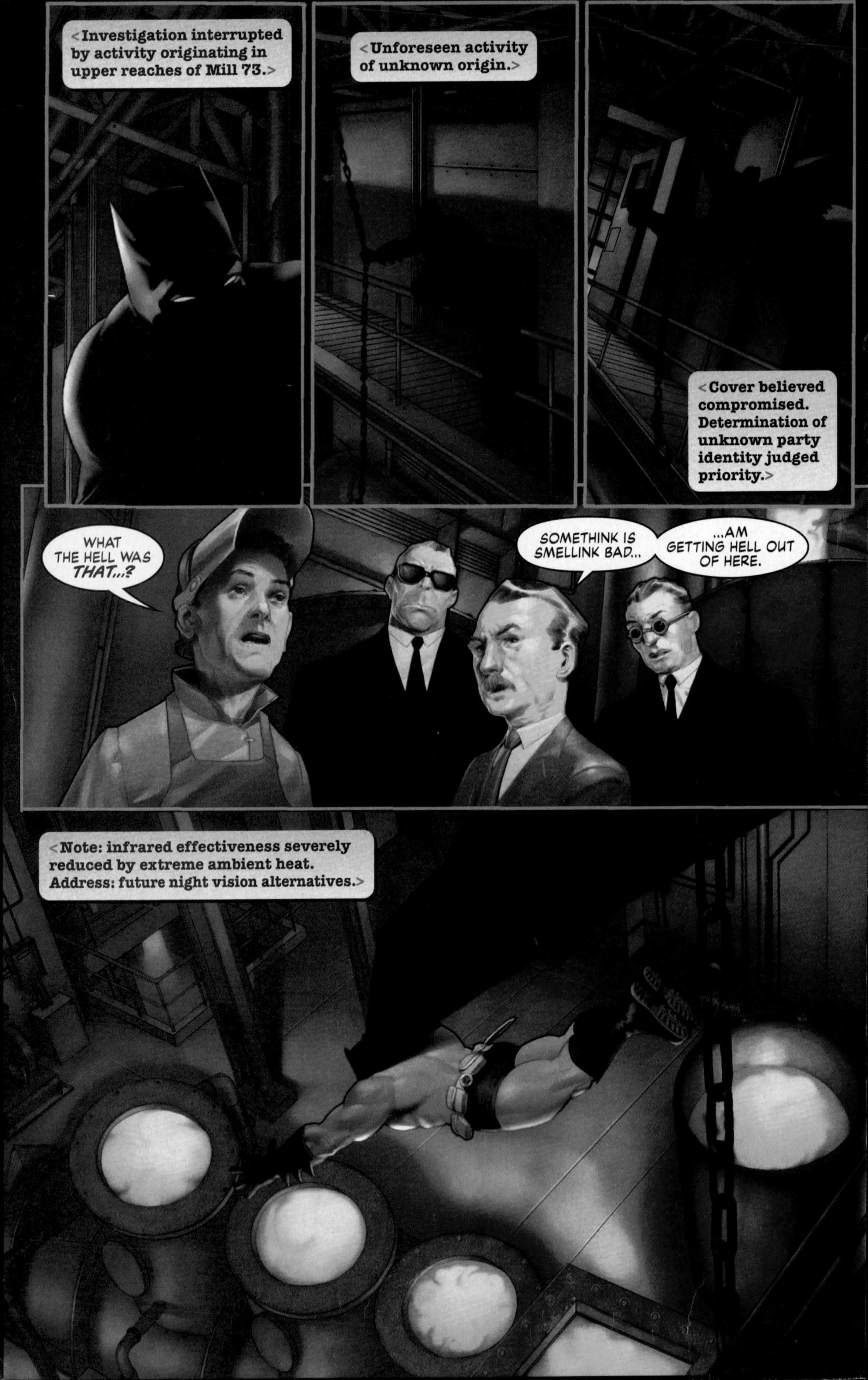

<Investigation interrupted by activity originating in upper reaches of Mill 73.>
<Unforeseen activity of unknown origin.>
<Cover believed compromised. Determination of unknown party identity judged priority.>
WHAT THE HELL WAS *THAT...?*
SOMETHINK IS SMELLINK BAD...
...AM GETTING HELL OUT OF HERE.
<Note: infrared effectiveness severely reduced by extreme ambient heat. Address: future night vision alternatives.>

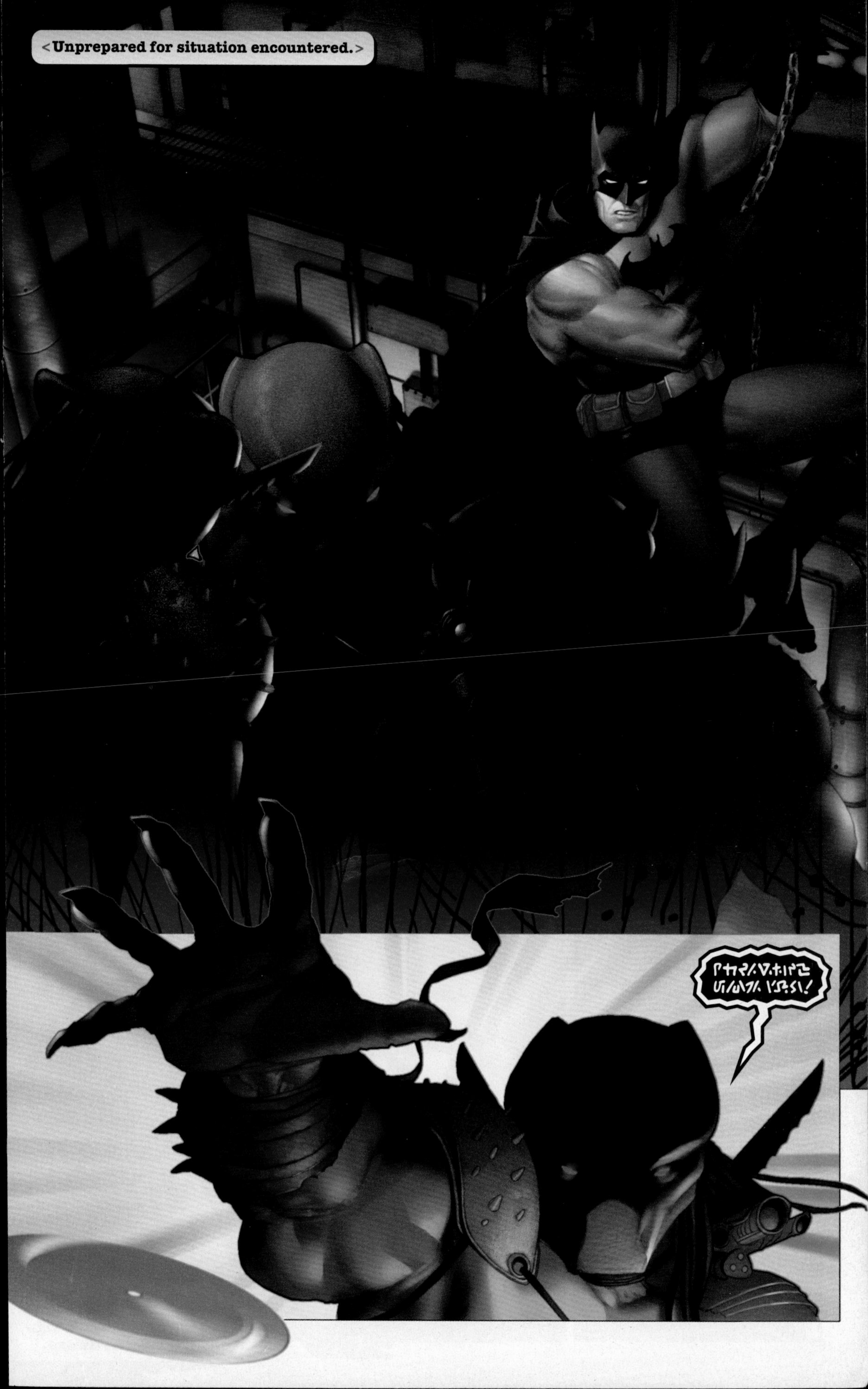
<Unprepared for situation encountered.>

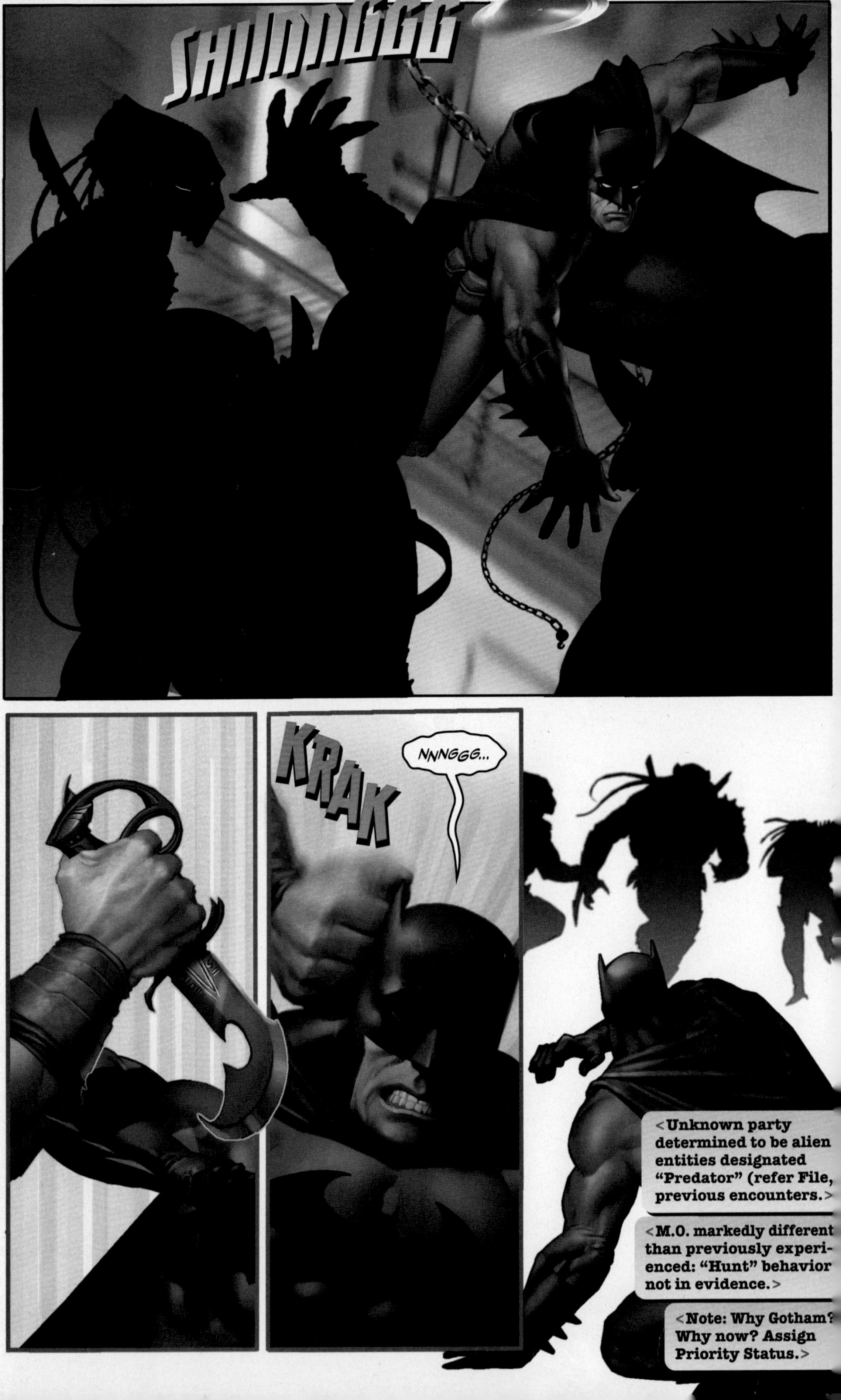
SHIMNGGG
KRAK
NNNGGG...
<Unknown party determined to be alien entities designated "Predator" (refer File, previous encounters.>
<M.O. markedly different than previously experienced: "Hunt" behavior not in evidence.>
<Note: Why Gotham? Why now? Assign Priority Status.>

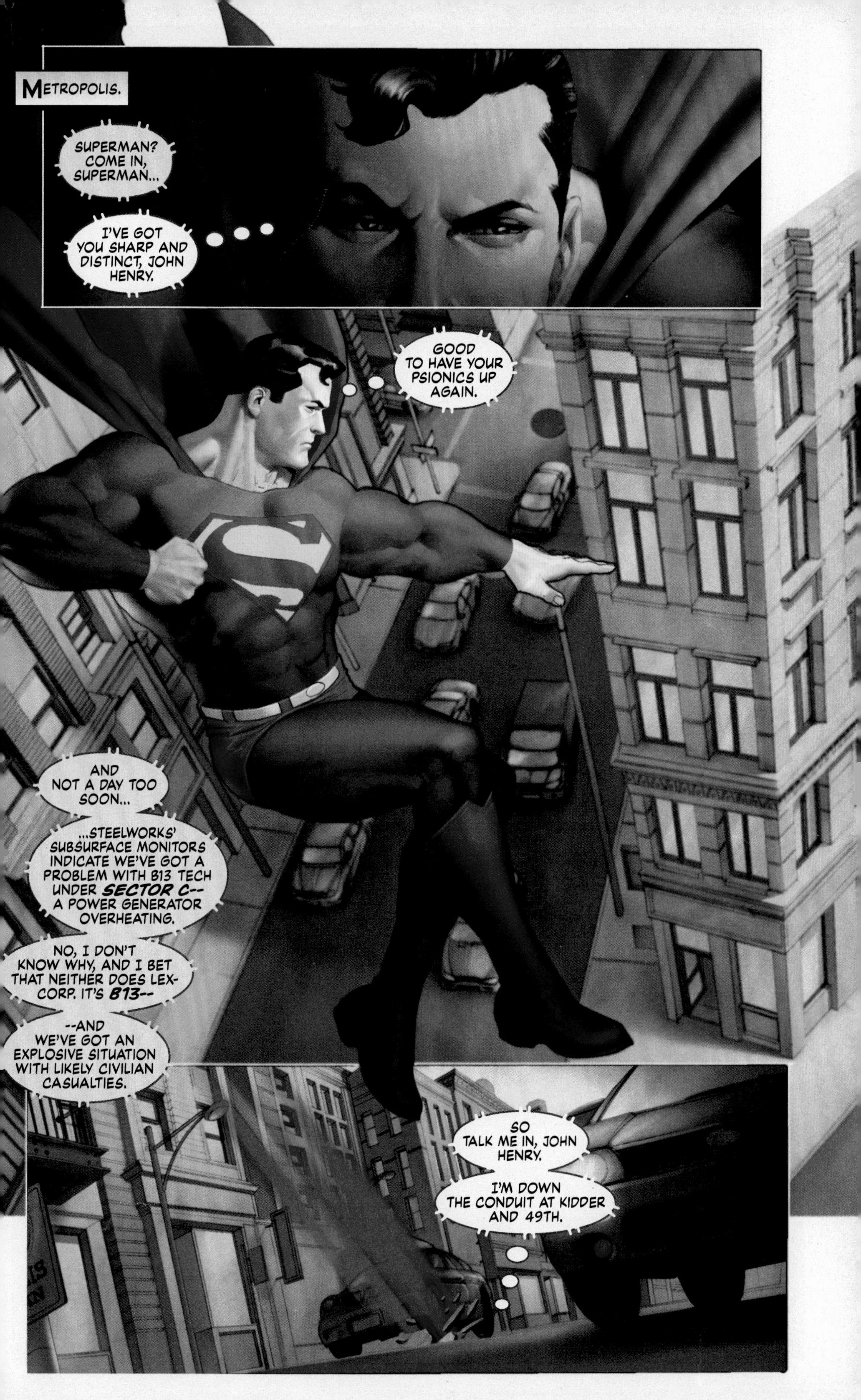
METROPOLIS.
SUPERMAN? COME IN, SUPERMAN...
I'VE GOT YOU SHARP AND DISTINCT, JOHN HENRY.
GOOD TO HAVE YOUR PSIONICS UP AGAIN.
AND NOT A DAY TOO SOON...
...STEELWORKS' SUBSURFACE MONITORS INDICATE WE'VE GOT A PROBLEM WITH B13 TECH UNDER SECTOR C-- A POWER GENERATOR OVERHEATING.
NO, I DON'T KNOW WHY, AND I BET THAT NEITHER DOES LEX-CORP. IT'S B13--
--AND WE'VE GOT AN EXPLOSIVE SITUATION WITH LIKELY CIVILIAN CASUALTIES.
SO TALK ME IN, JOHN HENRY.
I'M DOWN THE CONDUIT AT KIDDER AND 49TH.

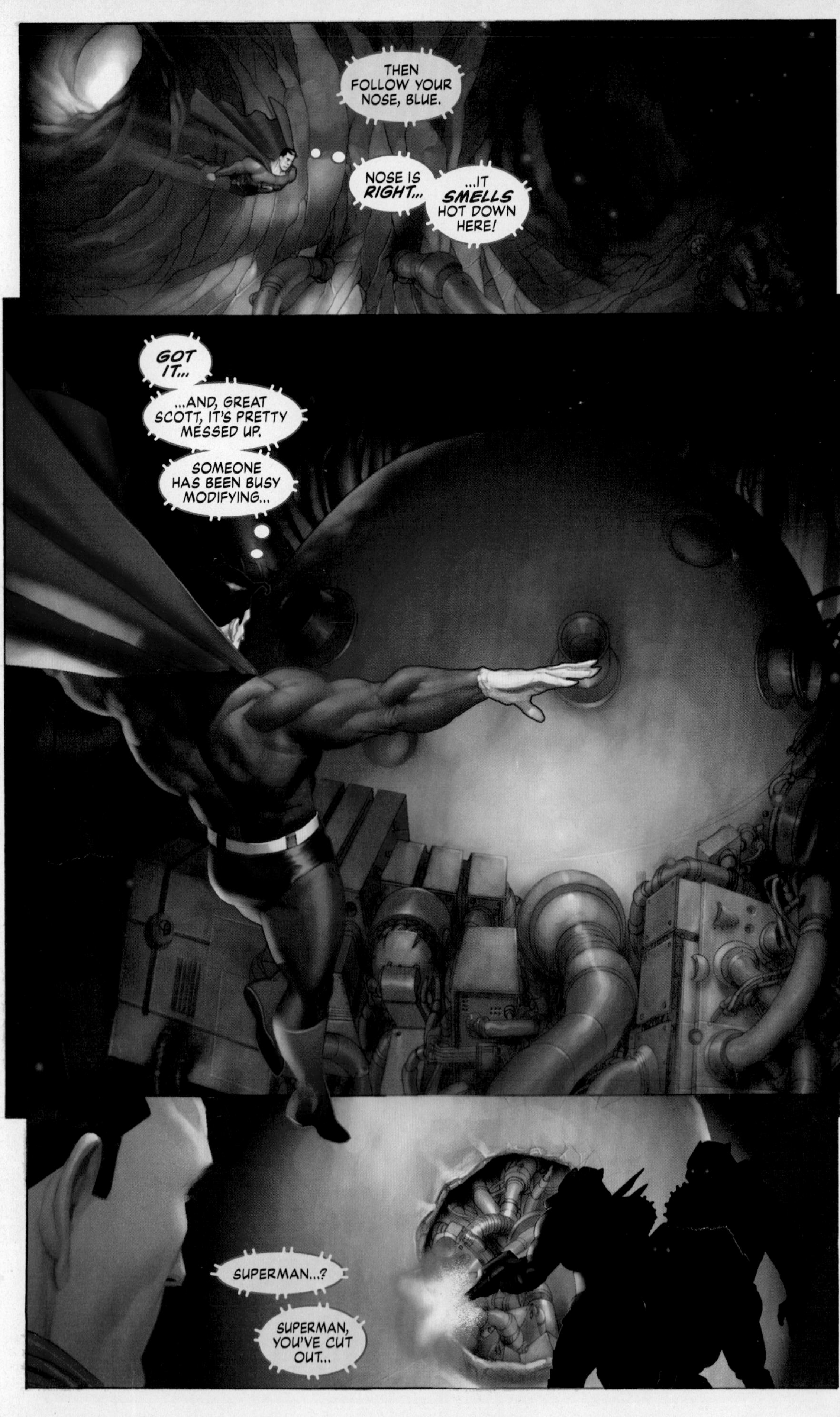
THEN FOLLOW YOUR NOSE, BLUE.
NOSE IS RIGHT...
...IT SMELLS HOT DOWN HERE!
GOT IT...
...AND, GREAT SCOTT, IT'S PRETTY MESSED UP.
SOMEONE HAS BEEN BUSY MODIFYING...
SUPERMAN...?
SUPERMAN, YOU'VE CUT OUT...

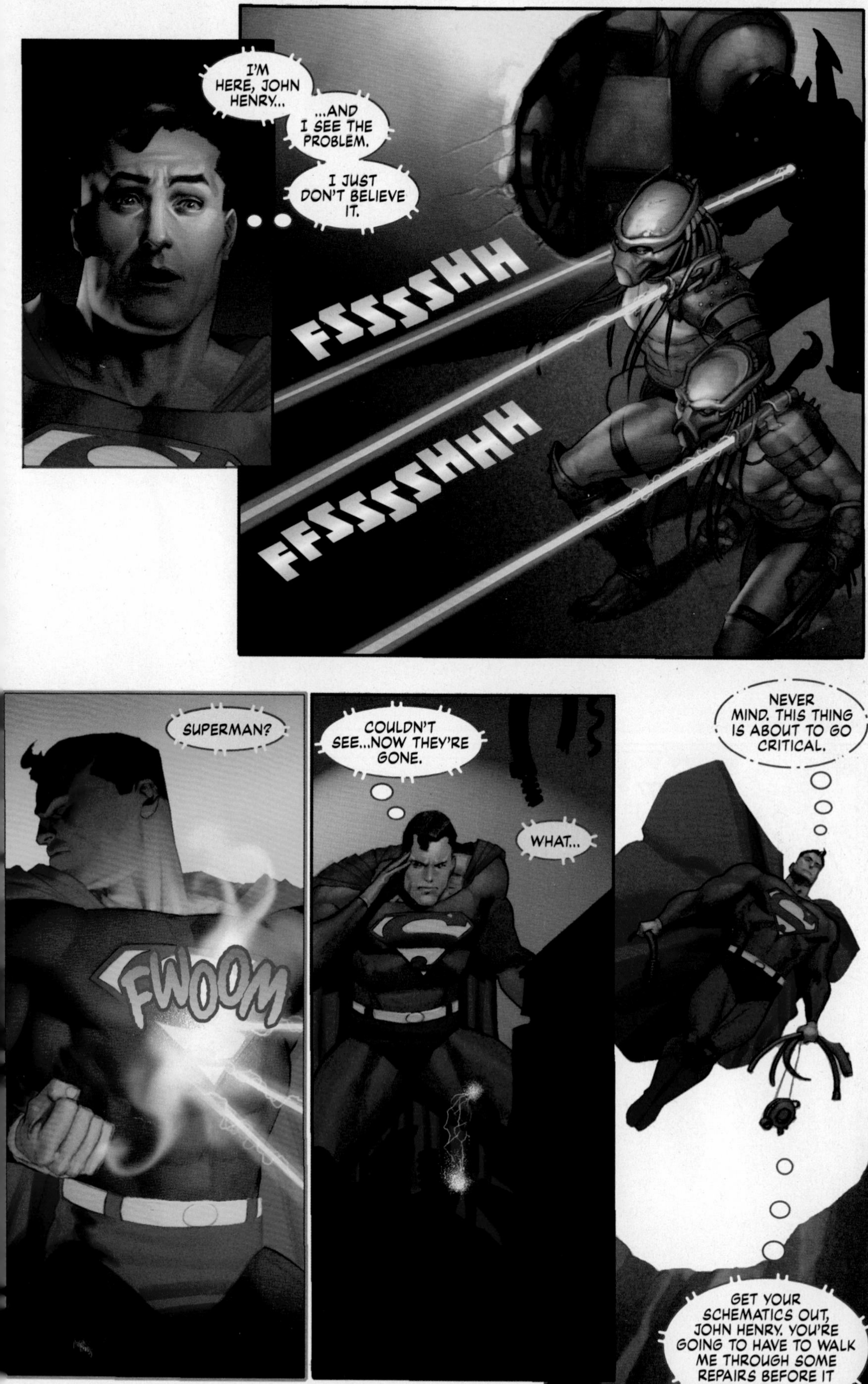
I'M HERE, JOHN HENRY...
...AND I SEE THE PROBLEM.
I JUST DON'T BELIEVE IT.
FSSSSHH
FFSSSSHHH
SUPERMAN?
FWOOM
COULDN'T SEE...NOW THEY'RE GONE.
WHAT...
NEVER MIND. THIS THING IS ABOUT TO GO CRITICAL.
GET YOUR SCHEMATICS OUT, JOHN HENRY. YOU'RE GOING TO HAVE TO WALK ME THROUGH SOME REPAIRS BEFORE IT GOES BOOM...

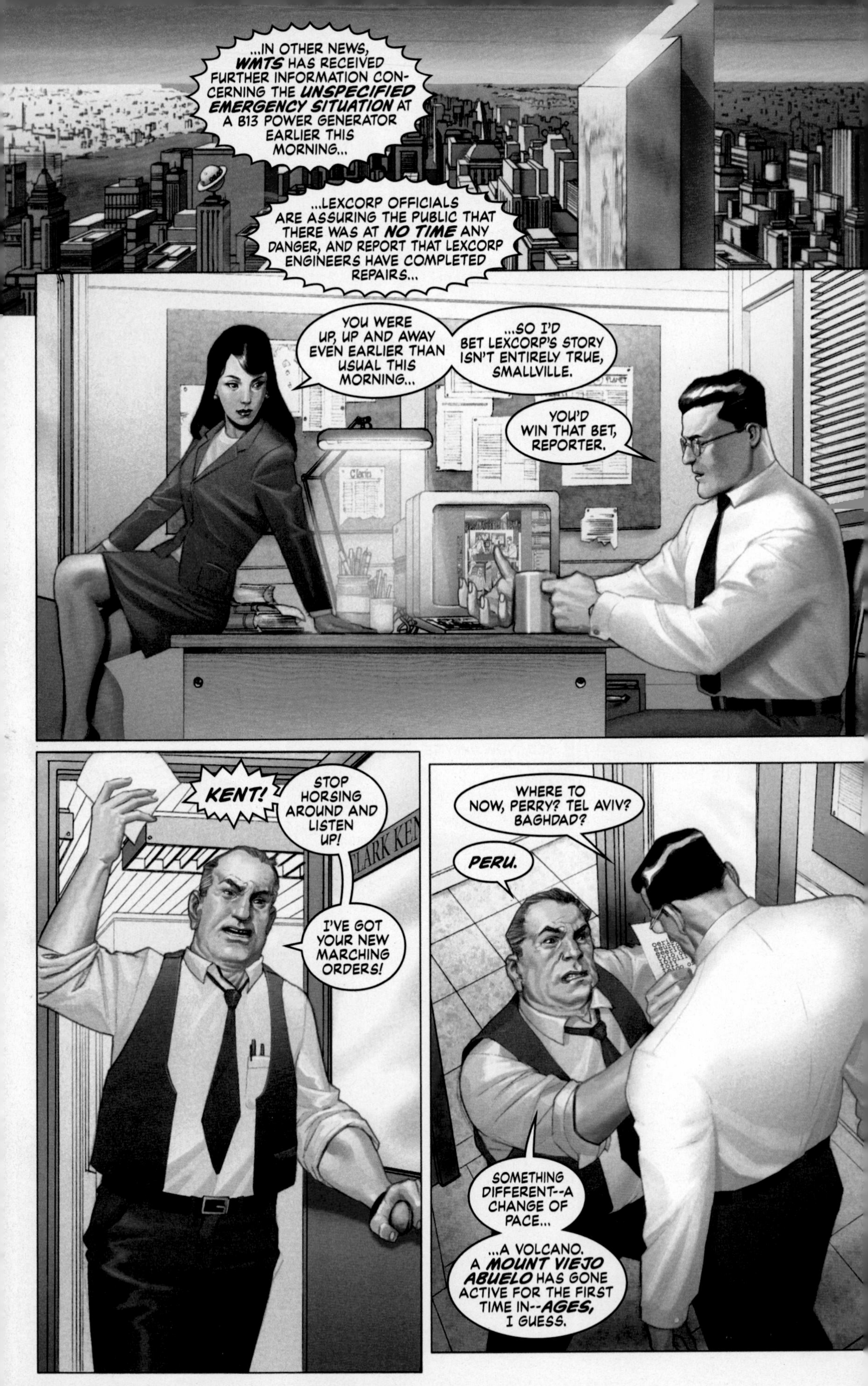
...IN OTHER NEWS, WMTS HAS RECEIVED FURTHER INFORMATION CON-CERNING THE UNSPECIFIED EMERGENCY SITUATION AT A B13 POWER GENERATOR EARLIER THIS MORNING...
...LEXCORP OFFICIALS ARE ASSURING THE PUBLIC THAT THERE WAS AT NO TIME ANY DANGER, AND REPORT THAT LEXCORP ENGINEERS HAVE COMPLETED REPAIRS...
YOU WERE UP, UP AND AWAY EVEN EARLIER THAN USUAL THIS MORNING...
...SO I'D BET LEXCORP'S STORY ISN'T ENTIRELY TRUE, SMALLVILLE.
YOU'D WIN THAT BET, REPORTER.
KENT!
STOP HORSING AROUND AND LISTEN UP!
I'VE GOT YOUR NEW MARCHING ORDERS!
WHERE TO NOW, PERRY? TEL AVIV? BAGHDAD?
PERU.
SOMETHING DIFFERENT--A CHANGE OF PACE...
...A VOLCANO. A MOUNT VIEJO ABUELO HAS GONE ACTIVE FOR THE FIRST TIME IN--AGES, I GUESS.

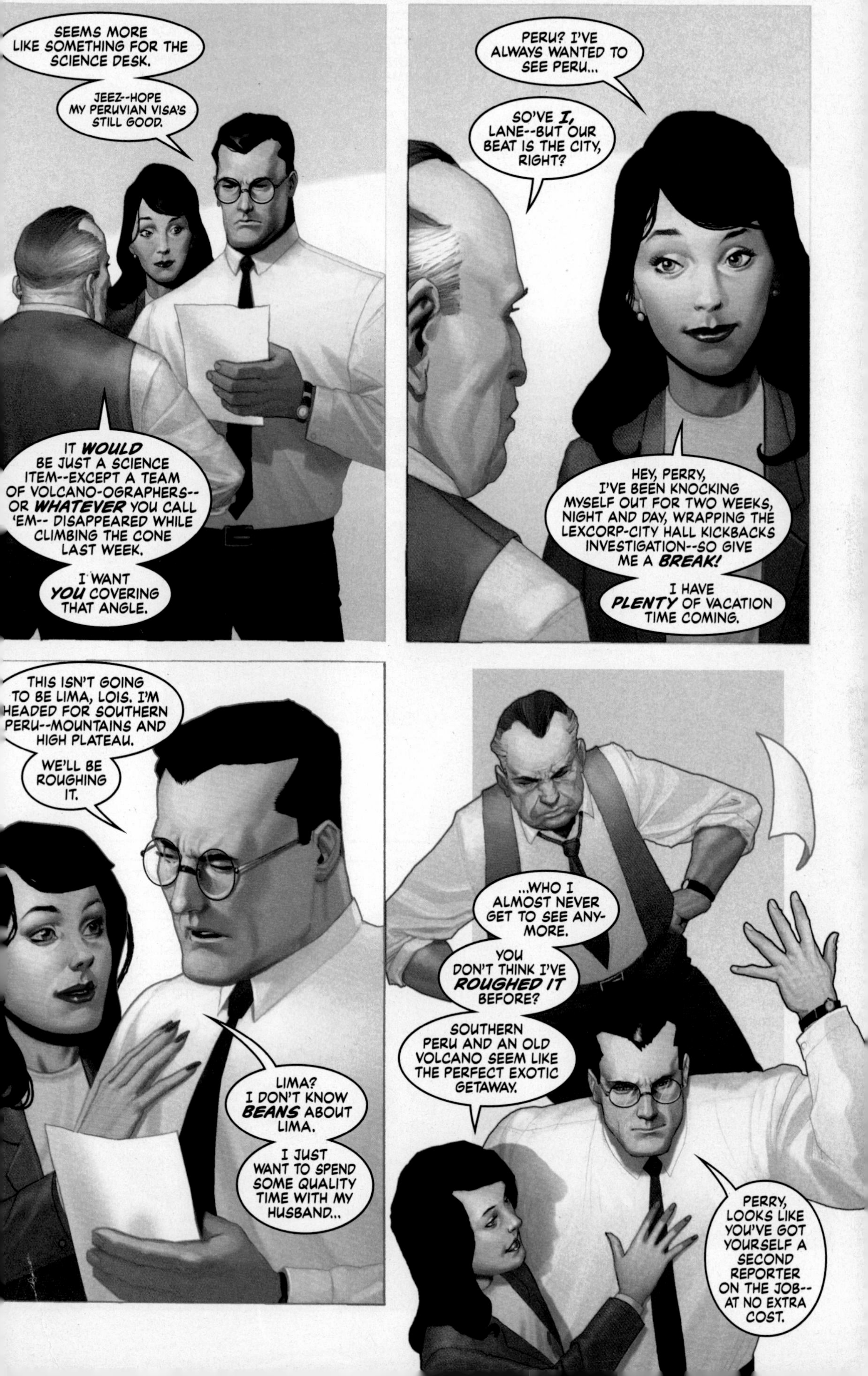
SEEMS MORE LIKE SOMETHING FOR THE SCIENCE DESK.
JEEZ--HOPE MY PERUVIAN VISA'S STILL GOOD.
IT WOULD BE JUST A SCIENCE ITEM--EXCEPT A TEAM OF VOLCANO-OGRAPHERS--OR WHATEVER YOU CALL 'EM-- DISAPPEARED WHILE CLIMBING THE CONE LAST WEEK.
I WANT YOU COVERING THAT ANGLE.
PERU? I'VE ALWAYS WANTED TO SEE PERU...
SO'VE I, LANE--BUT OUR BEAT IS THE CITY, RIGHT?
HEY, PERRY, I'VE BEEN KNOCKING MYSELF OUT FOR TWO WEEKS, NIGHT AND DAY, WRAPPING THE LEXCORP-CITY HALL KICKBACKS INVESTIGATION--SO GIVE ME A BREAK!
I HAVE PLENTY OF VACATION TIME COMING.
THIS ISN'T GOING TO BE LIMA, LOIS. I'M HEADED FOR SOUTHERN PERU--MOUNTAINS AND HIGH PLATEAU.
WE'LL BE ROUGHING IT.
LIMA? I DON'T KNOW BEANS ABOUT LIMA.
I JUST WANT TO SPEND SOME QUALITY TIME WITH MY HUSBAND...
...WHO I ALMOST NEVER GET TO SEE ANY-MORE.
YOU DON'T THINK I'VE ROUGHED IT BEFORE?
SOUTHERN PERU AND AN OLD VOLCANO SEEM LIKE THE PERFECT EXOTIC GETAWAY.
PERRY, LOOKS LIKE YOU'VE GOT YOURSELF A SECOND REPORTER ON THE JOB--AT NO EXTRA COST.

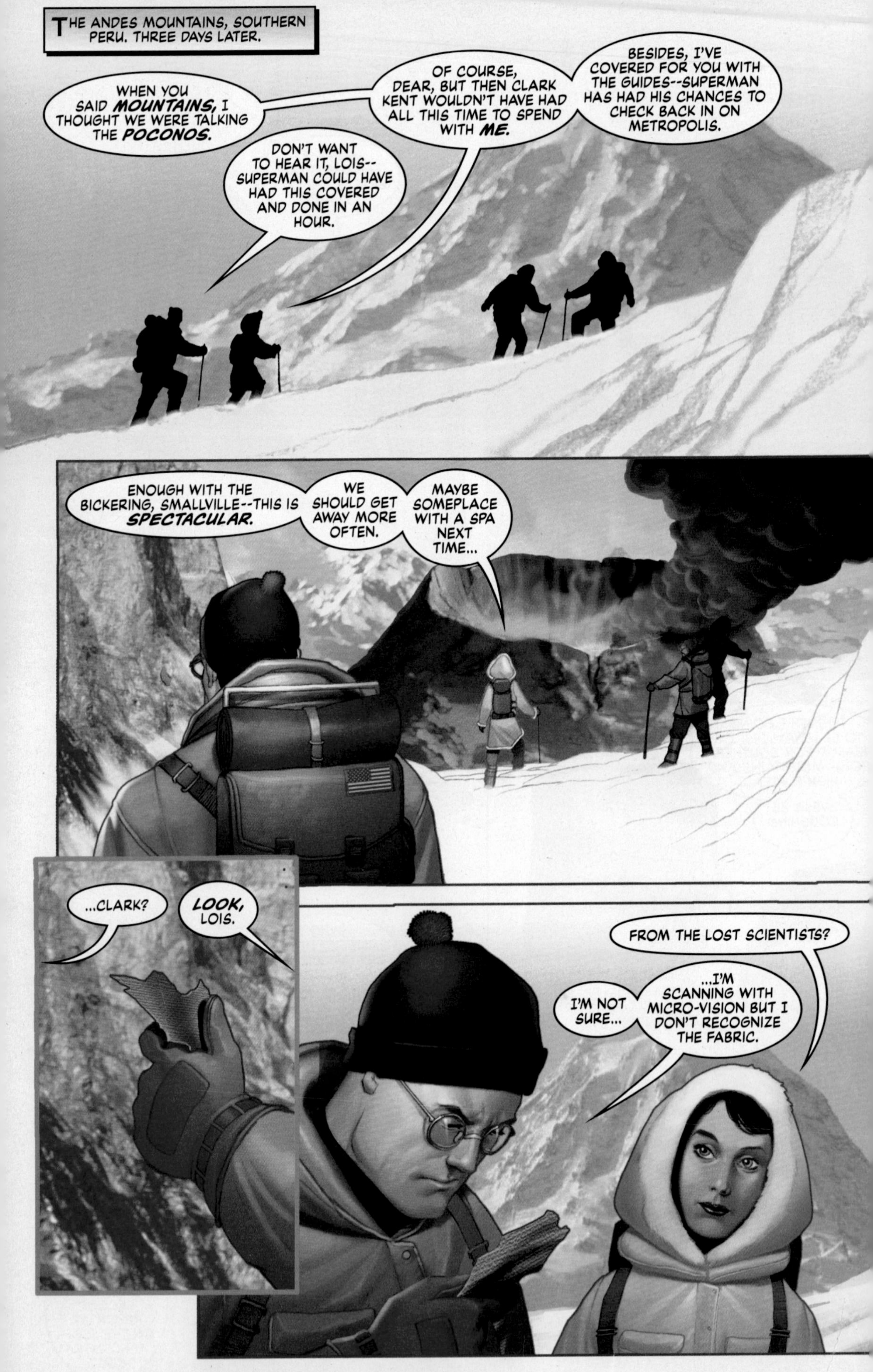
THE ANDES MOUNTAINS, SOUTHERN PERU. THREE DAYS LATER.
WHEN YOU SAID MOUNTAINS, I THOUGHT WE WERE TALKING THE POCONOS.
DON'T WANT TO HEAR IT, LOIS-- SUPERMAN COULD HAVE HAD THIS COVERED AND DONE IN AN HOUR.
OF COURSE, DEAR, BUT THEN CLARK KENT WOULDN'T HAVE HAD ALL THIS TIME TO SPEND WITH ME.
BESIDES, I'VE COVERED FOR YOU WITH THE GUIDES--SUPERMAN HAS HAD HIS CHANCES TO CHECK BACK IN ON METROPOLIS.
ENOUGH WITH THE BICKERING, SMALLVILLE--THIS IS SPECTACULAR.
WE SHOULD GET AWAY MORE OFTEN.
MAYBE SOMEPLACE WITH A SPA NEXT TIME...
...CLARK?
LOOK, LOIS.
FROM THE LOST SCIENTISTS?
I'M NOT SURE...
...I'M SCANNING WITH MICRO-VISION BUT I DON'T RECOGNIZE THE FABRIC.

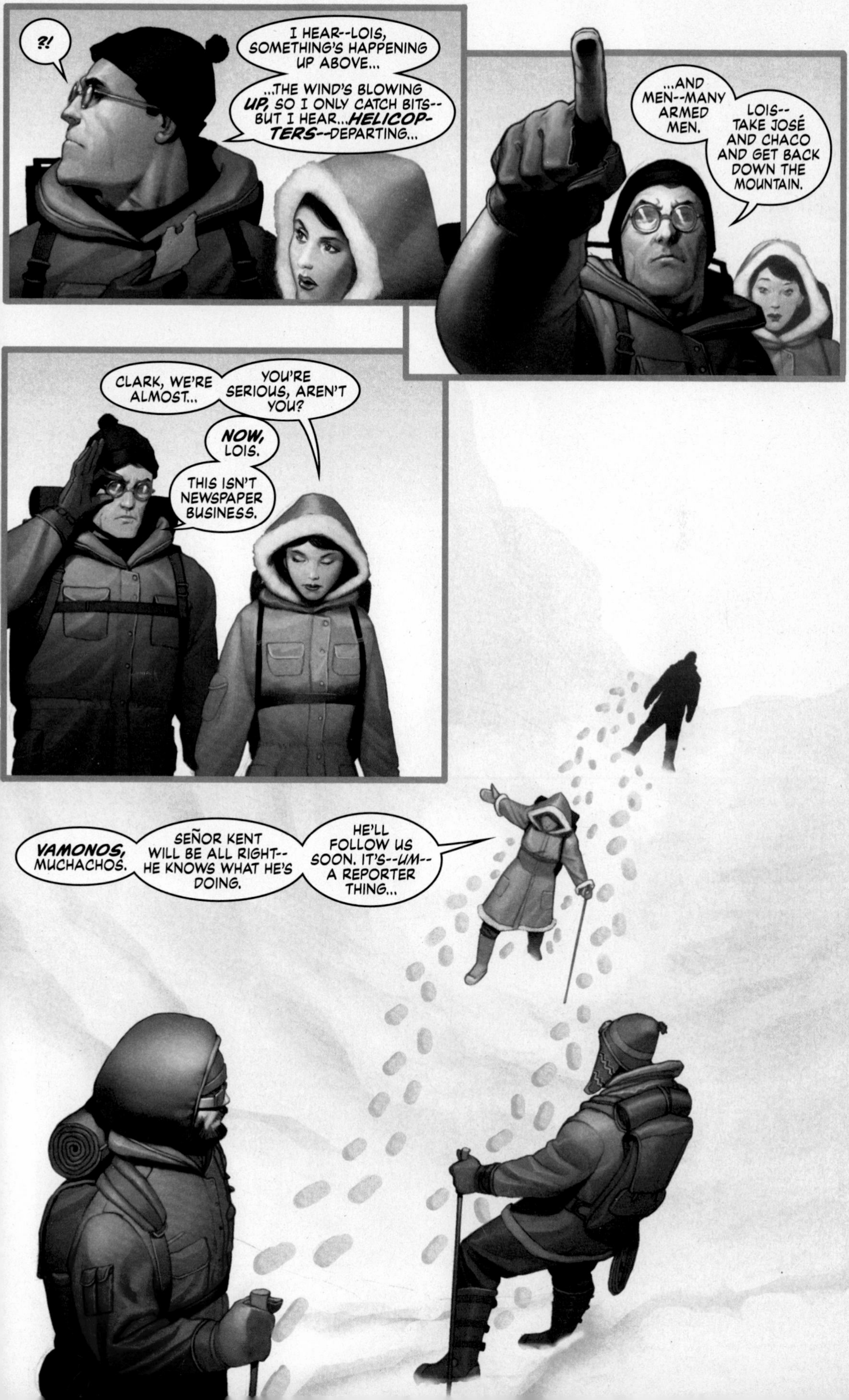
?!
I HEAR--LOIS, SOMETHING'S HAPPENING UP ABOVE...
...THE WIND'S BLOWING UP, SO I ONLY CATCH BITS--BUT I HEAR...HELICOPTERS--DEPARTING...
...AND MEN--MANY ARMED MEN.
LOIS--TAKE JOSÉ AND CHACO AND GET BACK DOWN THE MOUNTAIN.
CLARK, WE'RE ALMOST...
YOU'RE SERIOUS, AREN'T YOU?
NOW, LOIS.
THIS ISN'T NEWSPAPER BUSINESS.
VAMONOS, MUCHACHOS.
SEÑOR KENT WILL BE ALL RIGHT--HE KNOWS WHAT HE'S DOING.
HE'LL FOLLOW US SOON. IT'S--UM--A REPORTER THING...

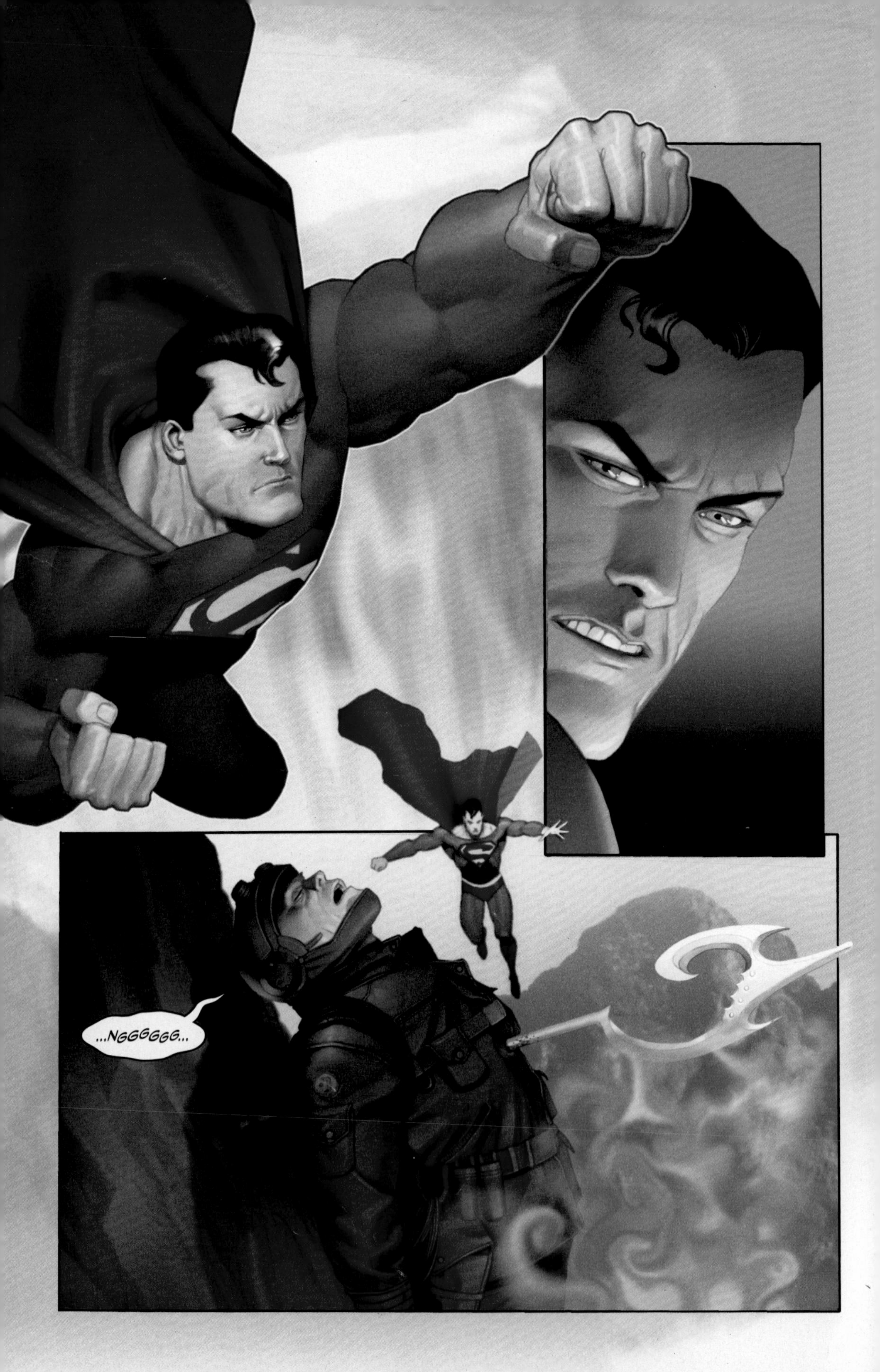
...NGGGGGG...

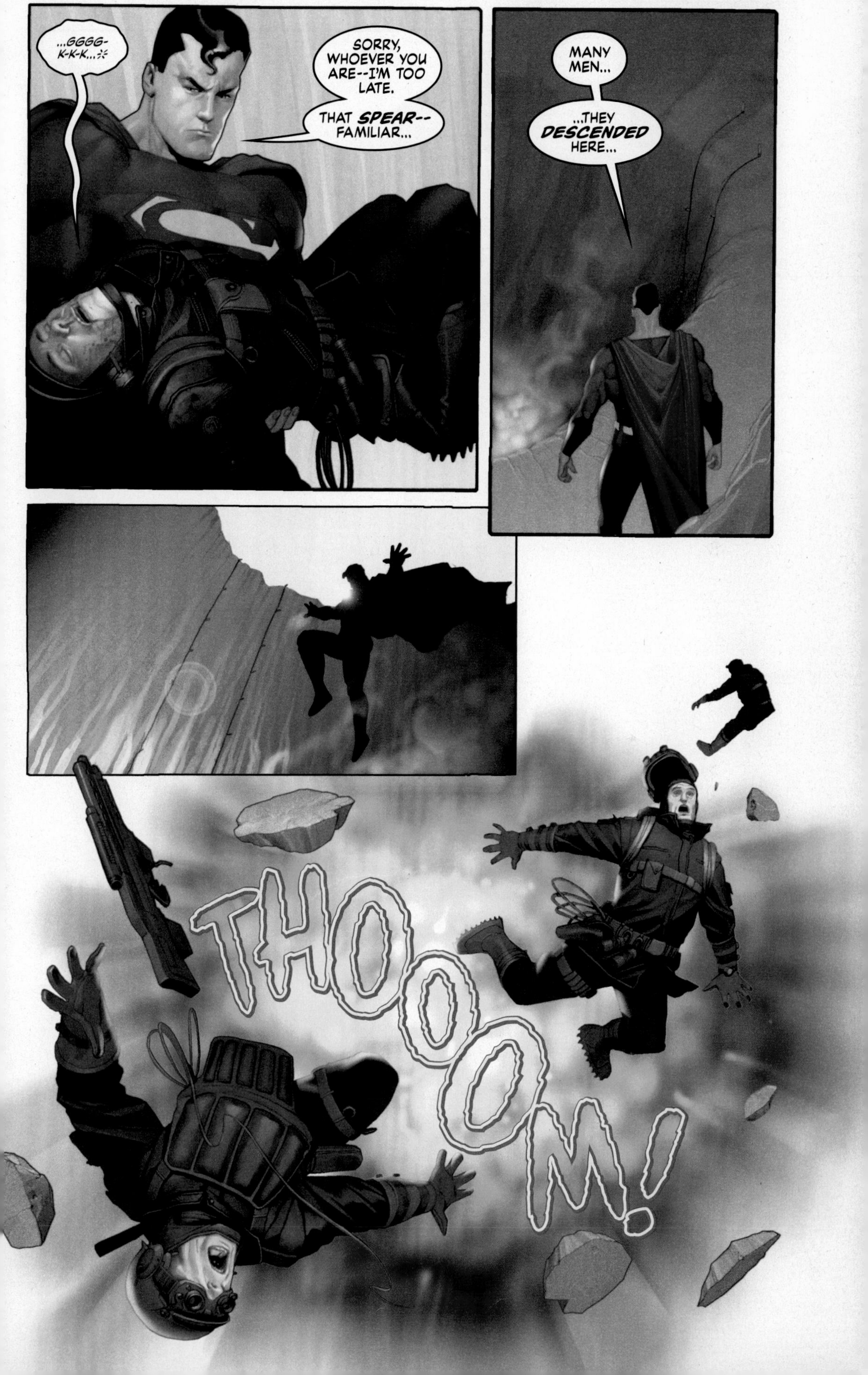
...GGGG-K-K-K...
SORRY, WHOEVER YOU ARE--I'M TOO LATE.
THAT SPEAR--FAMILIAR...
MANY MEN...
...THEY DESCENDED HERE...
THOOOOM!

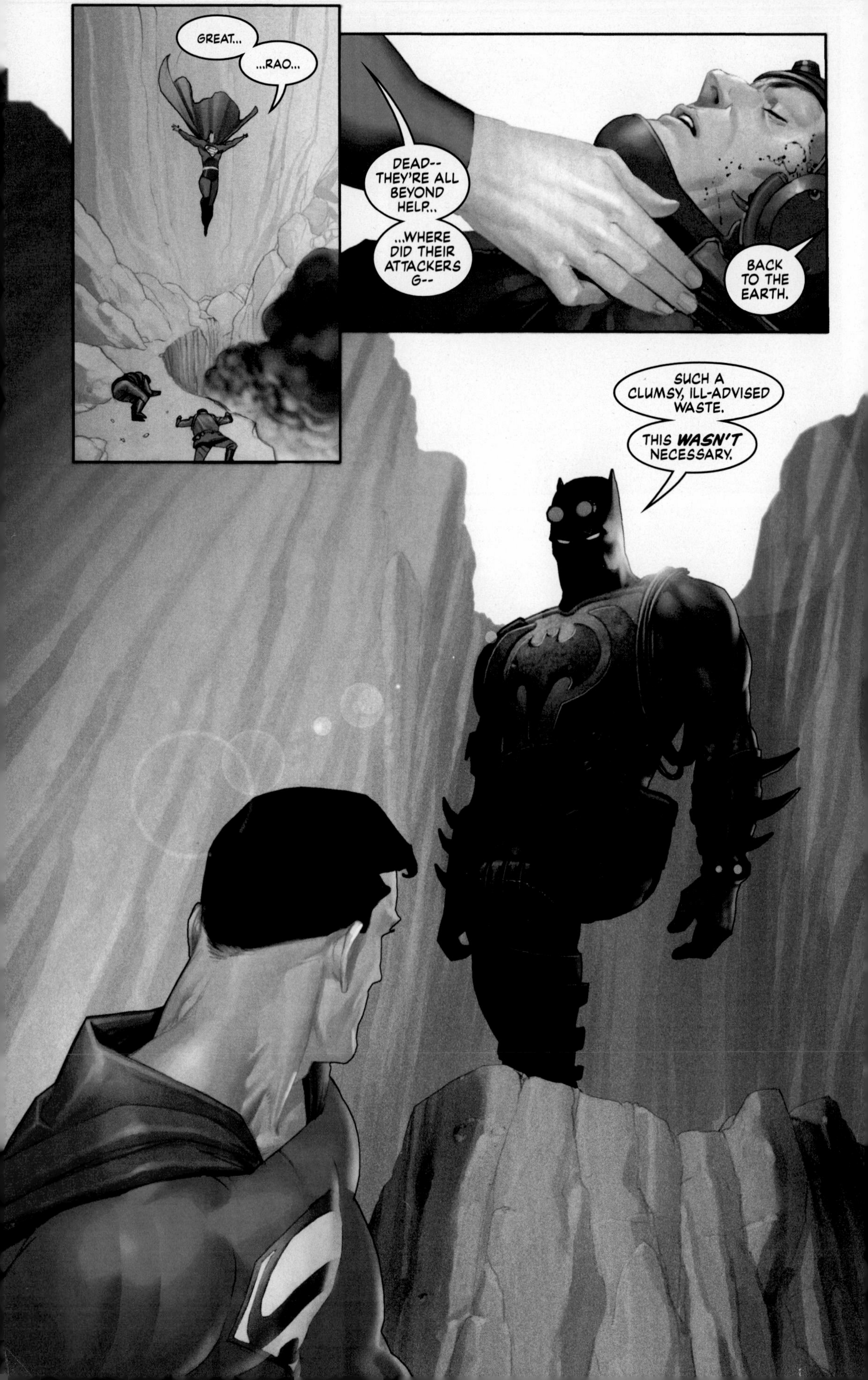
GREAT...
...RAO...
DEAD-- THEY'RE ALL BEYOND HELP...
...WHERE DID THEIR ATTACKERS G--
BACK TO THE EARTH.
SUCH A CLUMSY, ILL-ADVISED WASTE.
THIS WASN'T NECESSARY.

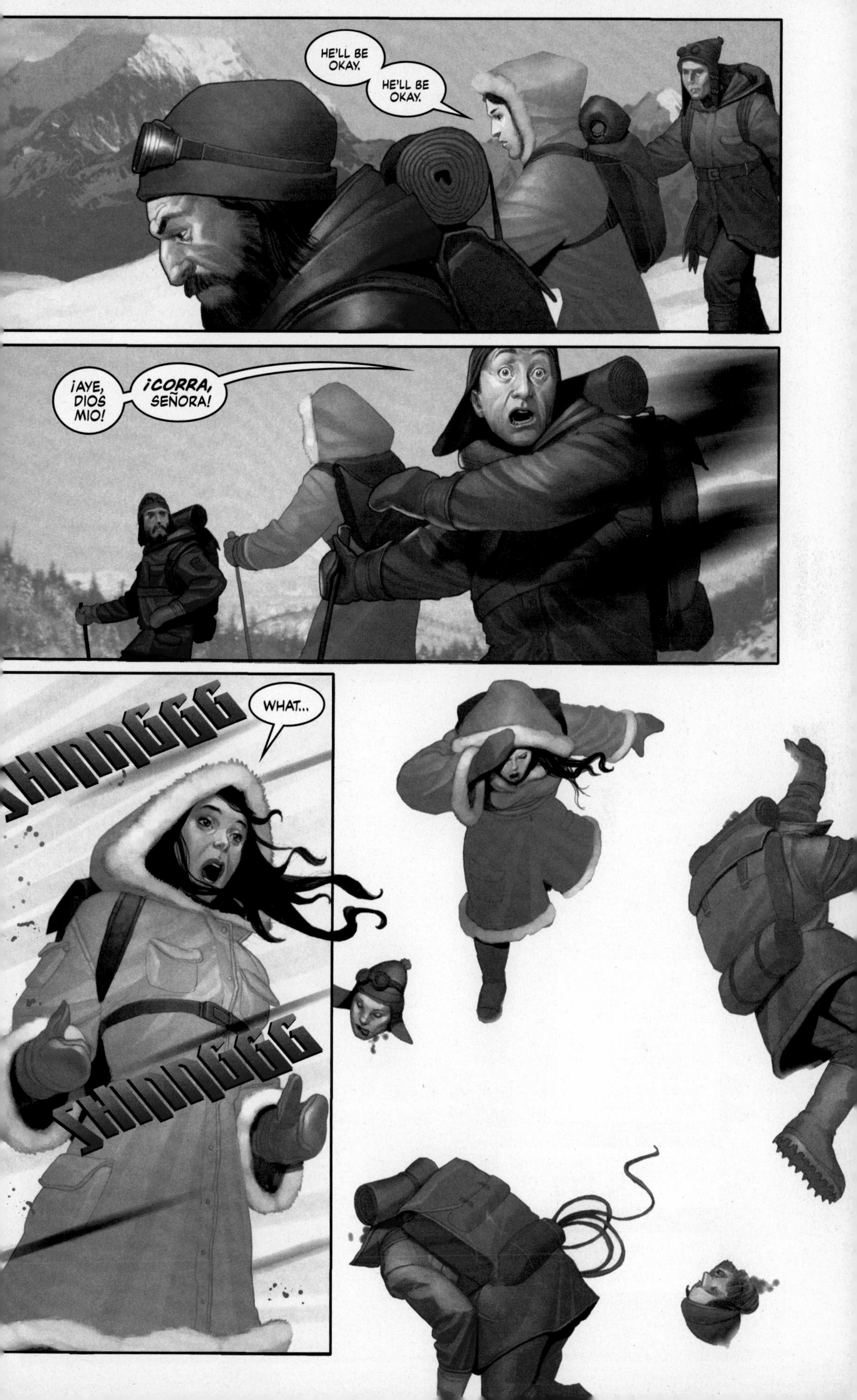

HE'LL BE OKAY.
HE'LL BE OKAY.
¡AYE, DIOS MIO!
¡CORRA, SEÑORA!
WHAT...
SHINGGG
SHINGGG

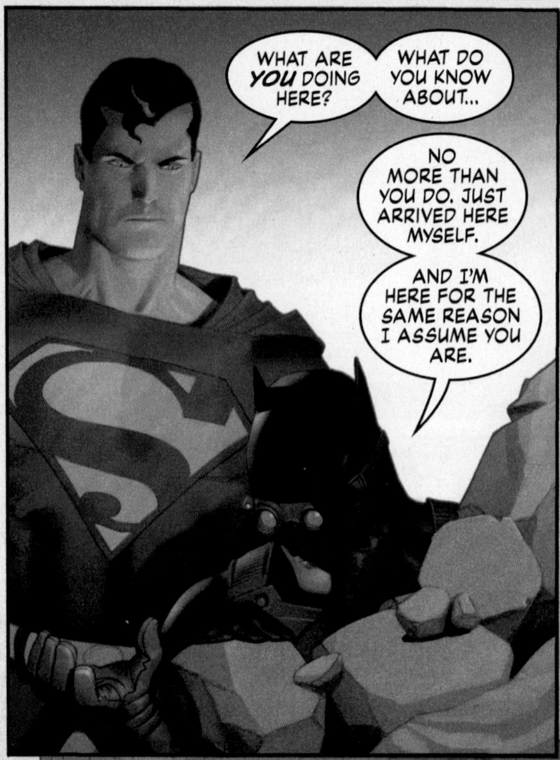
WHAT ARE YOU DOING HERE?
WHAT DO YOU KNOW ABOUT...
NO MORE THAN YOU DO. JUST ARRIVED HERE MYSELF.
AND I'M HERE FOR THE SAME REASON I ASSUME YOU ARE.

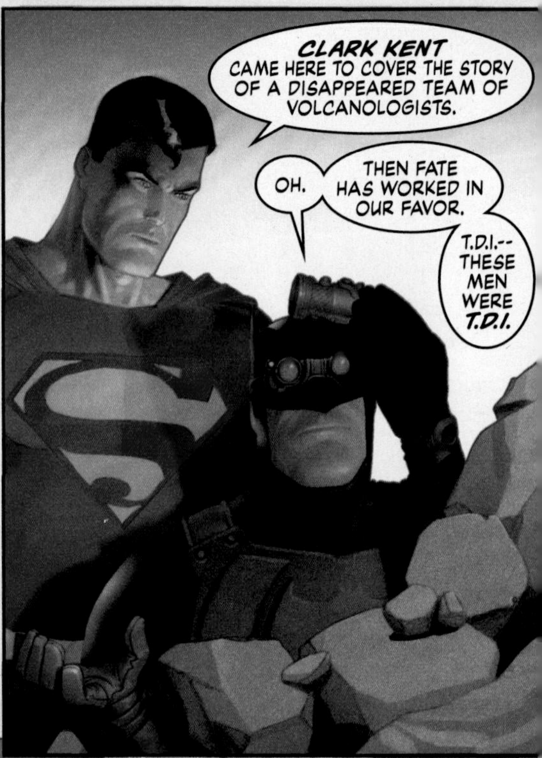
CLARK KENT CAME HERE TO COVER THE STORY OF A DISAPPEARED TEAM OF VOLCANOLOGISTS.
OH.
THEN FATE HAS WORKED IN OUR FAVOR.
T.D.I.--THESE MEN WERE T.D.I.

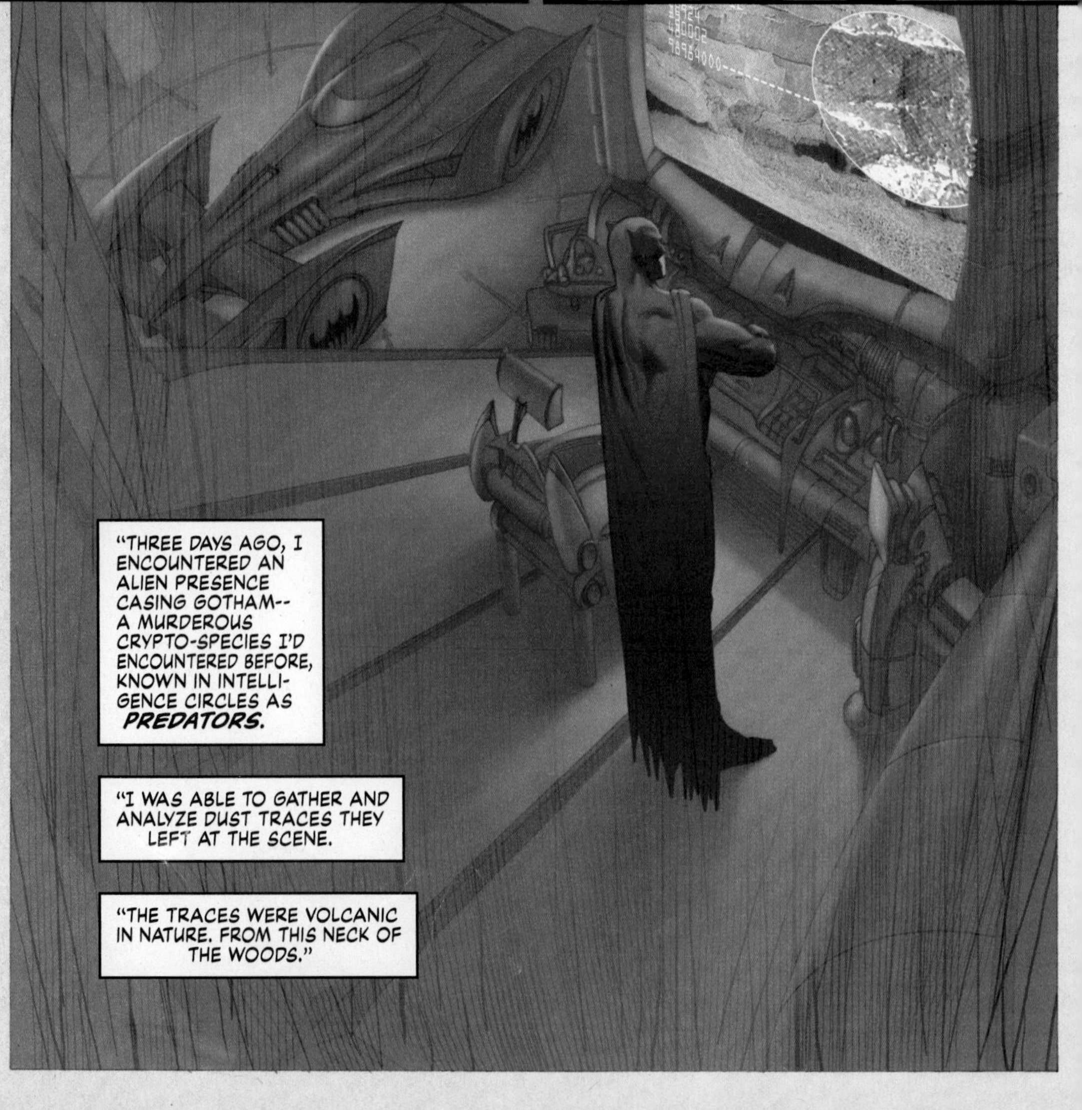
"THREE DAYS AGO, I ENCOUNTERED AN ALIEN PRESENCE CASING GOTHAM--A MURDEROUS CRYPTO-SPECIES I'D ENCOUNTERED BEFORE, KNOWN IN INTELLIGENCE CIRCLES AS PREDATORS.
"I WAS ABLE TO GATHER AND ANALYZE DUST TRACES THEY LEFT AT THE SCENE.
"THE TRACES WERE VOLCANIC IN NATURE. FROM THIS NECK OF THE WOODS."

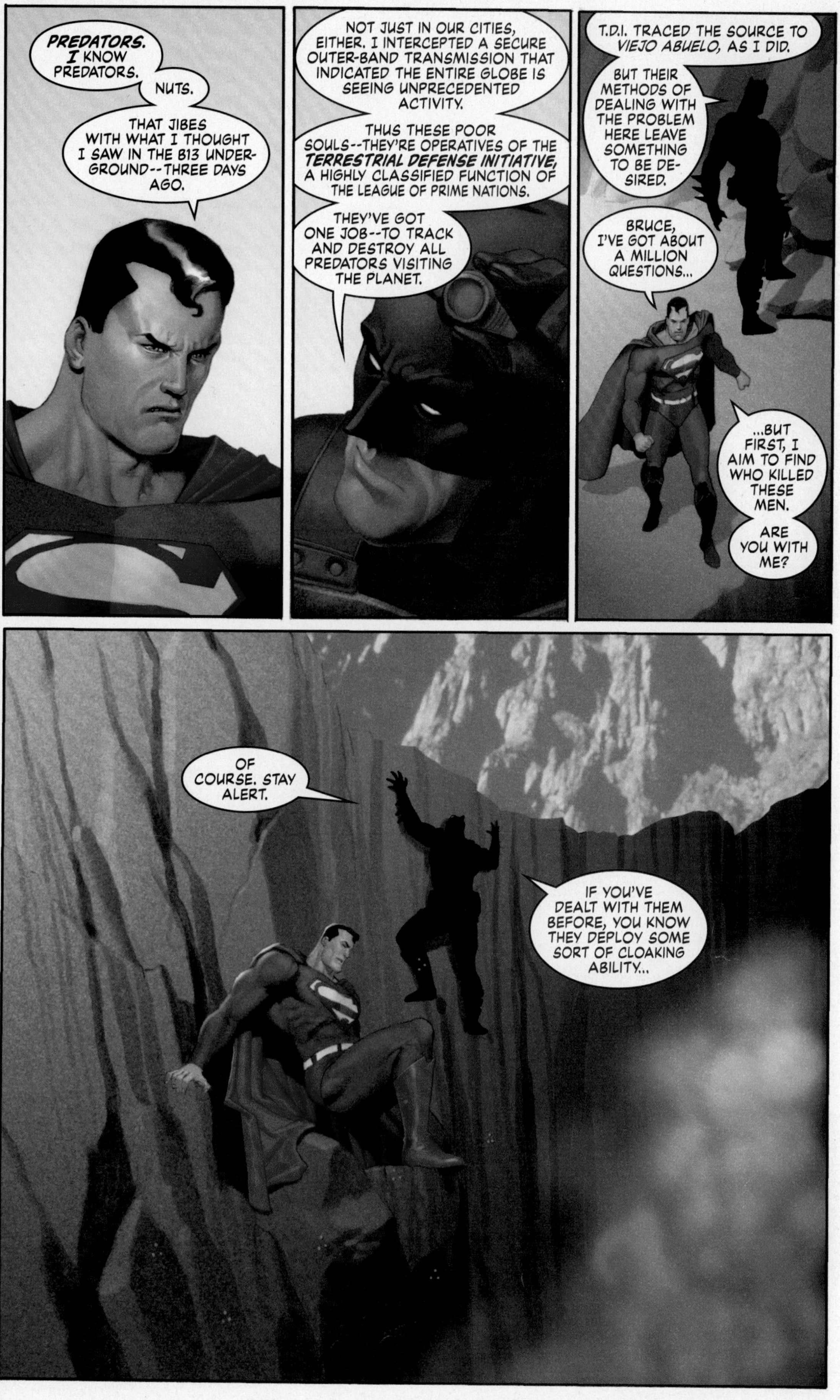
PREDATORS. I KNOW PREDATORS.
NUTS.
THAT JIBES WITH WHAT I THOUGHT I SAW IN THE B13 UNDER-GROUND--THREE DAYS AGO.
NOT JUST IN OUR CITIES, EITHER. I INTERCEPTED A SECURE OUTER-BAND TRANSMISSION THAT INDICATED THE ENTIRE GLOBE IS SEEING UNPRECEDENTED ACTIVITY.
THUS THESE POOR SOULS--THEY'RE OPERATIVES OF THE TERRESTRIAL DEFENSE INITIATIVE, A HIGHLY CLASSIFIED FUNCTION OF THE LEAGUE OF PRIME NATIONS.
THEY'VE GOT ONE JOB--TO TRACK AND DESTROY ALL PREDATORS VISITING THE PLANET.
T.D.I. TRACED THE SOURCE TO VIEJO ABUELO, AS I DID.
BUT THEIR METHODS OF DEALING WITH THE PROBLEM HERE LEAVE SOMETHING TO BE DE-SIRED.
BRUCE, I'VE GOT ABOUT A MILLION QUESTIONS...
...BUT FIRST, I AIM TO FIND WHO KILLED THESE MEN.
ARE YOU WITH ME?
OF COURSE. STAY ALERT.
IF YOU'VE DEALT WITH THEM BEFORE, YOU KNOW THEY DEPLOY SOME SORT OF CLOAKING ABILITY...

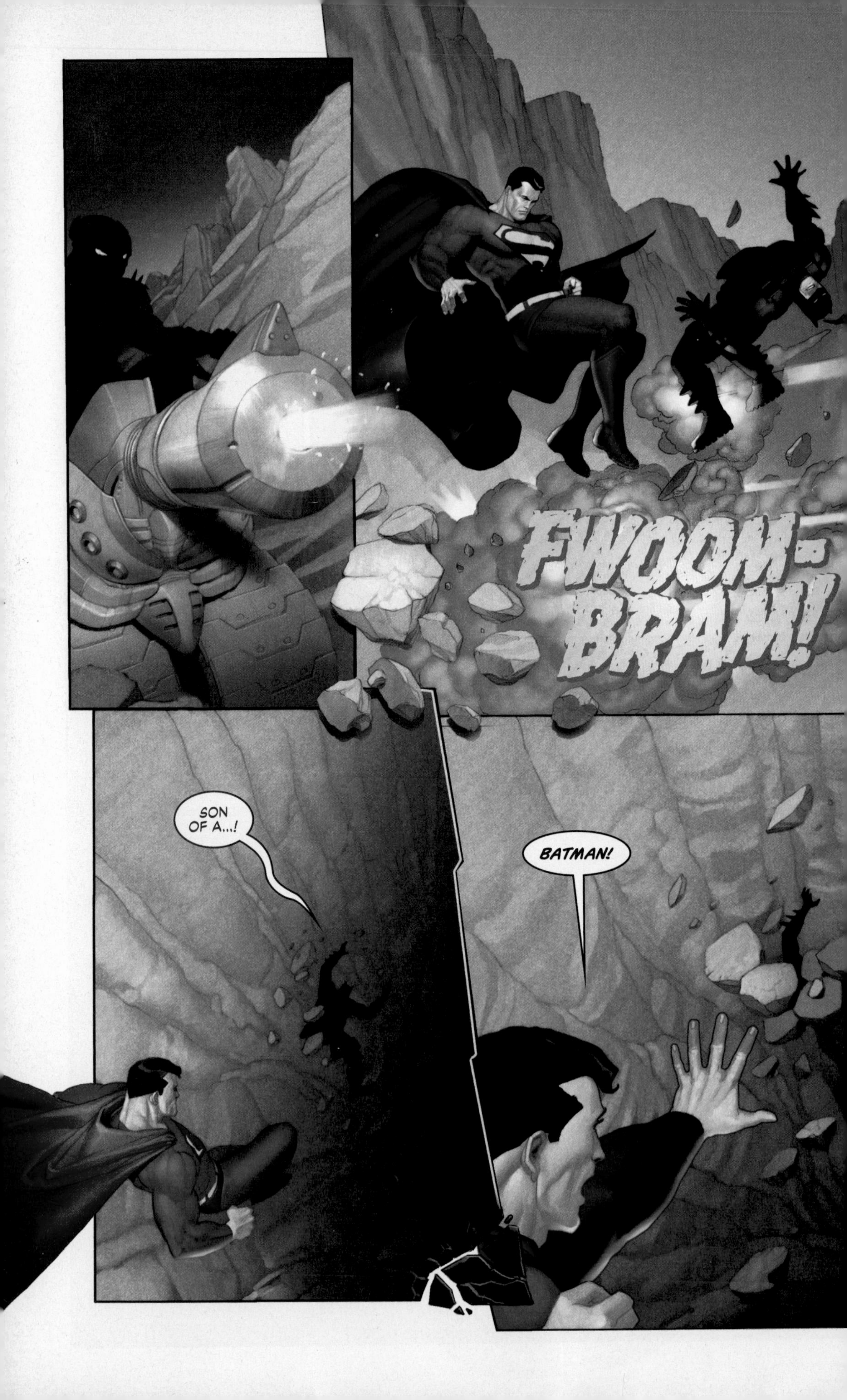
FWOOM-BRAM!
SON OF A...!
BATMAN!

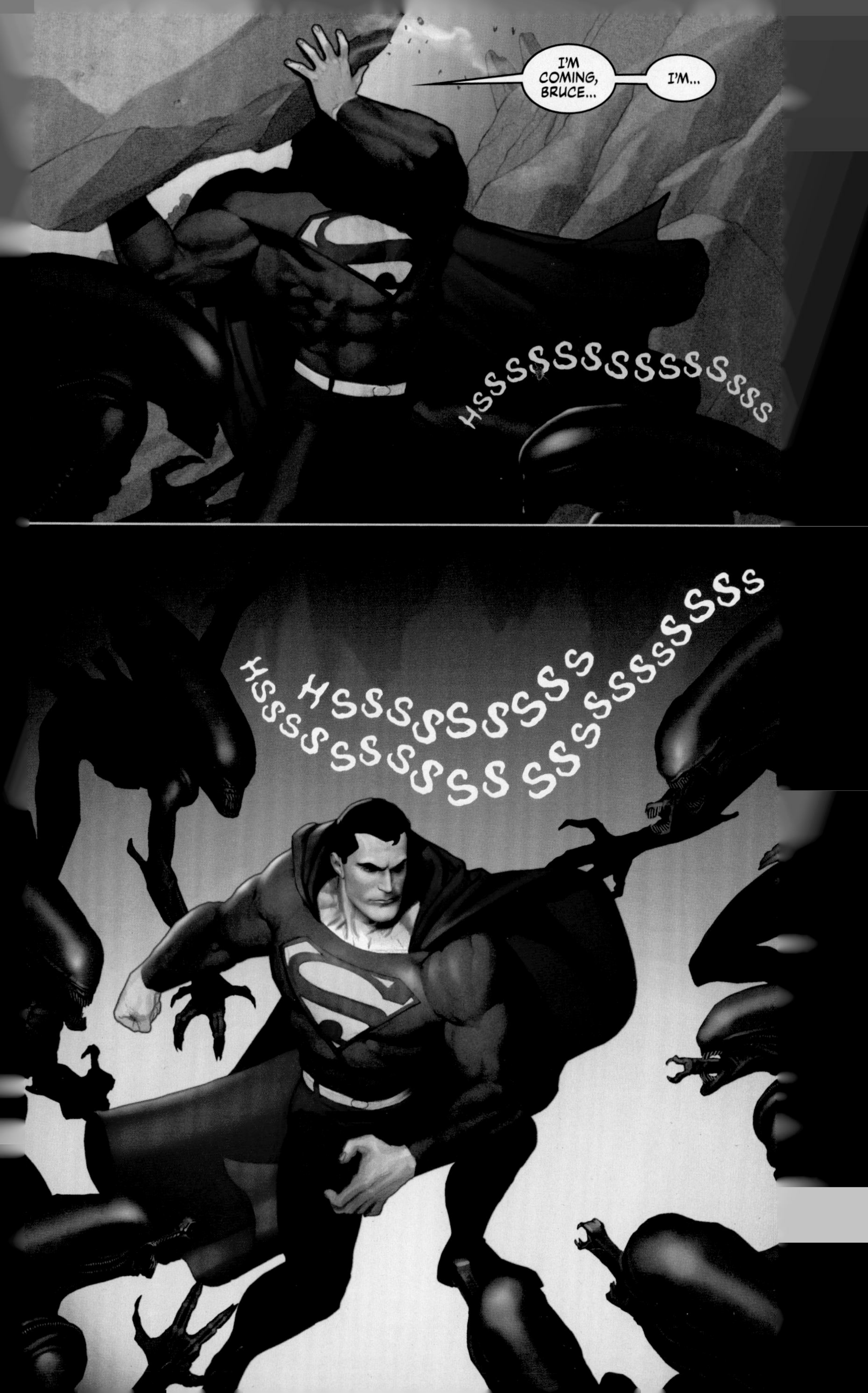
I'M COMING, BRUCE...
I'M...
HSSSSSSSSSSSSSSS
HSSSSSSSSS
HSSSSSSSSSSSSSSSSSSSSS

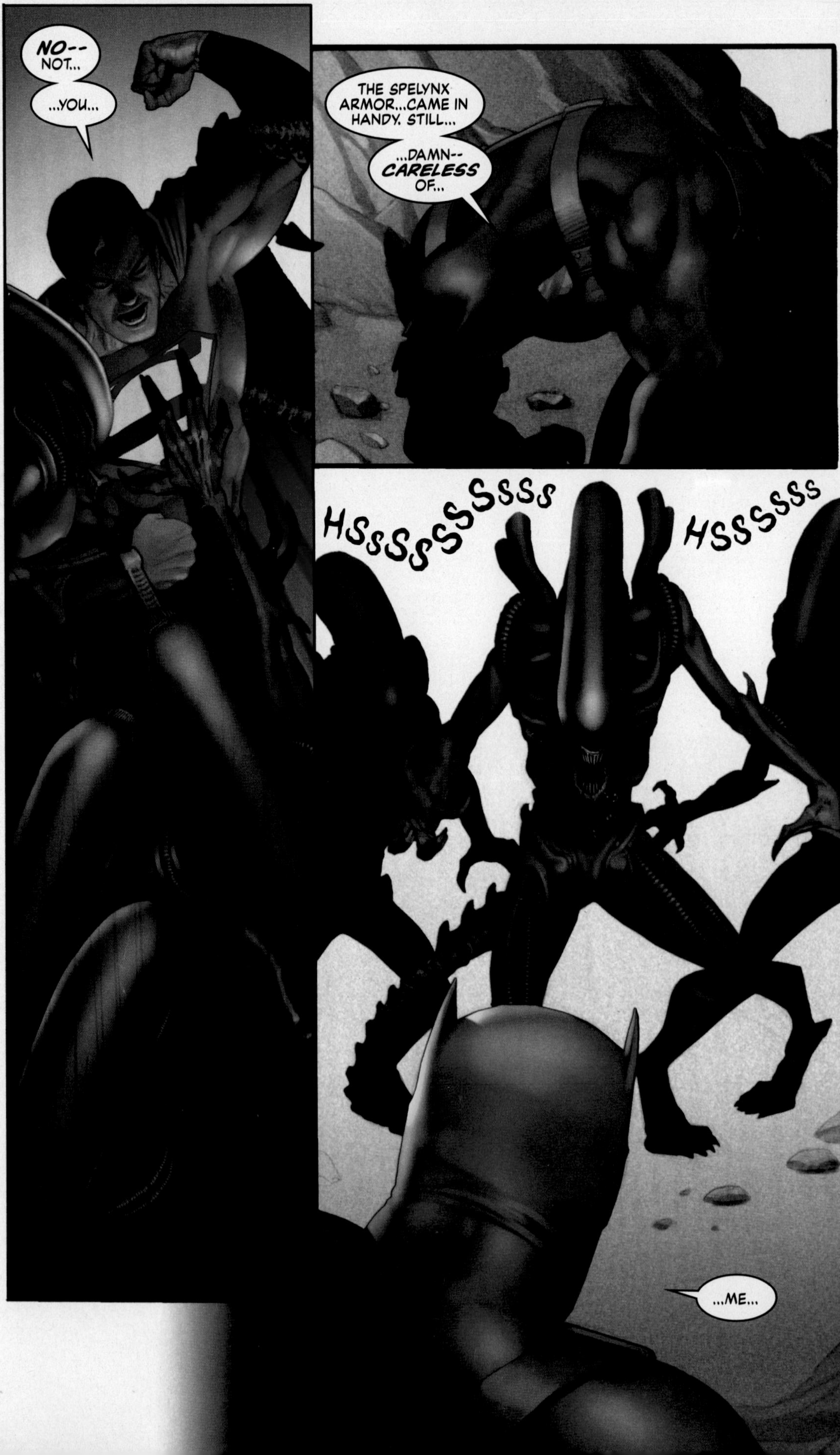
NO--
NOT...
...YOU...
THE SPELYNX ARMOR...CAME IN HANDY. STILL...
...DAMN-- CARELESS OF...
HSSSSSSSSSS
HSSSSSS
...ME...

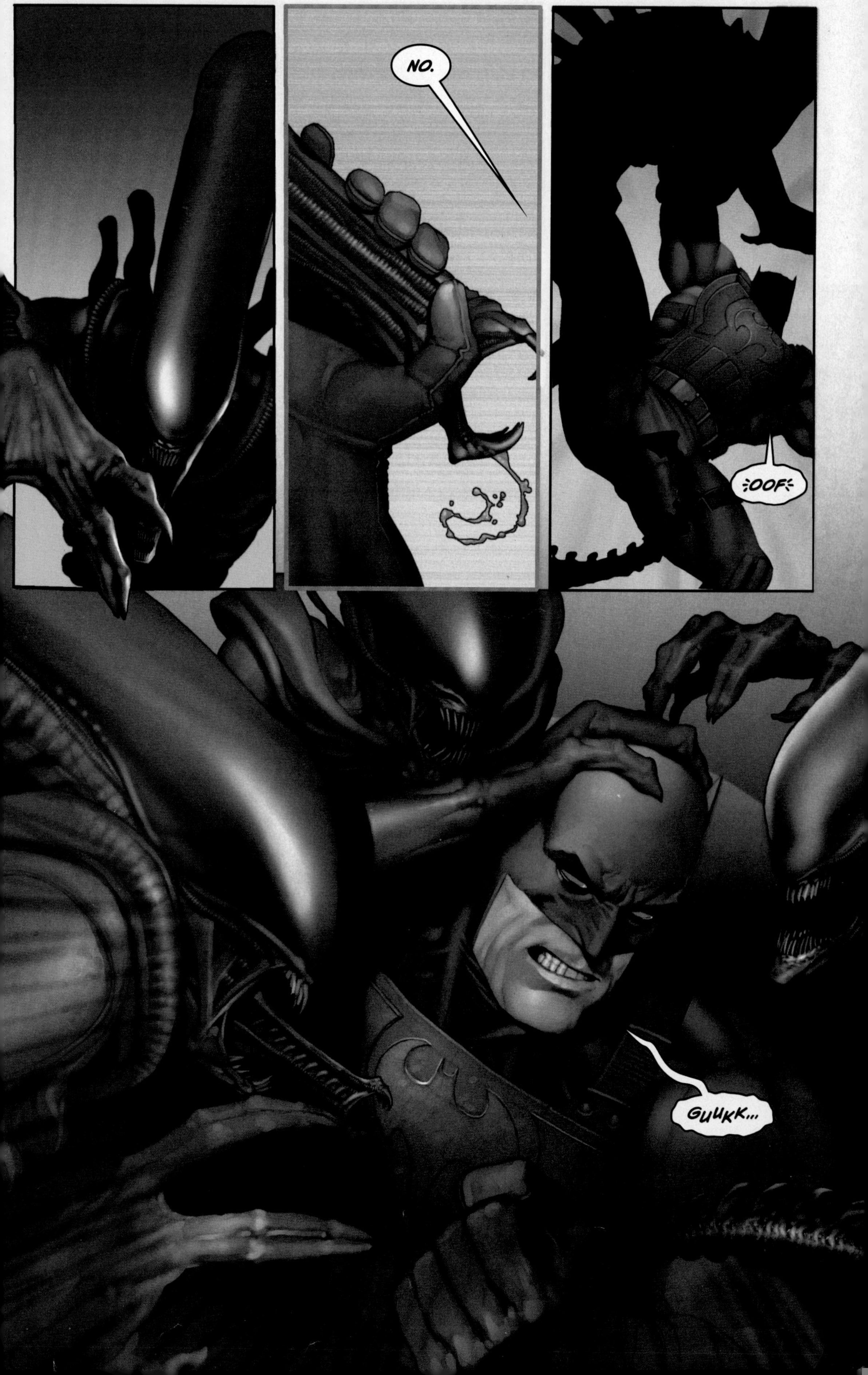
NO.
OOF
GUUKK...

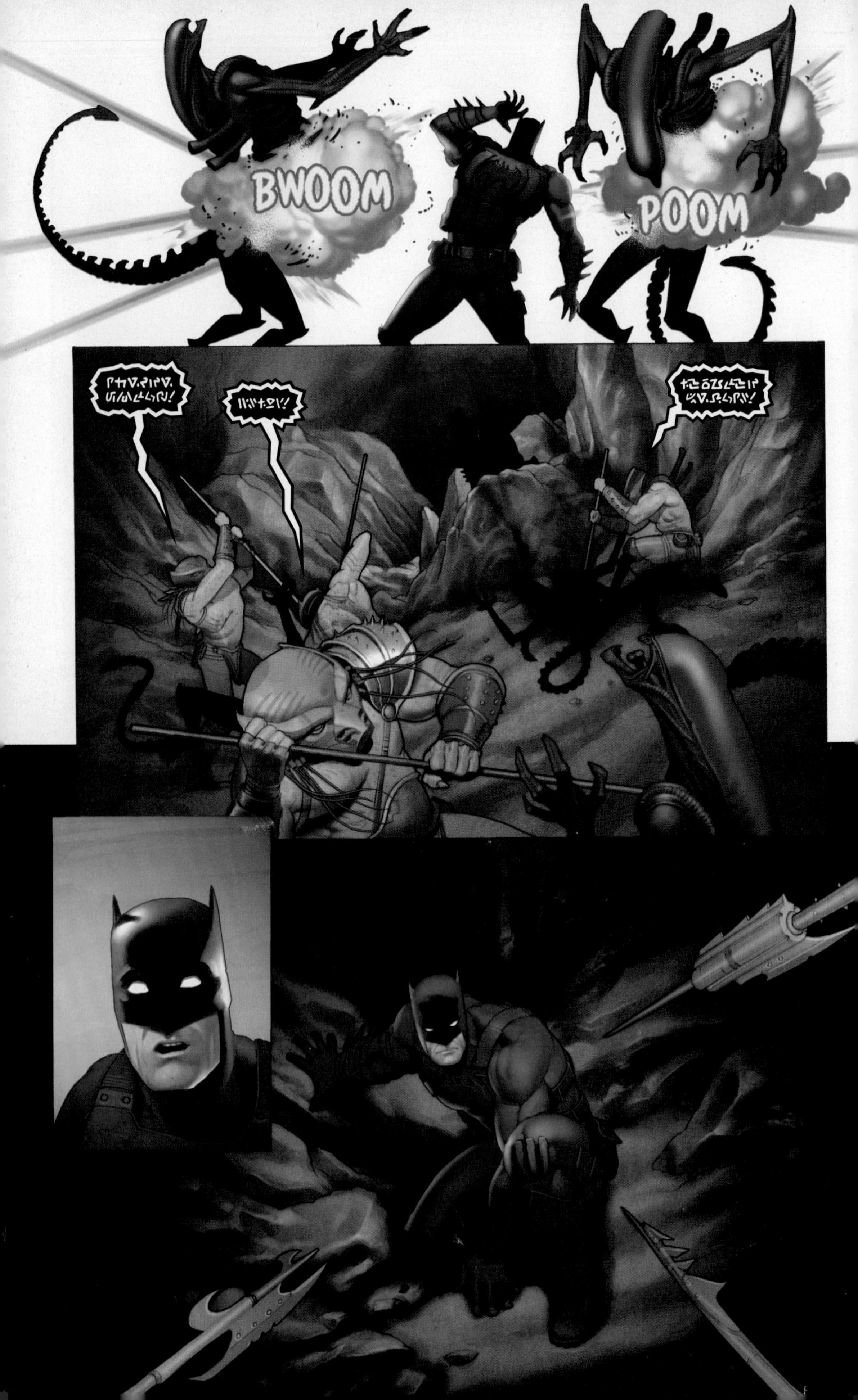
BWOOM
POOM

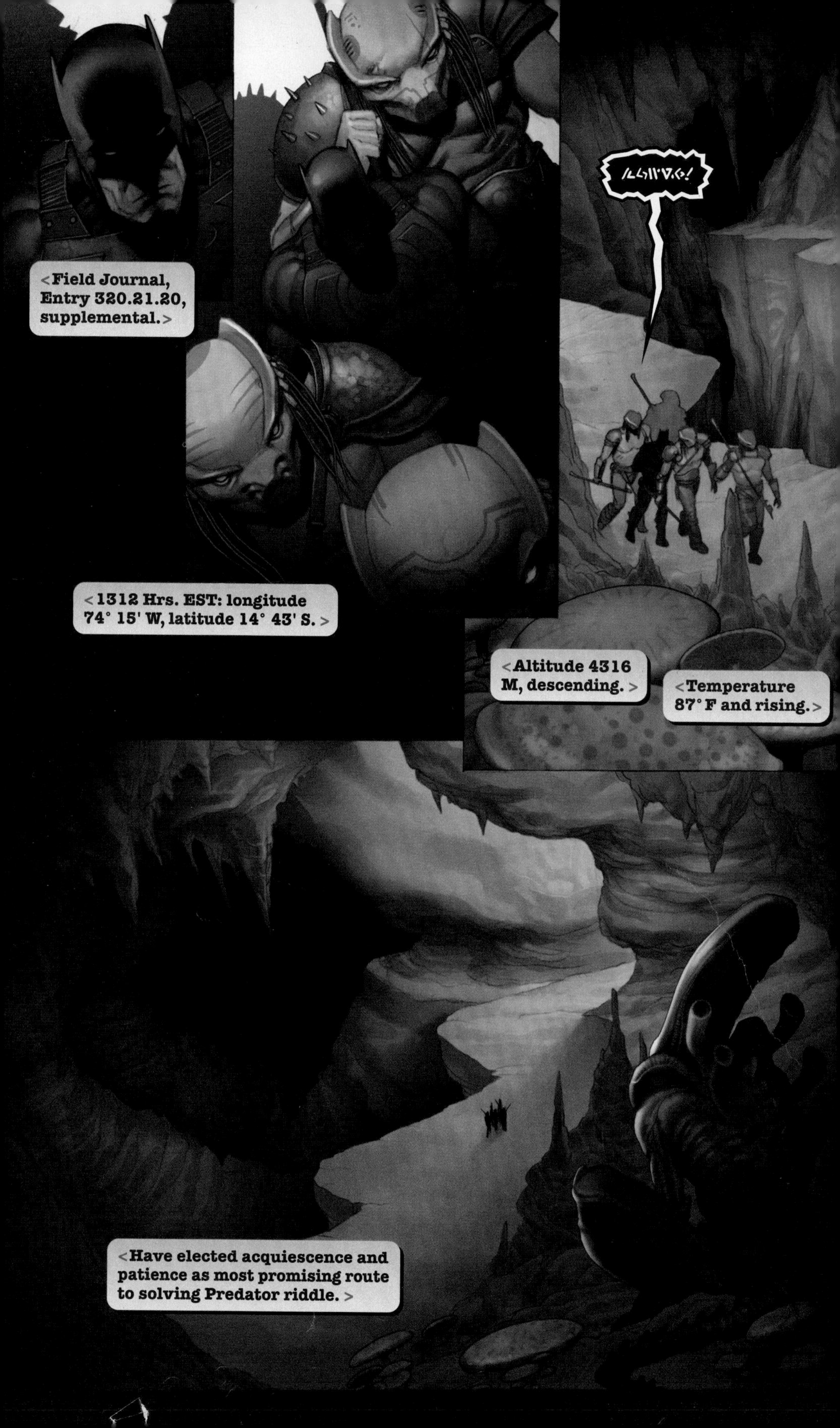
<Field Journal, Entry 320.21.20, supplemental.>
<1312 Hrs. EST: longitude 74° 15' W, latitude 14° 43' S.>
<Altitude 4316 M, descending.>
<Temperature 87° F and rising.>
<Have elected acquiescence and patience as most promising route to solving Predator riddle.>

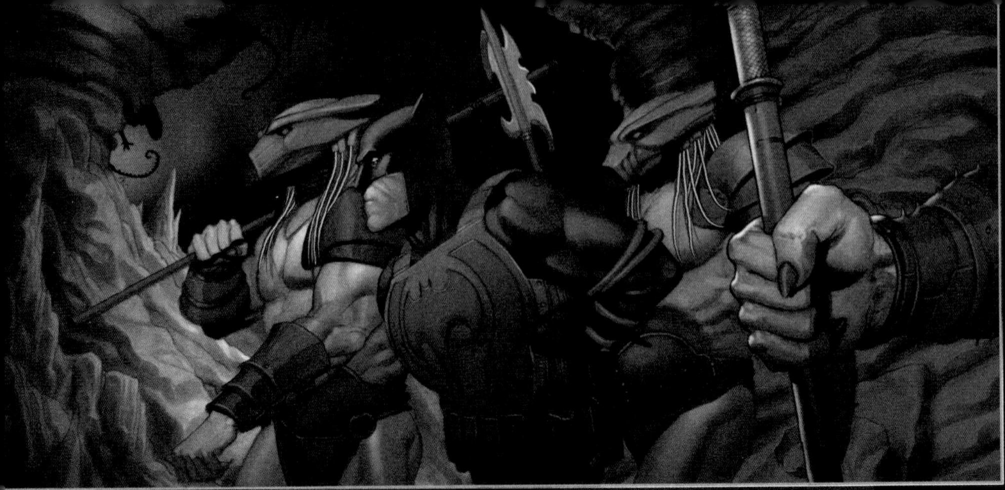

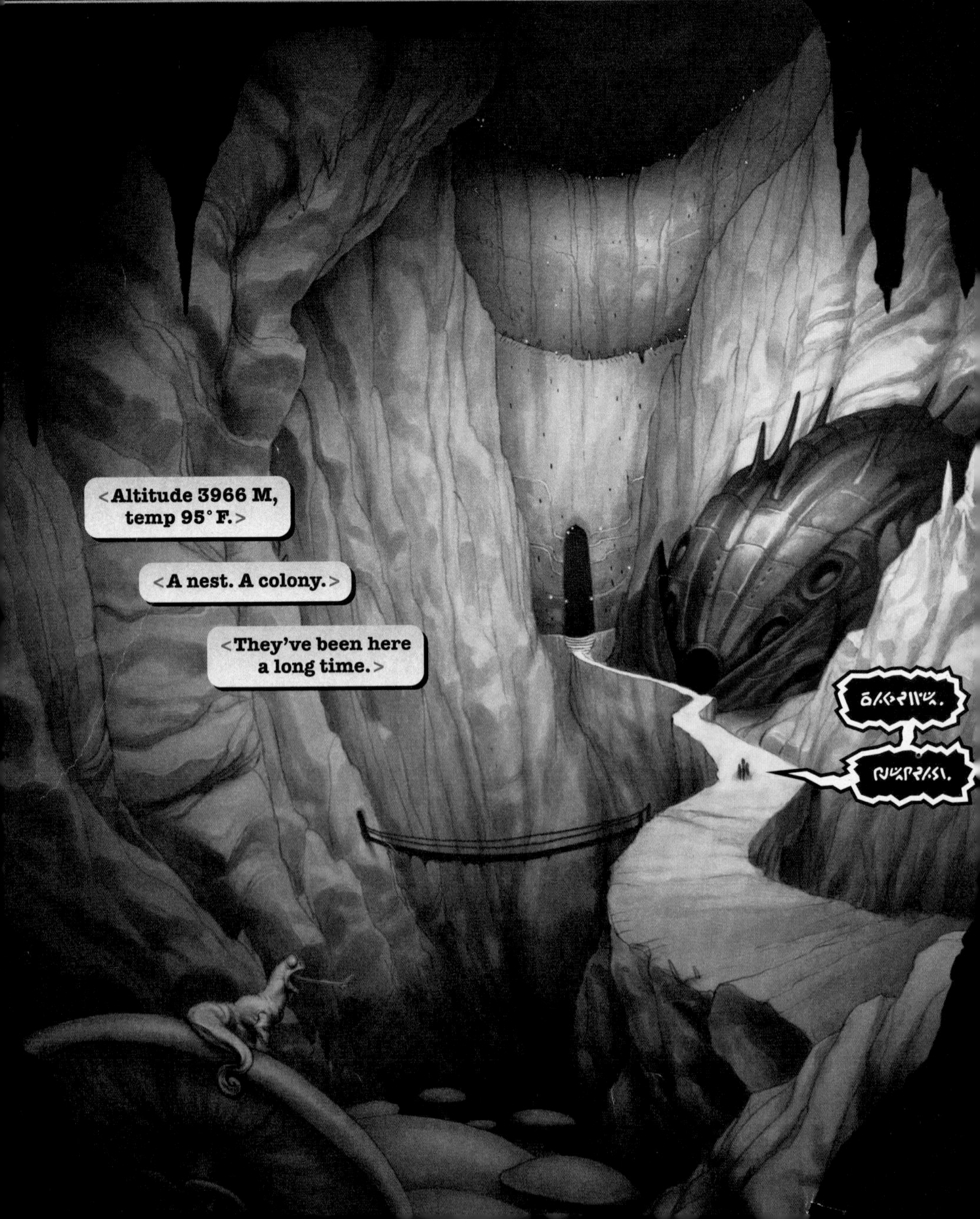
<Altitude 3966 M, temp 95° F.>
<A nest. A colony.>
<They've been here a long time.>

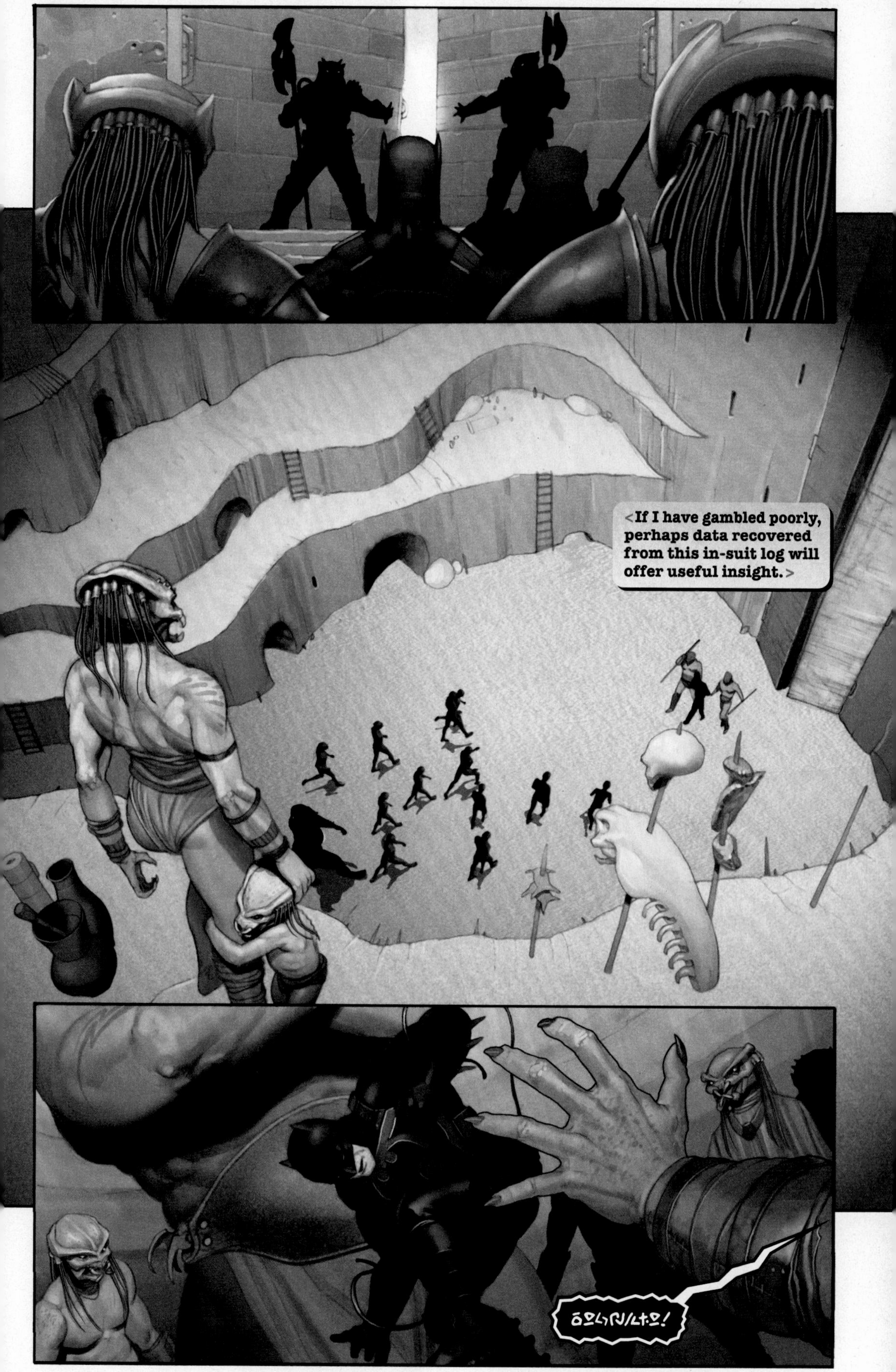
<If I have gambled poorly, perhaps data recovered from this in-suit log will offer useful insight.>

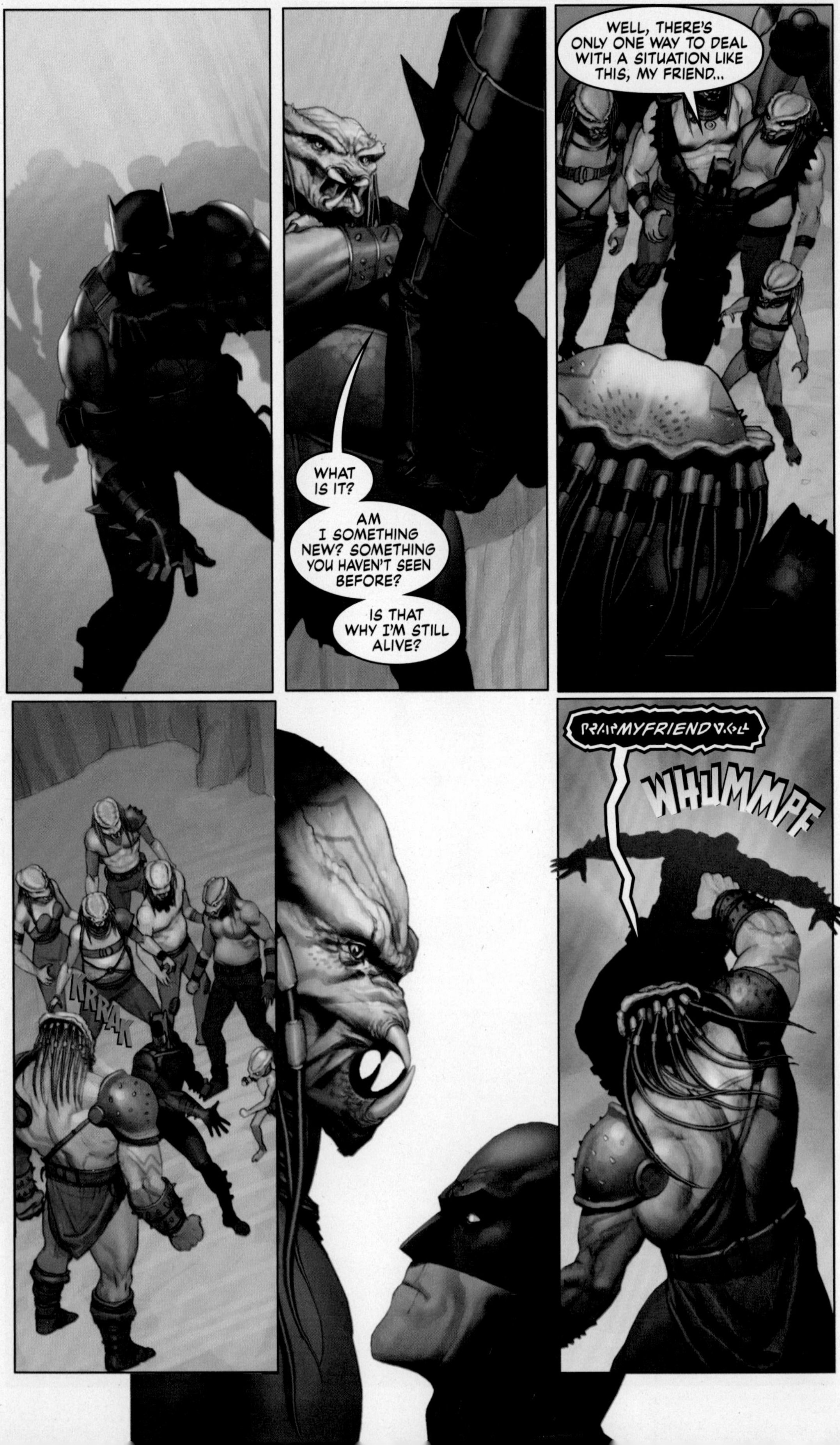
WHAT IS IT?
AM I SOMETHING NEW? SOMETHING YOU HAVEN'T SEEN BEFORE?
IS THAT WHY I'M STILL ALIVE?
WELL, THERE'S ONLY ONE WAY TO DEAL WITH A SITUATION LIKE THIS, MY FRIEND...
KRRAK
MYFRIEND
WHUMMPF

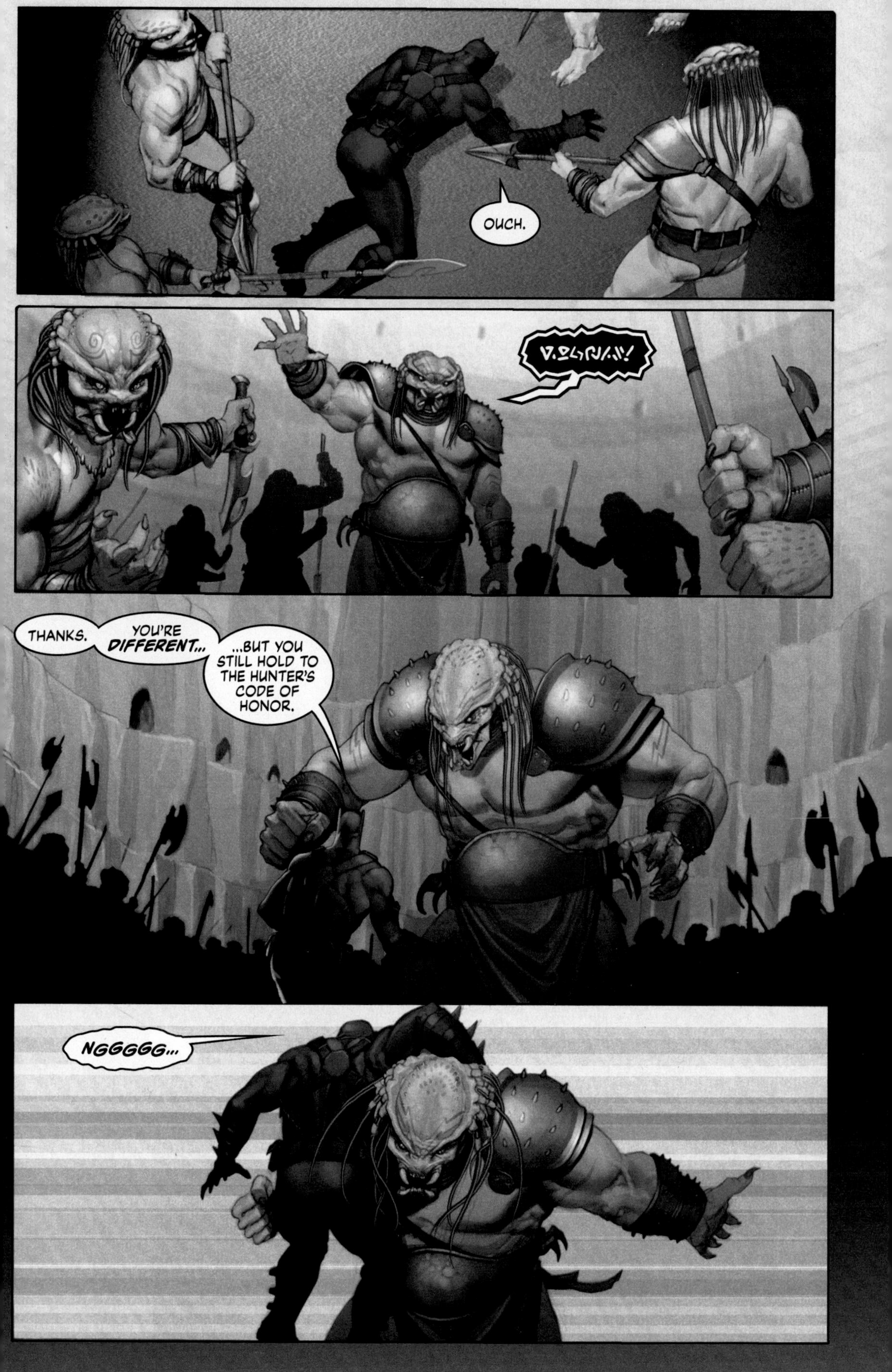
OUCH.
THANKS.
YOU'RE DIFFERENT...
...BUT YOU STILL HOLD TO THE HUNTER'S CODE OF HONOR.
NGGGGG...

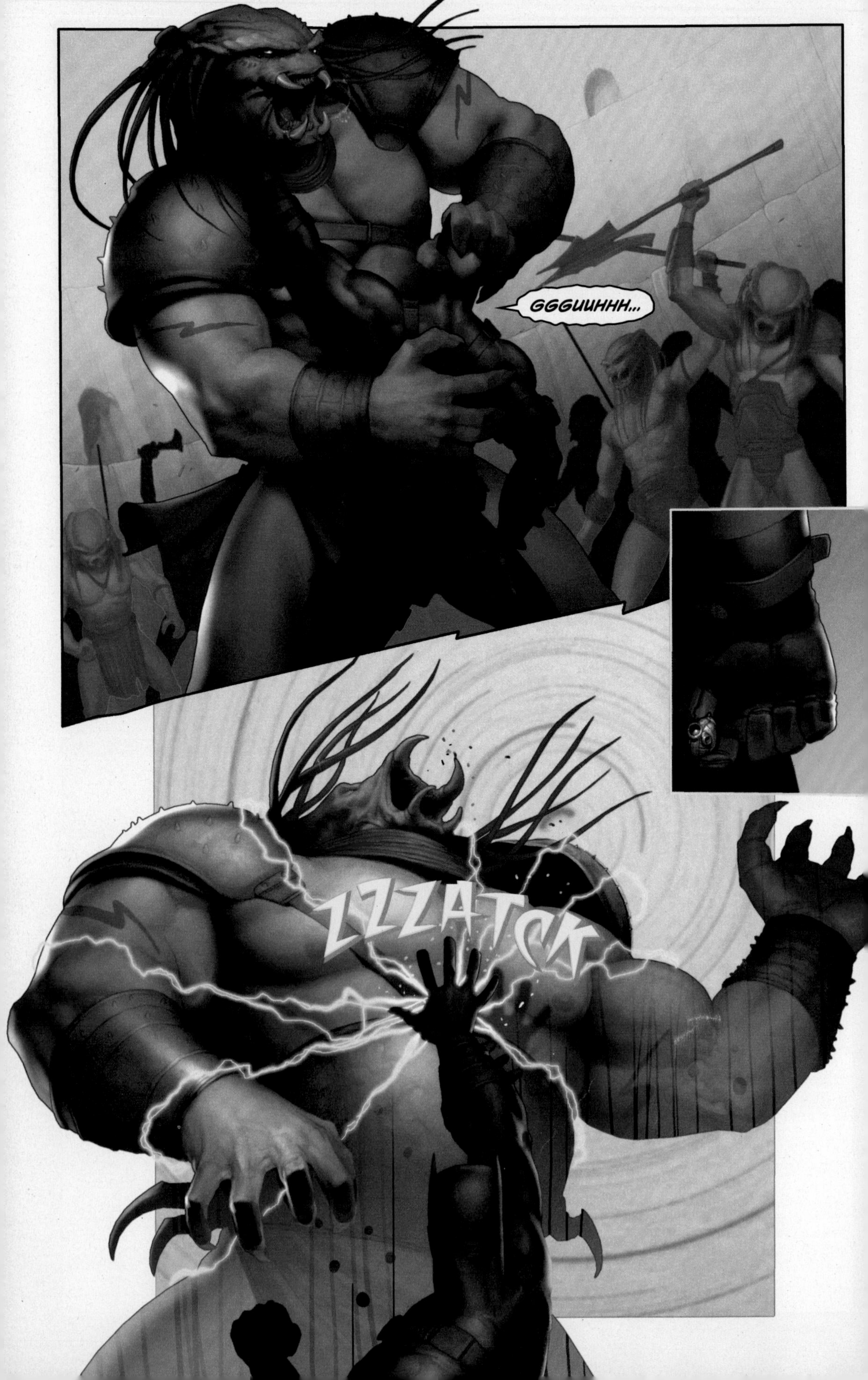
GGGUUHHH...
ZZZATCK

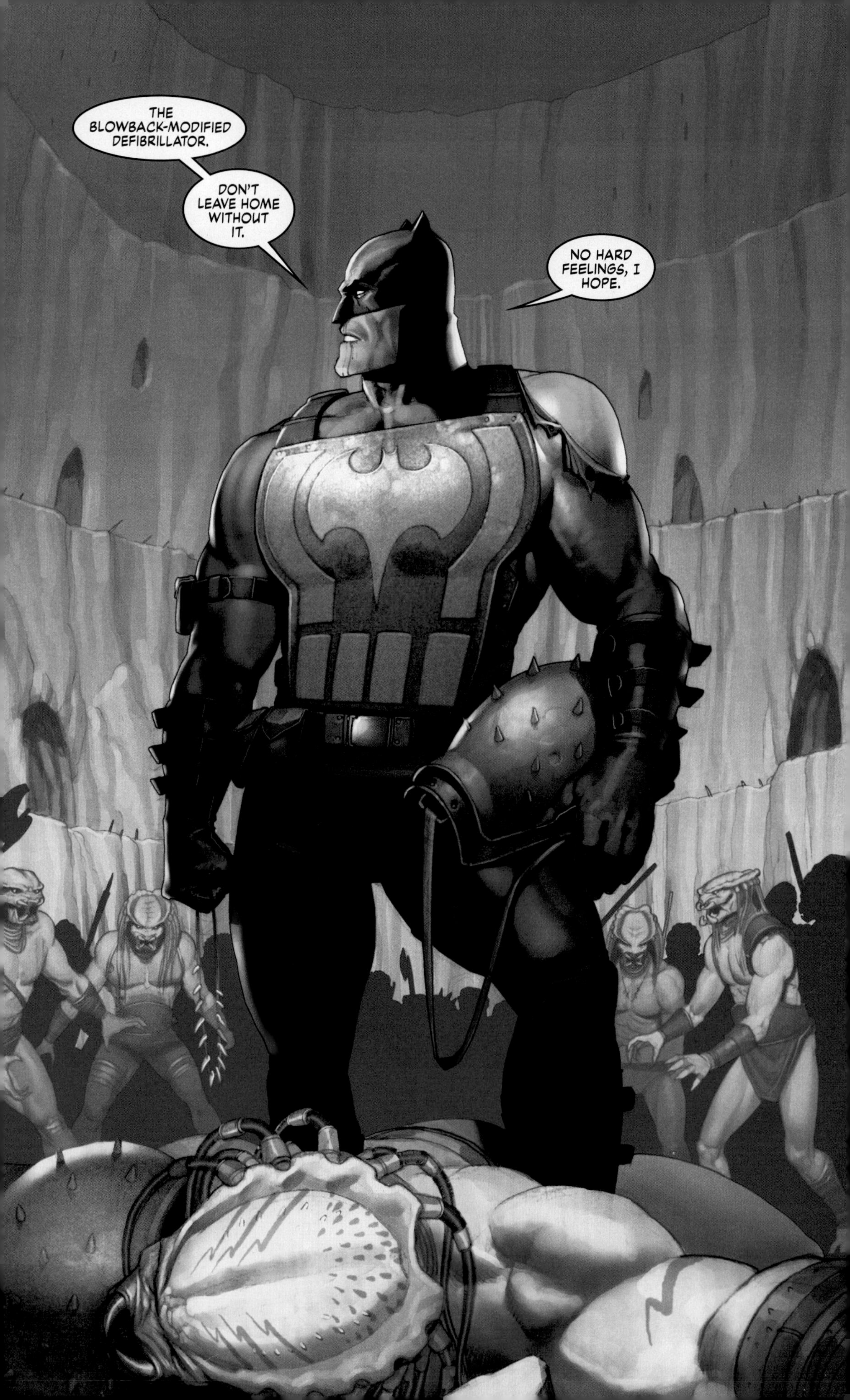
THE BLOWBACK-MODIFIED DEFIBRILLATOR.
DON'T LEAVE HOME WITHOUT IT.
NO HARD FEELINGS, I HOPE.

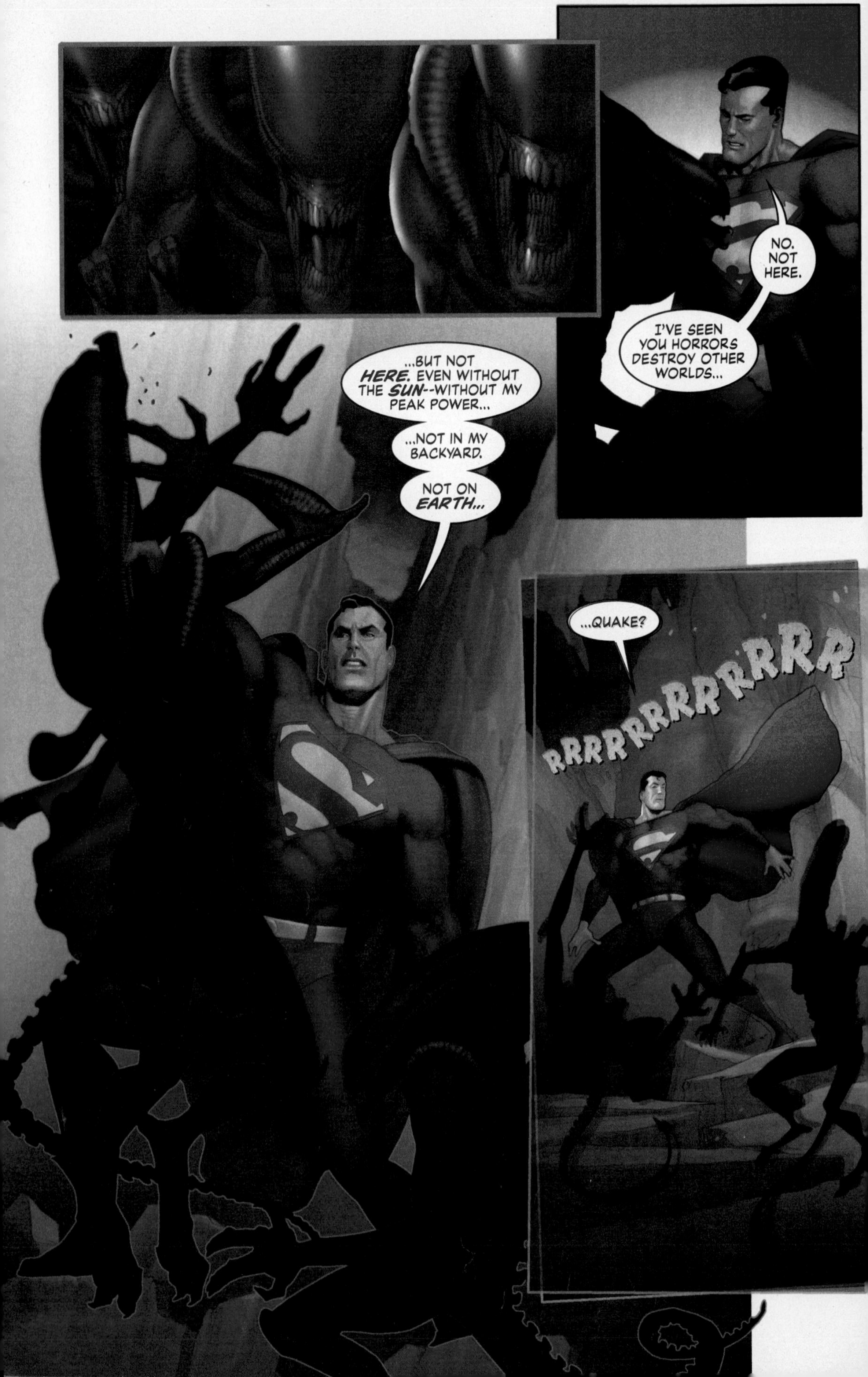
NO. NOT HERE.
I'VE SEEN YOU HORRORS DESTROY OTHER WORLDS...
...BUT NOT HERE. EVEN WITHOUT THE SUN--WITHOUT MY PEAK POWER...
...NOT IN MY BACKYARD.
NOT ON EARTH...
...QUAKE?
RRRRRRRRRRRRRR

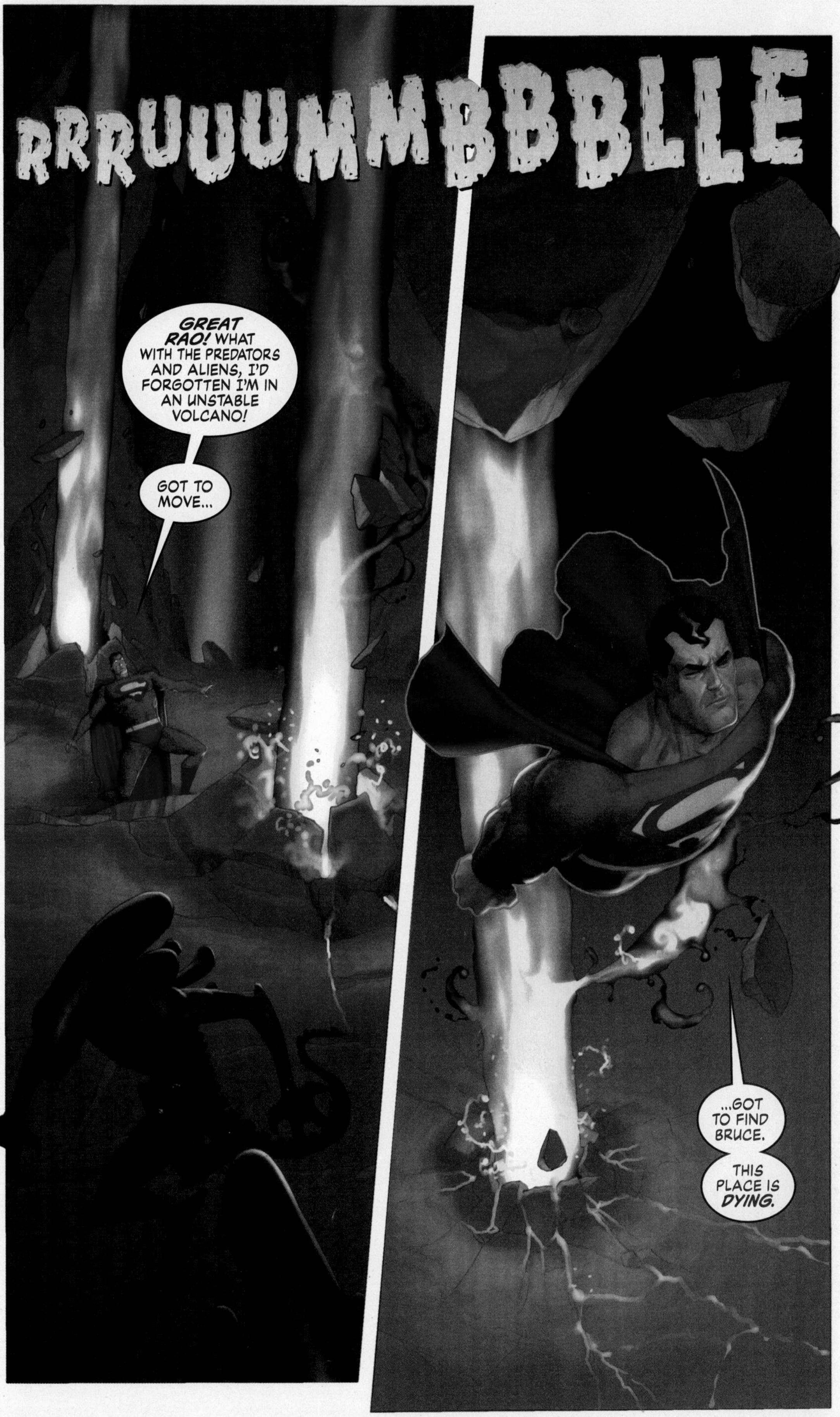
RRRUUUMMBBBLLE
GREAT RAO! WHAT WITH THE PREDATORS AND ALIENS, I'D FORGOTTEN I'M IN AN UNSTABLE VOLCANO!
GOT TO MOVE...
...GOT TO FIND BRUCE.
THIS PLACE IS DYING.

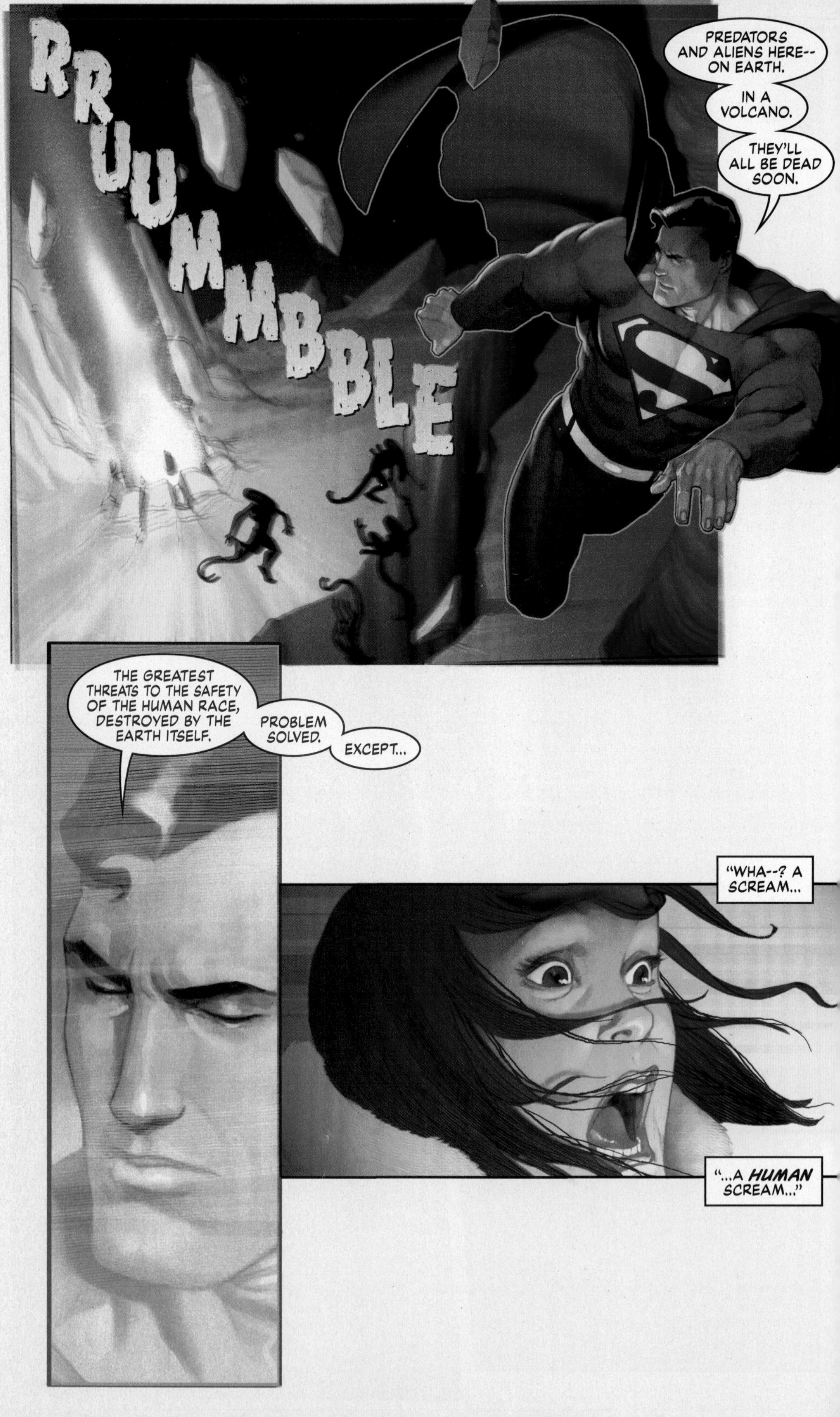
RRUUMMBBLE
PREDATORS AND ALIENS HERE-- ON EARTH.
IN A VOLCANO.
THEY'LL ALL BE DEAD SOON.
THE GREATEST THREATS TO THE SAFETY OF THE HUMAN RACE, DESTROYED BY THE EARTH ITSELF.
PROBLEM SOLVED.
EXCEPT...
"WHA--? A SCREAM...
"...A *HUMAN* SCREAM..."

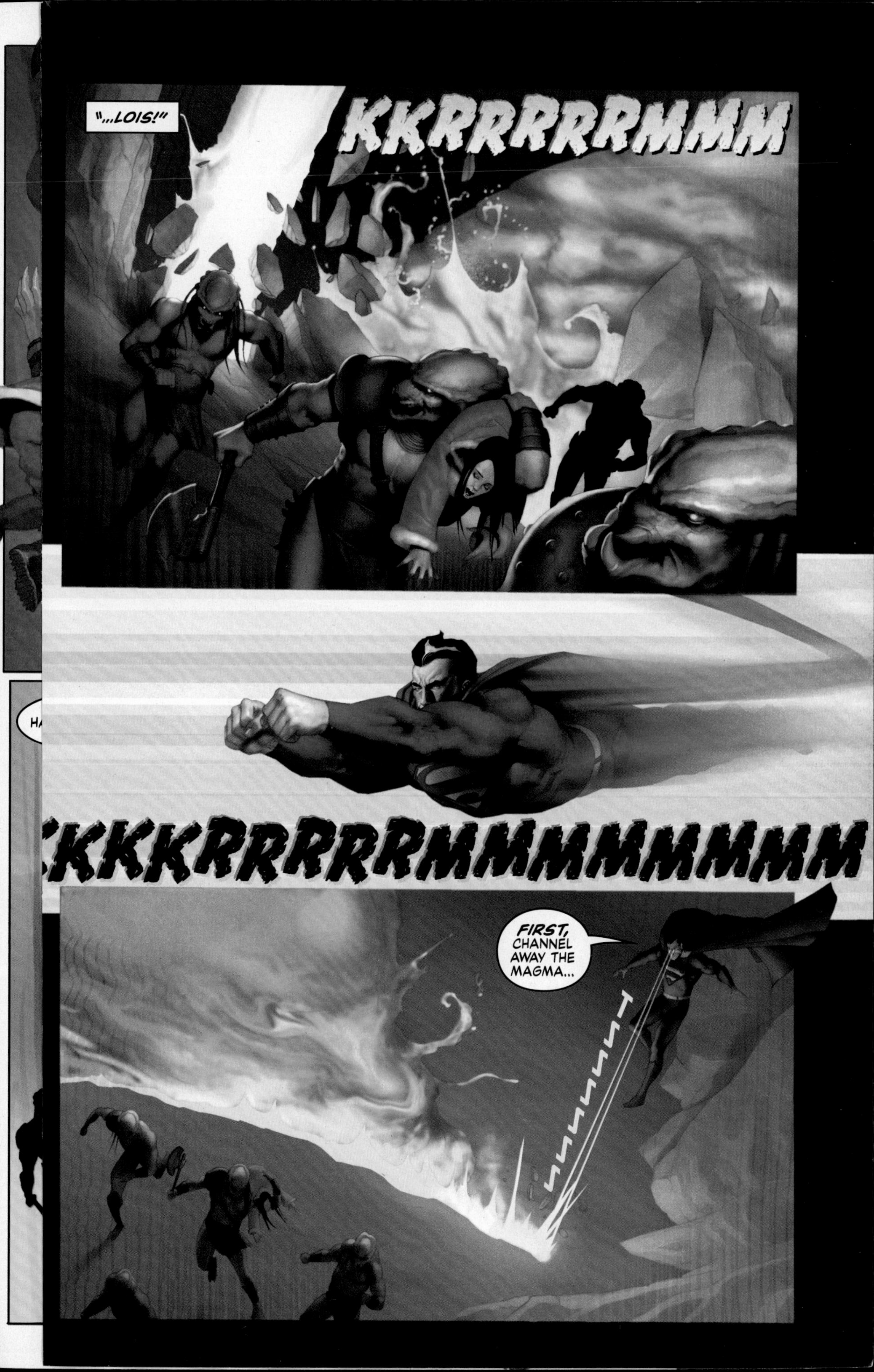
"...LOIS!"
KKRRRRRMMM
KKKRRRRRMMMMMMM
FIRST, CHANNEL AWAY THE MAGMA...

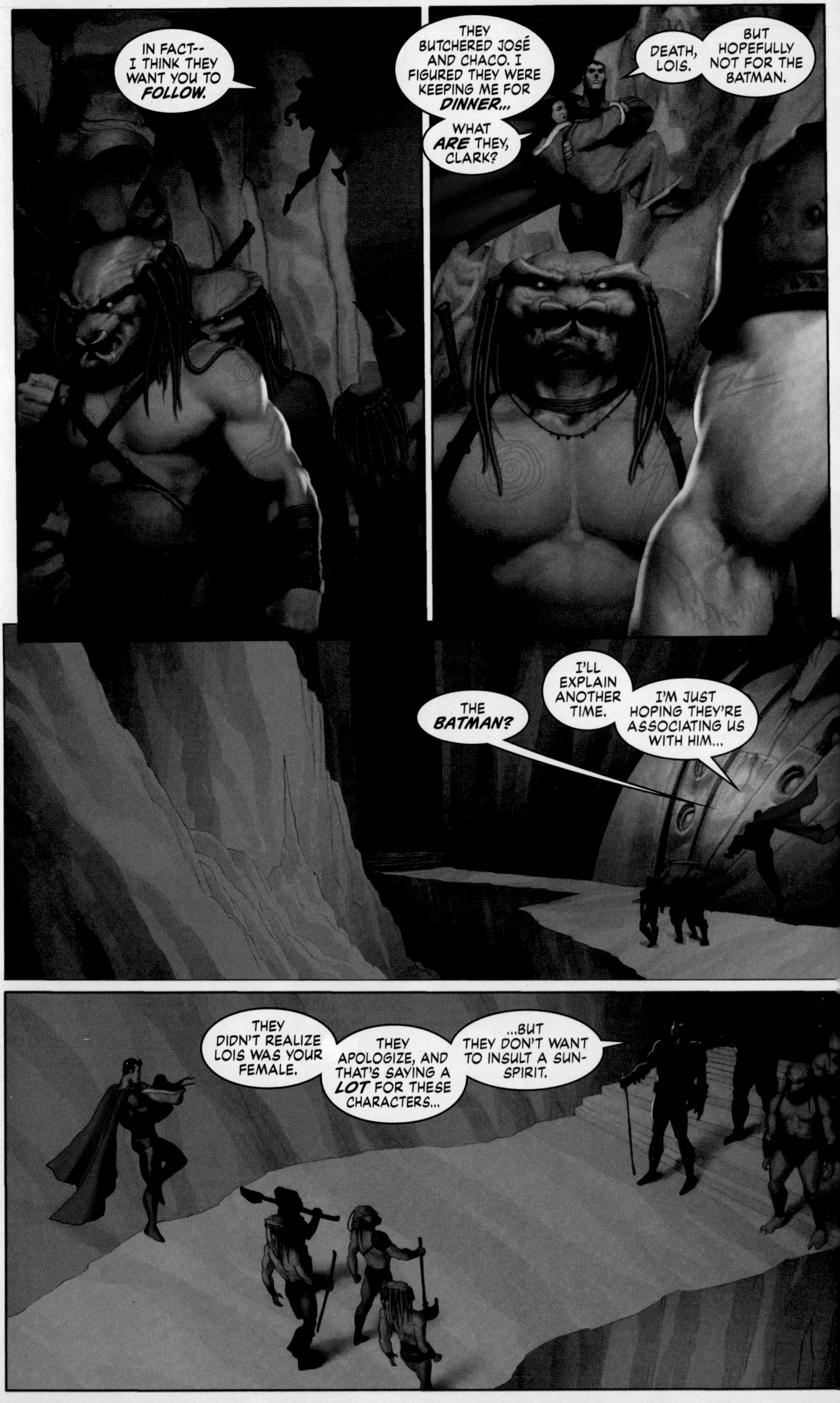
IN FACT-- I THINK THEY WANT YOU TO FOLLOW.
THEY BUTCHERED JOSÉ AND CHACO. I FIGURED THEY WERE KEEPING ME FOR DINNER...
WHAT ARE THEY, CLARK?
DEATH, LOIS.
BUT HOPEFULLY NOT FOR THE BATMAN.
THE BATMAN?
I'LL EXPLAIN ANOTHER TIME.
I'M JUST HOPING THEY'RE ASSOCIATING US WITH HIM...
THEY DIDN'T REALIZE LOIS WAS YOUR FEMALE.
THEY APOLOGIZE, AND THAT'S SAYING A LOT FOR THESE CHARACTERS...
...BUT THEY DON'T WANT TO INSULT A SUN-SPIRIT.

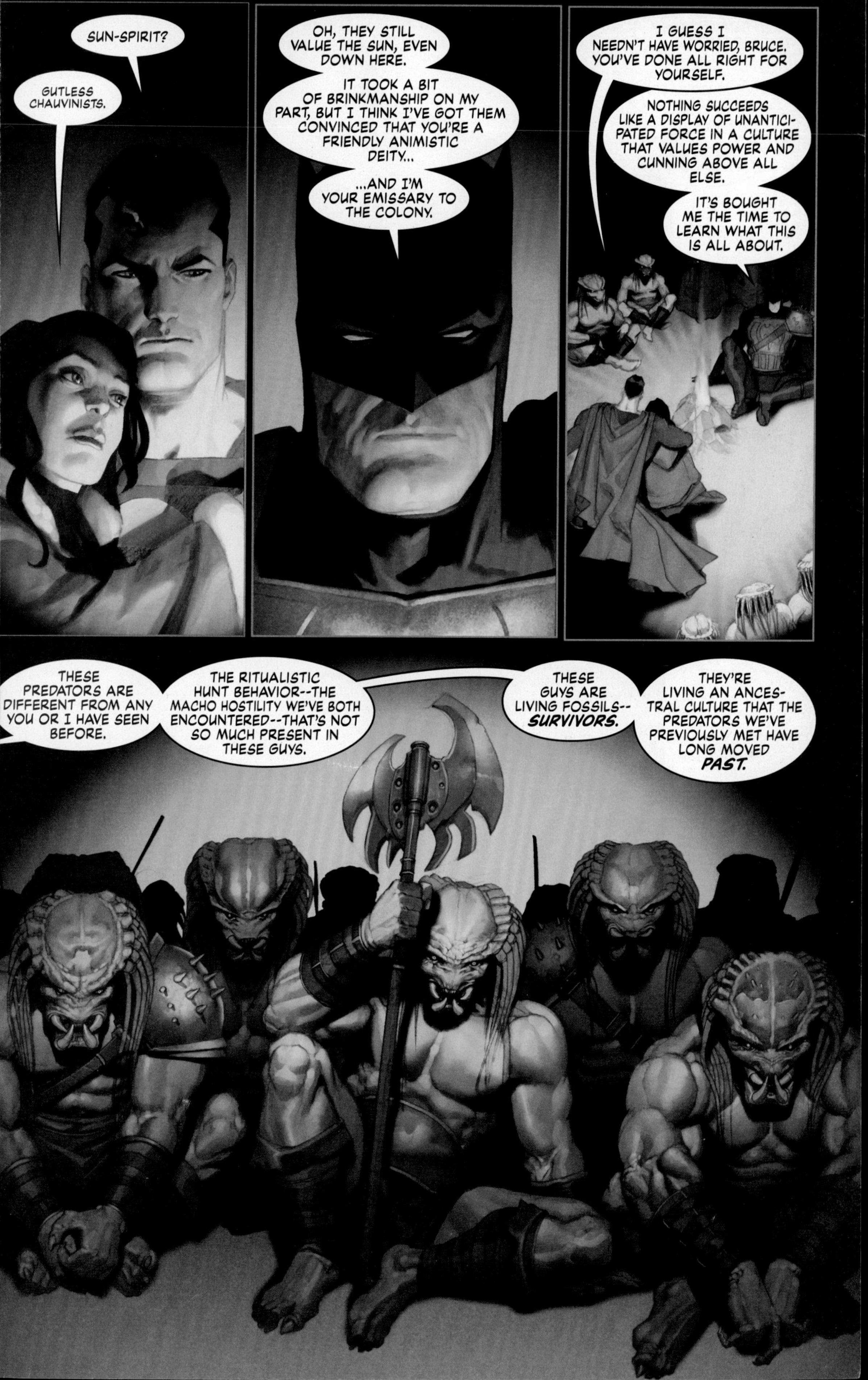
SUN-SPIRIT?
GUTLESS CHAUVINISTS.
OH, THEY STILL VALUE THE SUN, EVEN DOWN HERE.
IT TOOK A BIT OF BRINKMANSHIP ON MY PART, BUT I THINK I'VE GOT THEM CONVINCED THAT YOU'RE A FRIENDLY ANIMISTIC DEITY...
...AND I'M YOUR EMISSARY TO THE COLONY.
I GUESS I NEEDN'T HAVE WORRIED, BRUCE. YOU'VE DONE ALL RIGHT FOR YOURSELF.
NOTHING SUCCEEDS LIKE A DISPLAY OF UNANTICIPATED FORCE IN A CULTURE THAT VALUES POWER AND CUNNING ABOVE ALL ELSE.
IT'S BOUGHT ME THE TIME TO LEARN WHAT THIS IS ALL ABOUT.
THESE PREDATORS ARE DIFFERENT FROM ANY YOU OR I HAVE SEEN BEFORE.
THE RITUALISTIC HUNT BEHAVIOR--THE MACHO HOSTILITY WE'VE BOTH ENCOUNTERED--THAT'S NOT SO MUCH PRESENT IN THESE GUYS.
THESE GUYS ARE LIVING FOSSILS-- *SURVIVORS.*
THEY'RE LIVING AN ANCESTRAL CULTURE THAT THE PREDATORS WE'VE PREVIOUSLY MET HAVE LONG MOVED *PAST.*

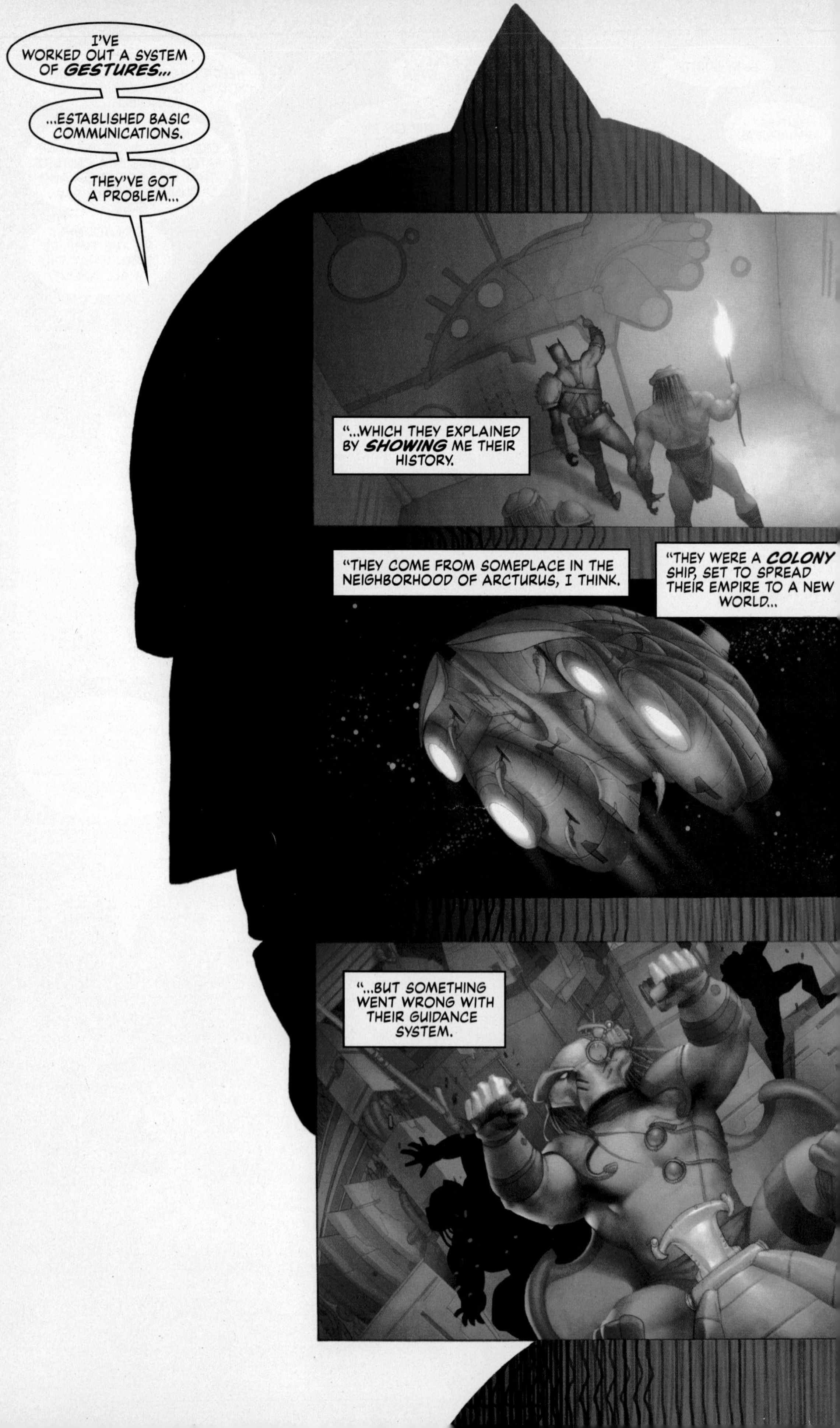
I'VE WORKED OUT A SYSTEM OF GESTURES...
...ESTABLISHED BASIC COMMUNICATIONS.
THEY'VE GOT A PROBLEM...
"...WHICH THEY EXPLAINED BY SHOWING ME THEIR HISTORY.
"THEY COME FROM SOMEPLACE IN THE NEIGHBORHOOD OF ARCTURUS, I THINK.
"THEY WERE A COLONY SHIP, SET TO SPREAD THEIR EMPIRE TO A NEW WORLD...
"...BUT SOMETHING WENT WRONG WITH THEIR GUIDANCE SYSTEM.

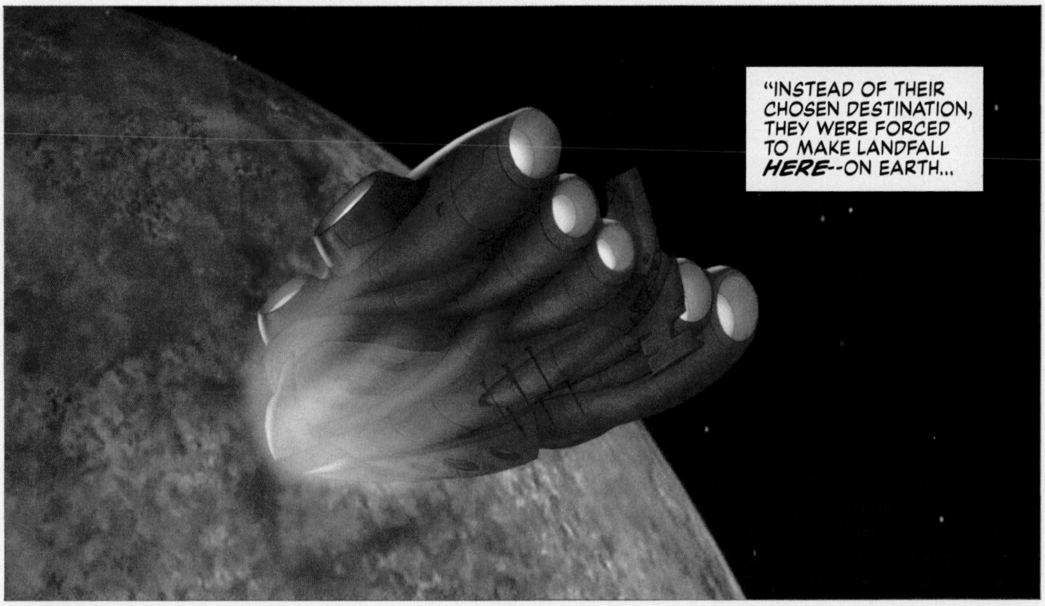
"INSTEAD OF THEIR CHOSEN DESTINATION, THEY WERE FORCED TO MAKE LANDFALL *HERE*--ON EARTH...

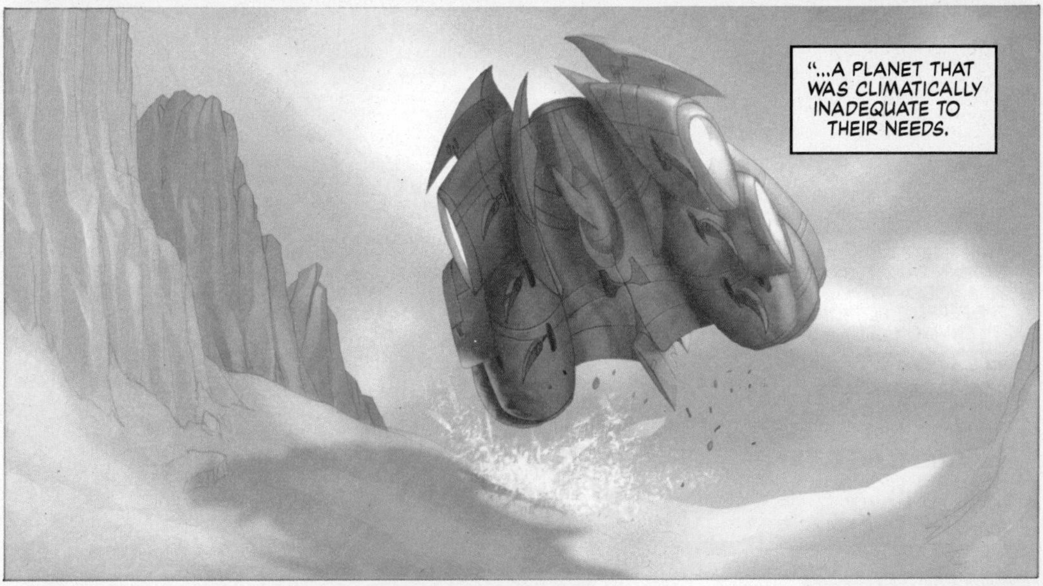
"...A PLANET THAT WAS CLIMATICALLY INADEQUATE TO THEIR NEEDS.

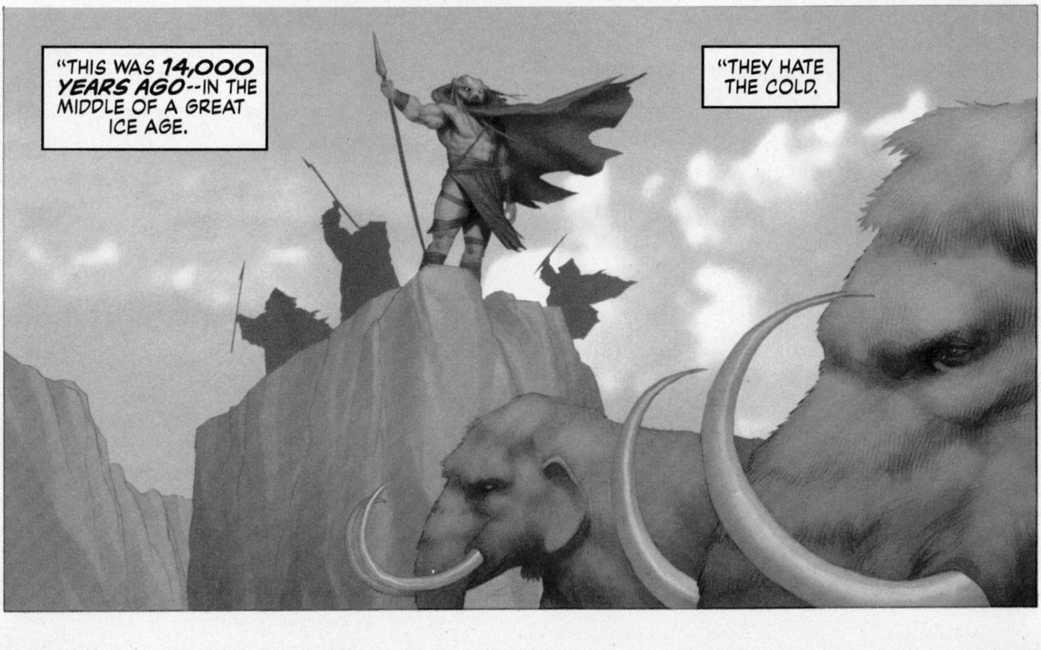
"THIS WAS **14,000 YEARS AGO**--IN THE MIDDLE OF A GREAT ICE AGE.
"THEY HATE THE COLD.

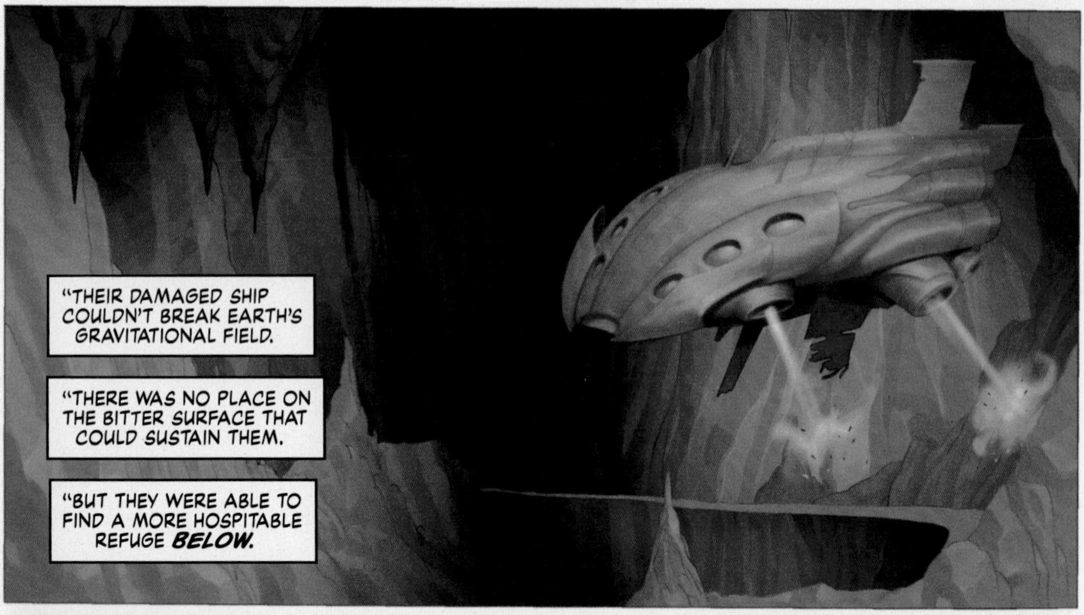
"THEIR DAMAGED SHIP COULDN'T BREAK EARTH'S GRAVITATIONAL FIELD.
"THERE WAS NO PLACE ON THE BITTER SURFACE THAT COULD SUSTAIN THEM.
"BUT THEY WERE ABLE TO FIND A MORE HOSPITABLE REFUGE BELOW.

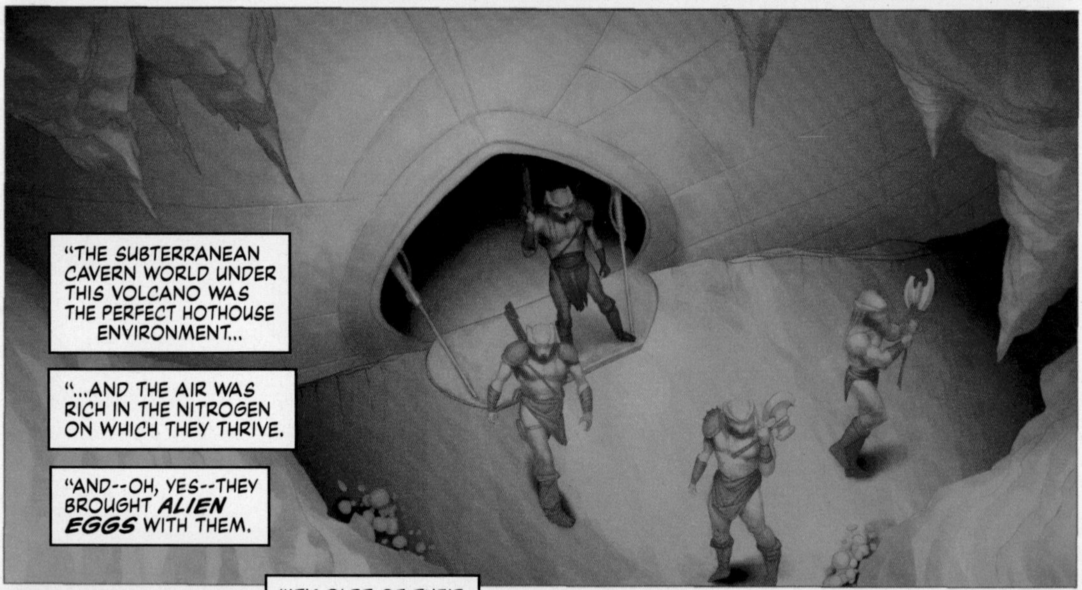
"THE SUBTERRANEAN CAVERN WORLD UNDER THIS VOLCANO WAS THE PERFECT HOTHOUSE ENVIRONMENT...
"...AND THE AIR WAS RICH IN THE NITROGEN ON WHICH THEY THRIVE.
"AND--OH, YES--THEY BROUGHT ALIEN EGGS WITH THEM.

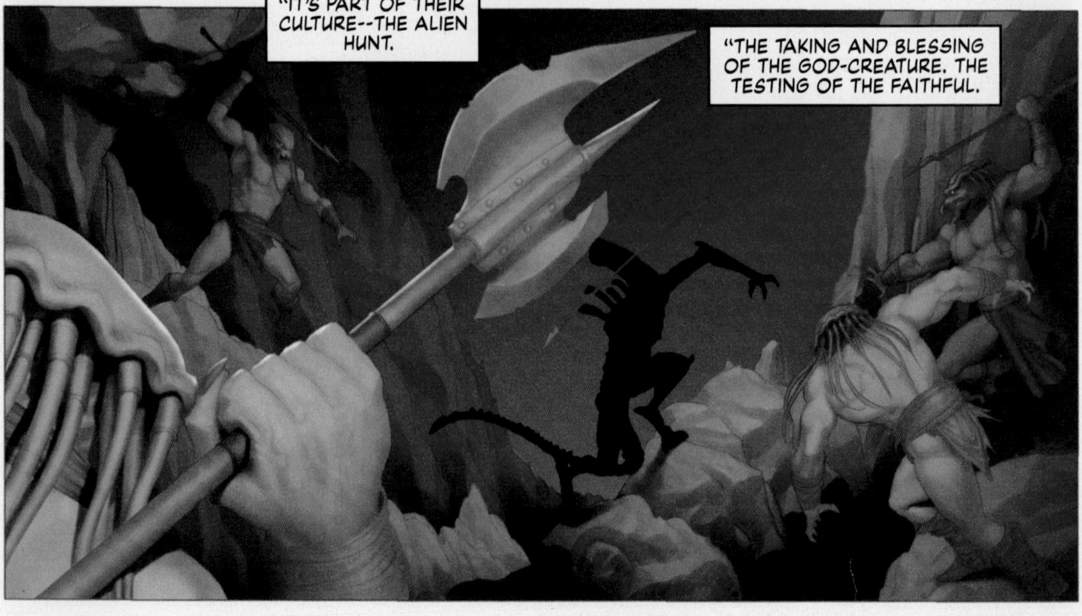
"IT'S PART OF THEIR CULTURE--THE ALIEN HUNT.
"THE TAKING AND BLESSING OF THE GOD-CREATURE. THE TESTING OF THE FAITHFUL.

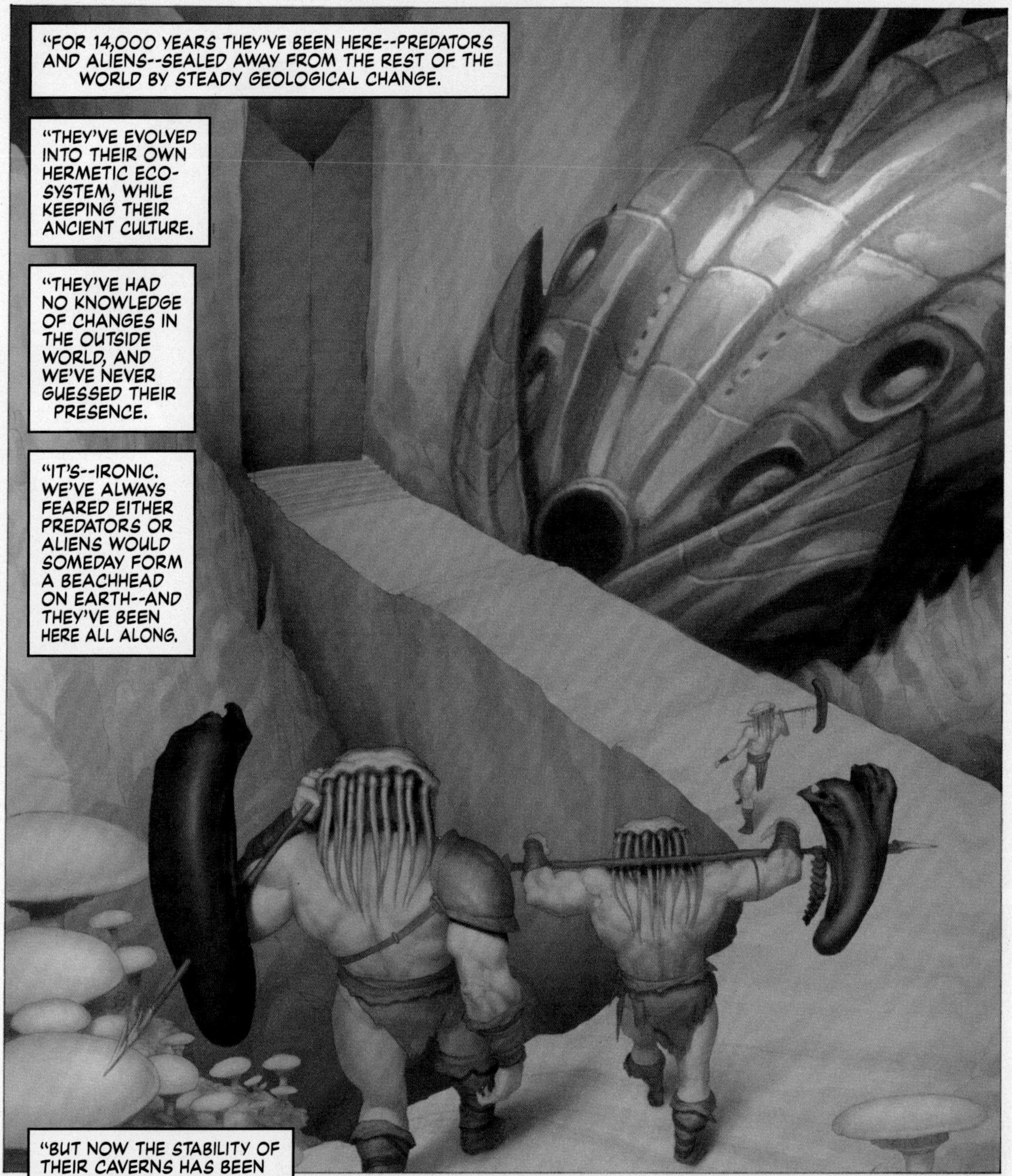

"FOR 14,000 YEARS THEY'VE BEEN HERE--PREDATORS AND ALIENS--SEALED AWAY FROM THE REST OF THE WORLD BY STEADY GEOLOGICAL CHANGE.
"THEY'VE EVOLVED INTO THEIR OWN HERMETIC ECO-SYSTEM, WHILE KEEPING THEIR ANCIENT CULTURE.
"THEY'VE HAD NO KNOWLEDGE OF CHANGES IN THE OUTSIDE WORLD, AND WE'VE NEVER GUESSED THEIR PRESENCE.
"IT'S--IRONIC. WE'VE ALWAYS FEARED EITHER PREDATORS OR ALIENS WOULD SOMEDAY FORM A BEACHHEAD ON EARTH--AND THEY'VE BEEN HERE ALL ALONG.

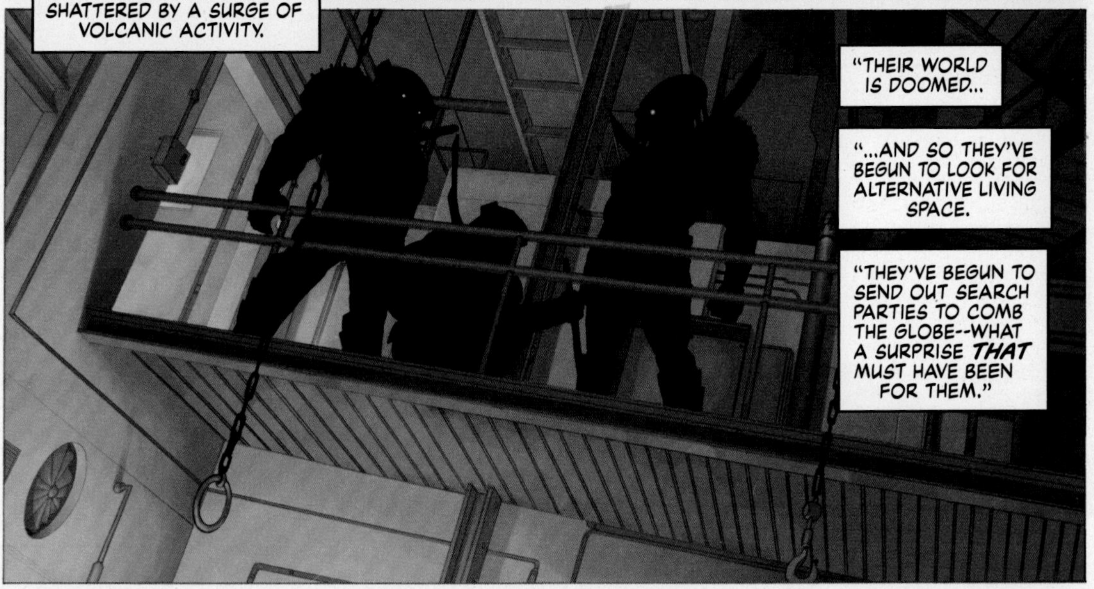

"BUT NOW THE STABILITY OF THEIR CAVERNS HAS BEEN SHATTERED BY A SURGE OF VOLCANIC ACTIVITY.
"THEIR WORLD IS DOOMED...
"...AND SO THEY'VE BEGUN TO LOOK FOR ALTERNATIVE LIVING SPACE.
"THEY'VE BEGUN TO SEND OUT SEARCH PARTIES TO COMB THE GLOBE--WHAT A SURPRISE *THAT* MUST HAVE BEEN FOR THEM."

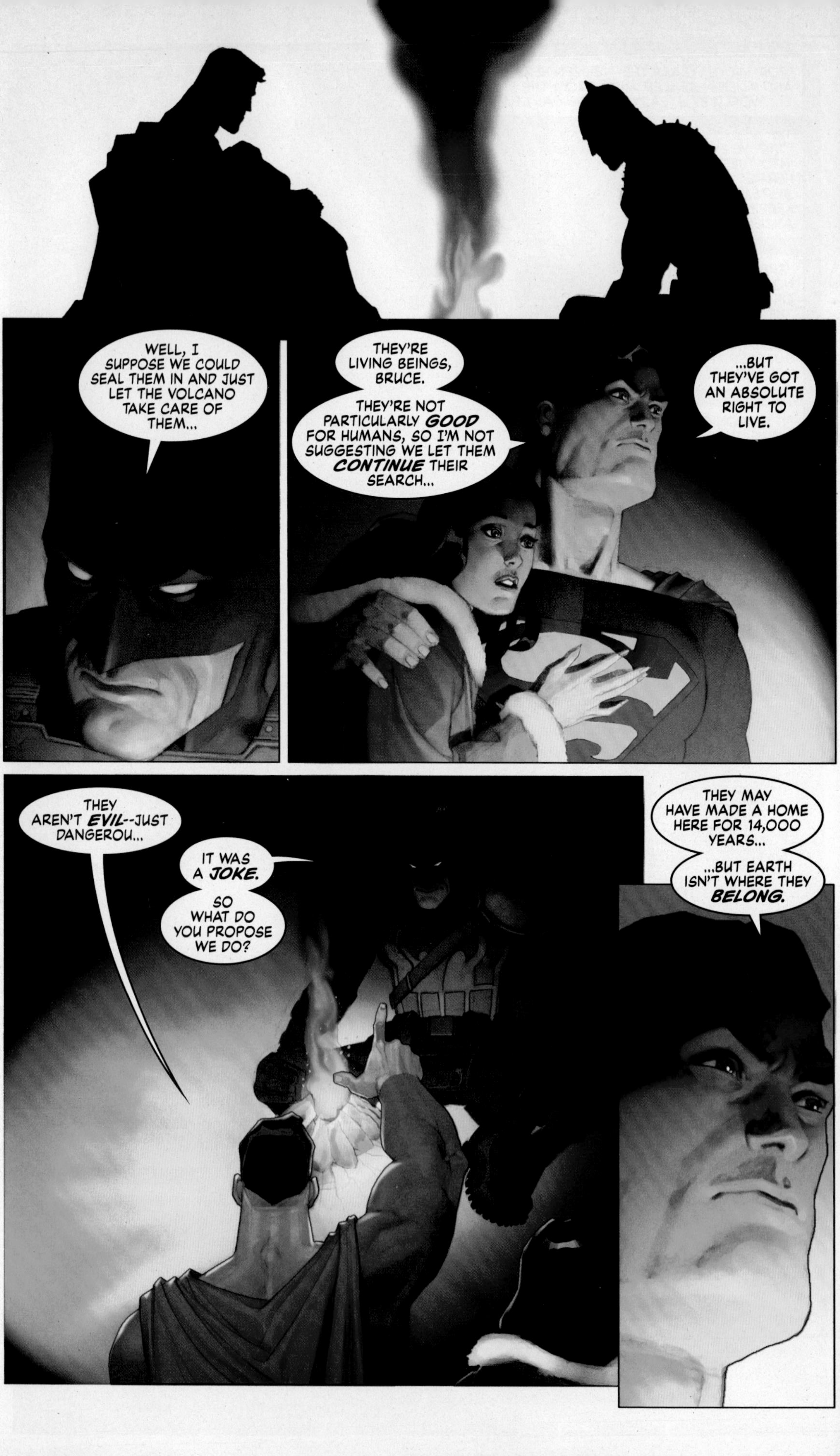
WELL, I SUPPOSE WE COULD SEAL THEM IN AND JUST LET THE VOLCANO TAKE CARE OF THEM...
THEY'RE LIVING BEINGS, BRUCE.
THEY'RE NOT PARTICULARLY GOOD FOR HUMANS, SO I'M NOT SUGGESTING WE LET THEM CONTINUE THEIR SEARCH...
...BUT THEY'VE GOT AN ABSOLUTE RIGHT TO LIVE.
THEY AREN'T EVIL--JUST DANGEROU...
IT WAS A JOKE.
SO WHAT DO YOU PROPOSE WE DO?
THEY MAY HAVE MADE A HOME HERE FOR 14,000 YEARS...
...BUT EARTH ISN'T WHERE THEY BELONG.

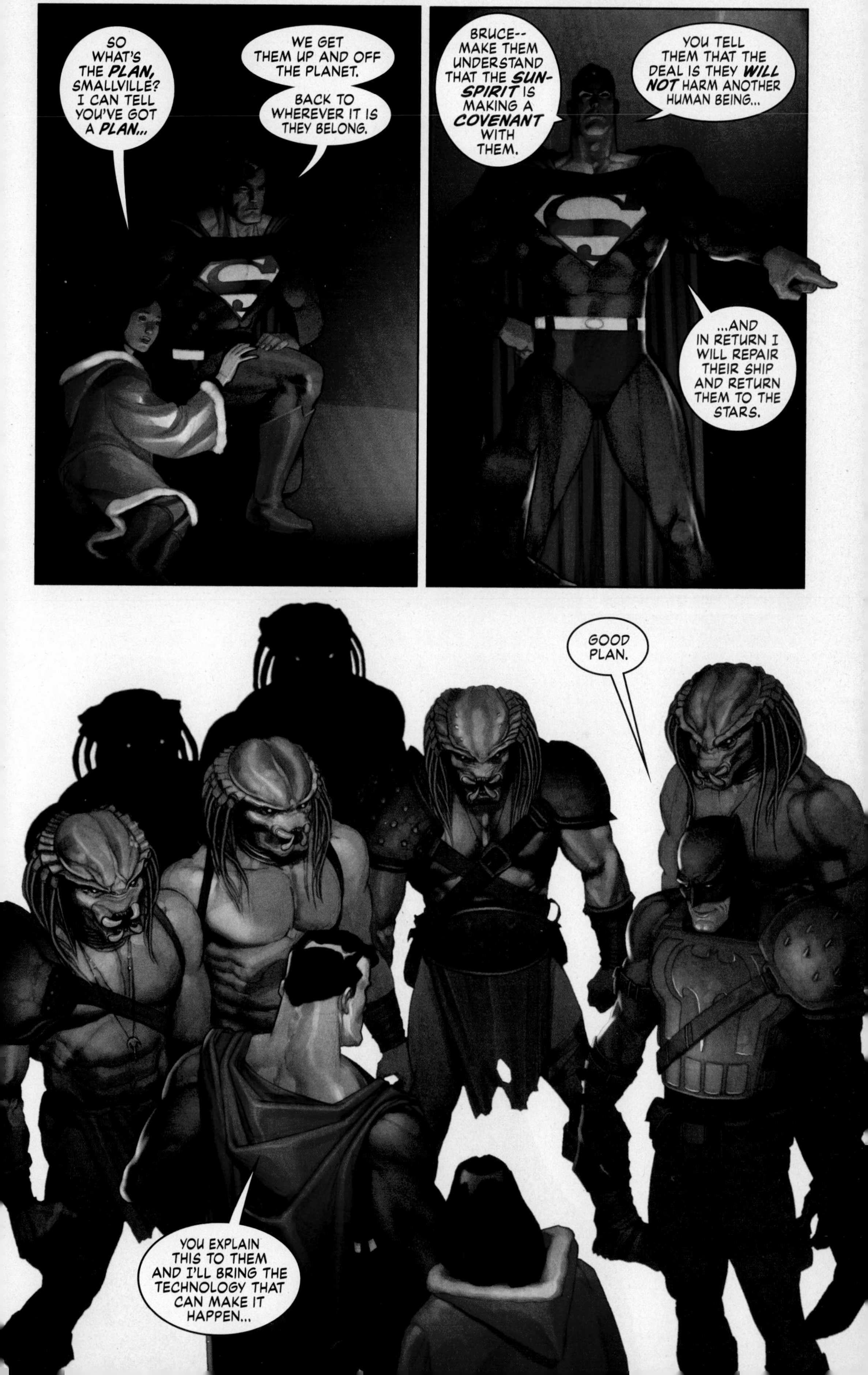
SO WHAT'S THE PLAN, SMALLVILLE? I CAN TELL YOU'VE GOT A PLAN...
WE GET THEM UP AND OFF THE PLANET.
BACK TO WHEREVER IT IS THEY BELONG.
BRUCE-- MAKE THEM UNDERSTAND THAT THE SUN-SPIRIT IS MAKING A COVENANT WITH THEM.
YOU TELL THEM THAT THE DEAL IS THEY WILL NOT HARM ANOTHER HUMAN BEING...
...AND IN RETURN I WILL REPAIR THEIR SHIP AND RETURN THEM TO THE STARS.
GOOD PLAN.
YOU EXPLAIN THIS TO THEM AND I'LL BRING THE TECHNOLOGY THAT CAN MAKE IT HAPPEN...

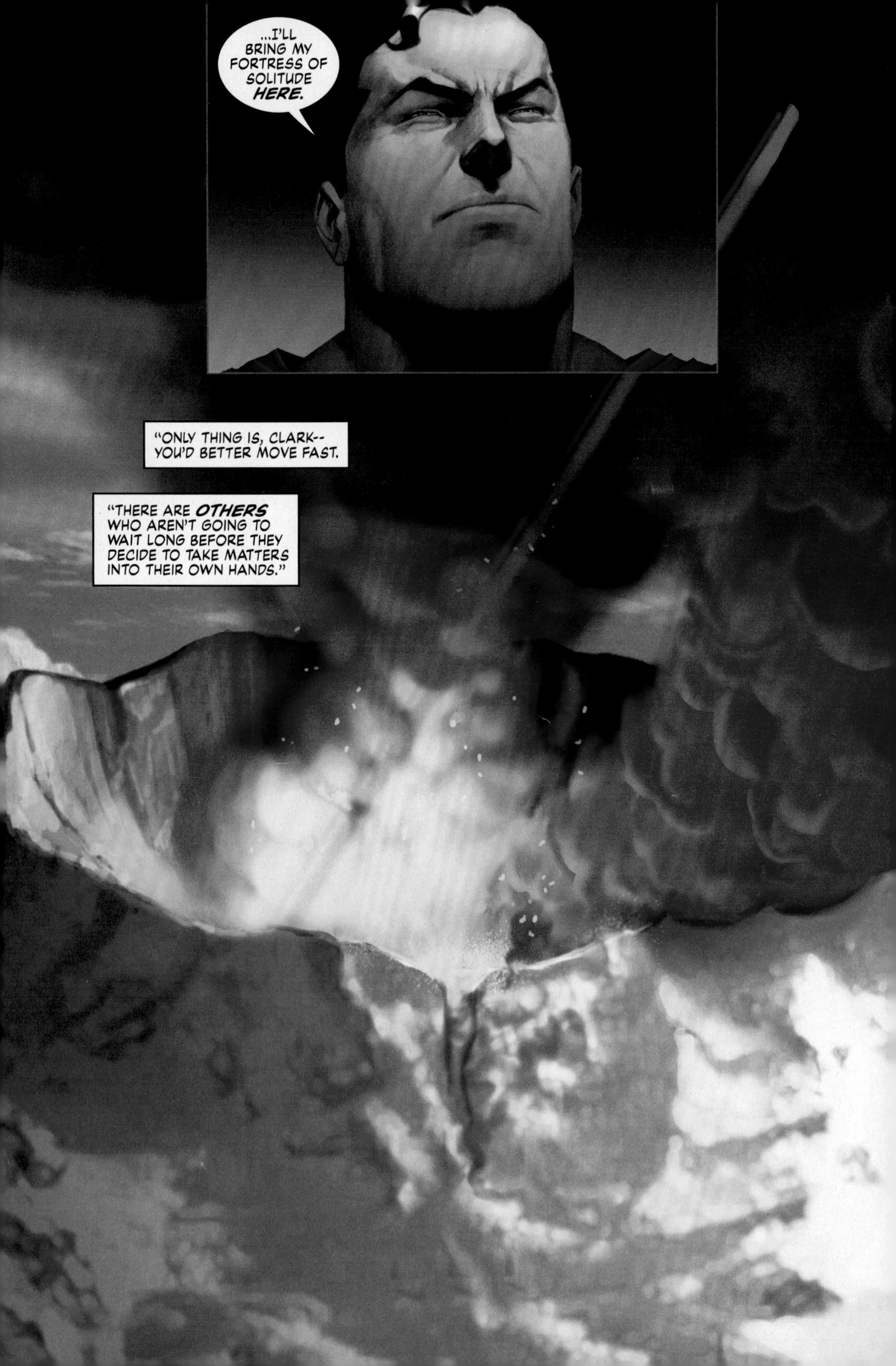
...I'LL BRING MY FORTRESS OF SOLITUDE *HERE.*
"ONLY THING IS, CLARK-- YOU'D BETTER MOVE FAST.
"THERE ARE *OTHERS* WHO AREN'T GOING TO WAIT LONG BEFORE THEY DECIDE TO TAKE MATTERS INTO THEIR OWN HANDS."

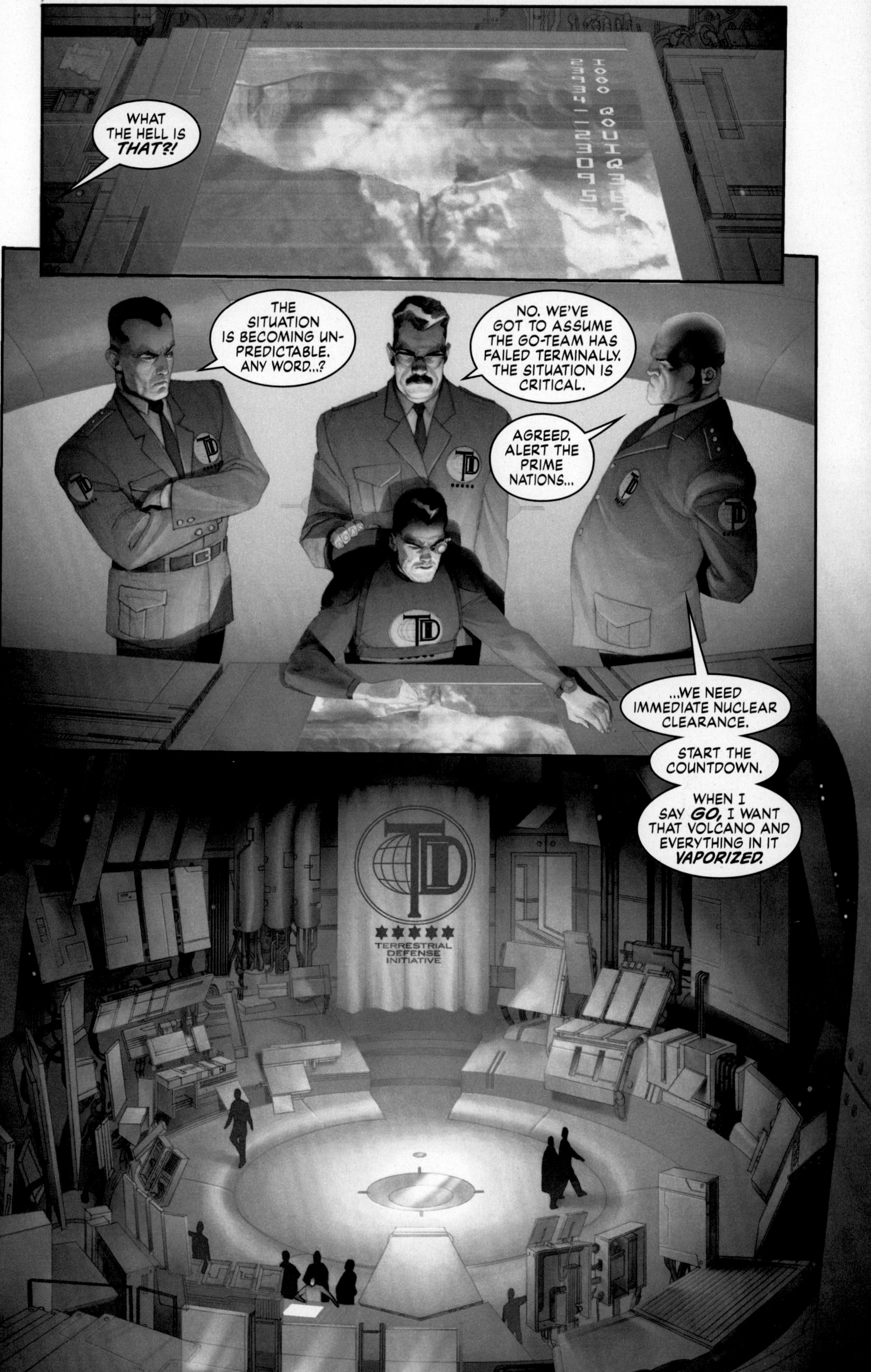
WHAT THE HELL IS *THAT?!*
THE SITUATION IS BECOMING UN-PREDICTABLE. ANY WORD...?
NO. WE'VE GOT TO ASSUME THE GO-TEAM HAS FAILED TERMINALLY. THE SITUATION IS CRITICAL.
AGREED. ALERT THE PRIME NATIONS...
...WE NEED IMMEDIATE NUCLEAR CLEARANCE.
START THE COUNTDOWN.
WHEN I SAY *GO,* I WANT THAT VOLCANO AND EVERYTHING IN IT *VAPORIZED.*
TERRESTRIAL DEFENSE INITIATIVE

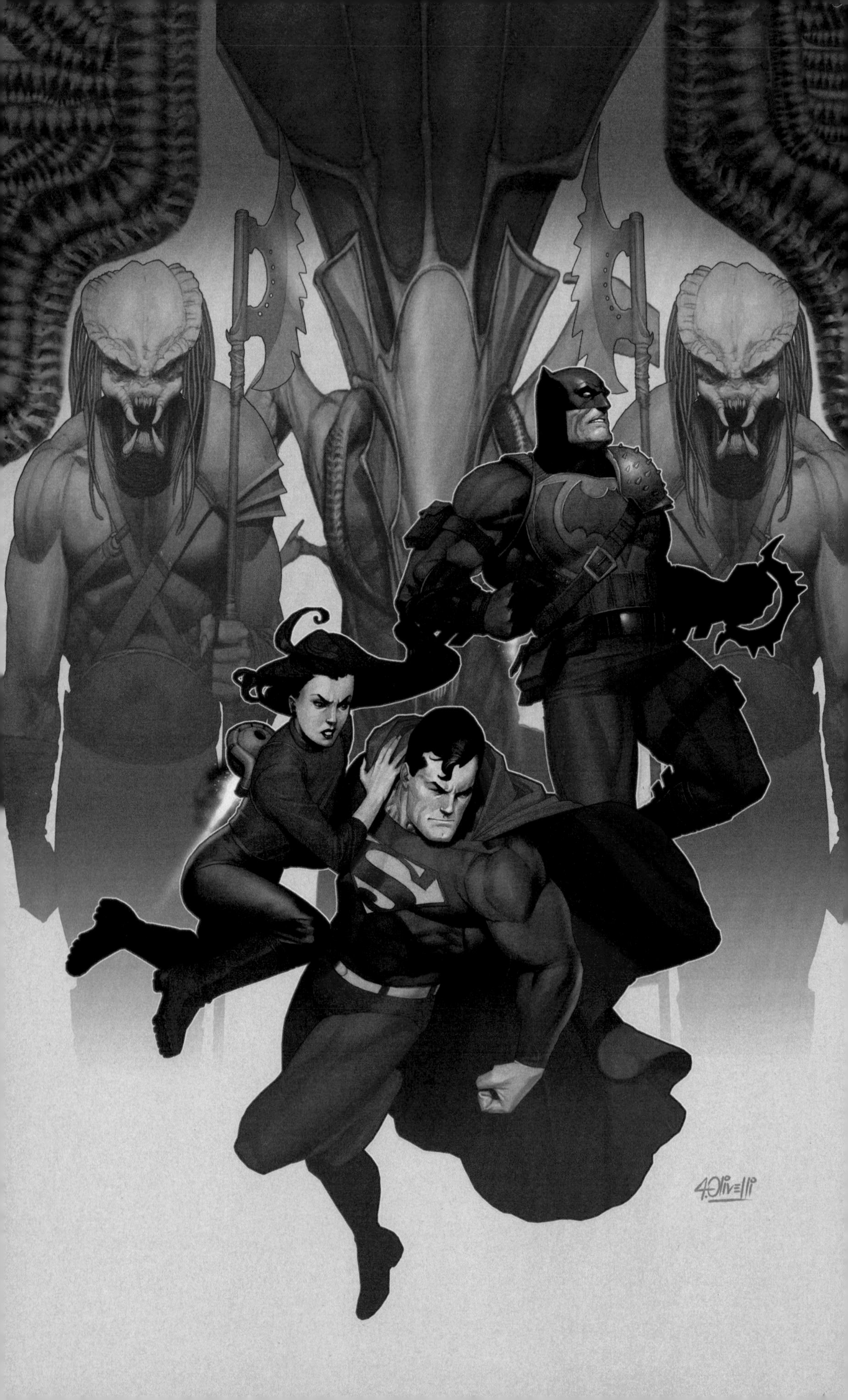

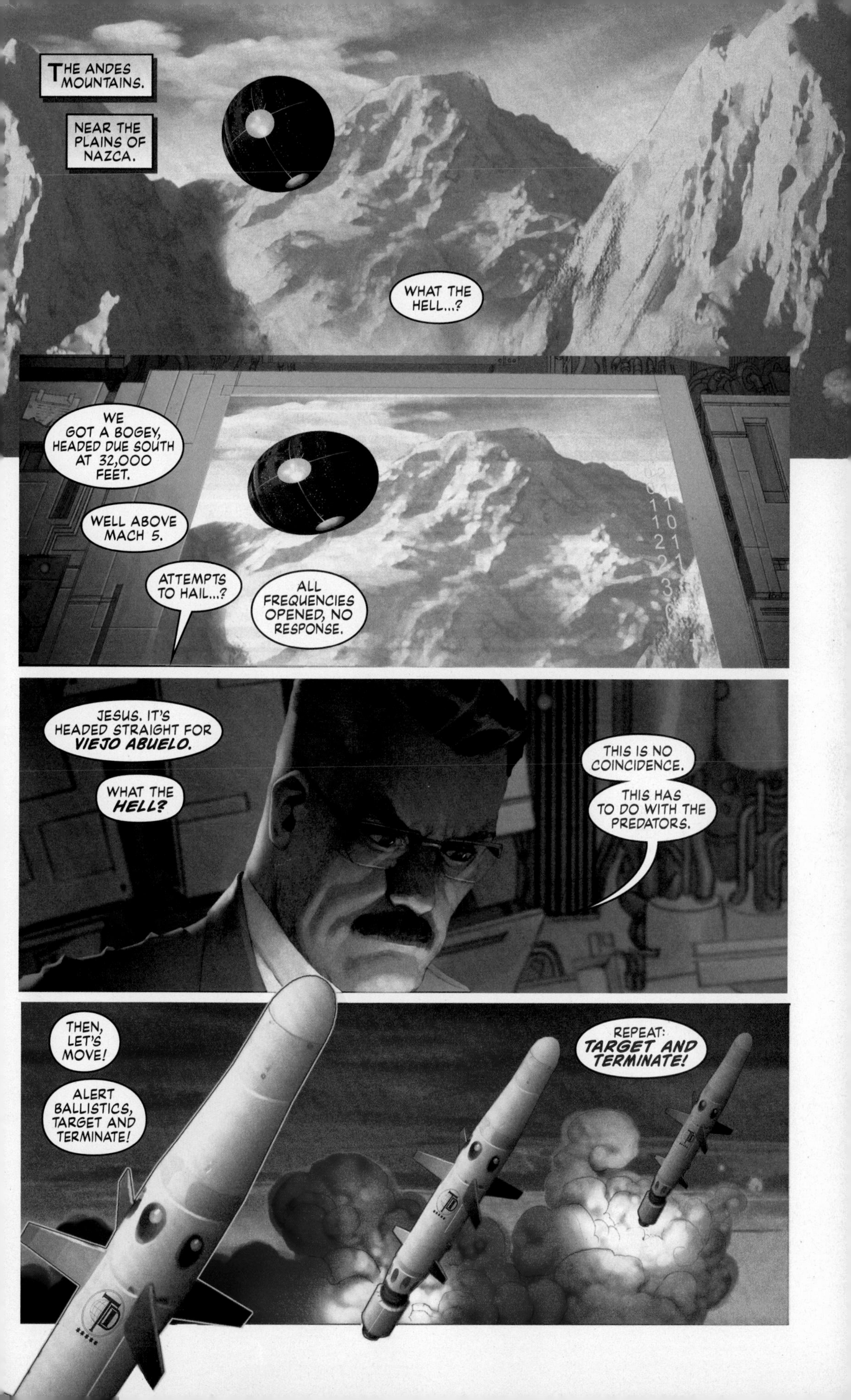
THE ANDES MOUNTAINS.
NEAR THE PLAINS OF NAZCA.
WHAT THE HELL...?
WE GOT A BOGEY, HEADED DUE SOUTH AT 32,000 FEET.
WELL ABOVE MACH 5.
ATTEMPTS TO HAIL...?
ALL FREQUENCIES OPENED, NO RESPONSE.
JESUS. IT'S HEADED STRAIGHT FOR VIEJO ABUELO.
WHAT THE HELL?
THIS IS NO COINCIDENCE.
THIS HAS TO DO WITH THE PREDATORS.
THEN, LET'S MOVE!
ALERT BALLISTICS, TARGET AND TERMINATE!
REPEAT: TARGET AND TERMINATE!

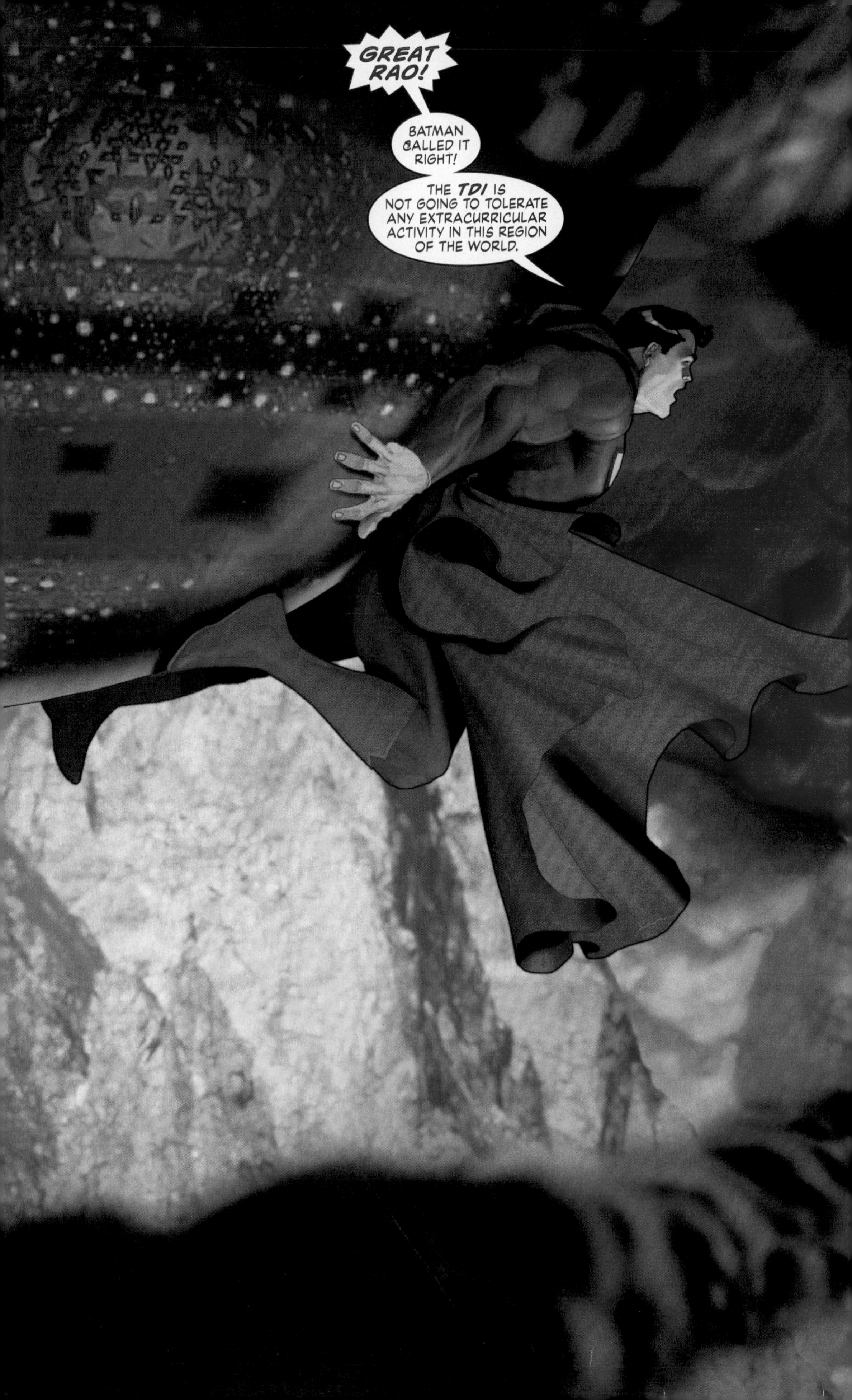
GREAT RAO!
BATMAN CALLED IT RIGHT!
THE TDI IS NOT GOING TO TOLERATE ANY EXTRACURRICULAR ACTIVITY IN THIS REGION OF THE WORLD.

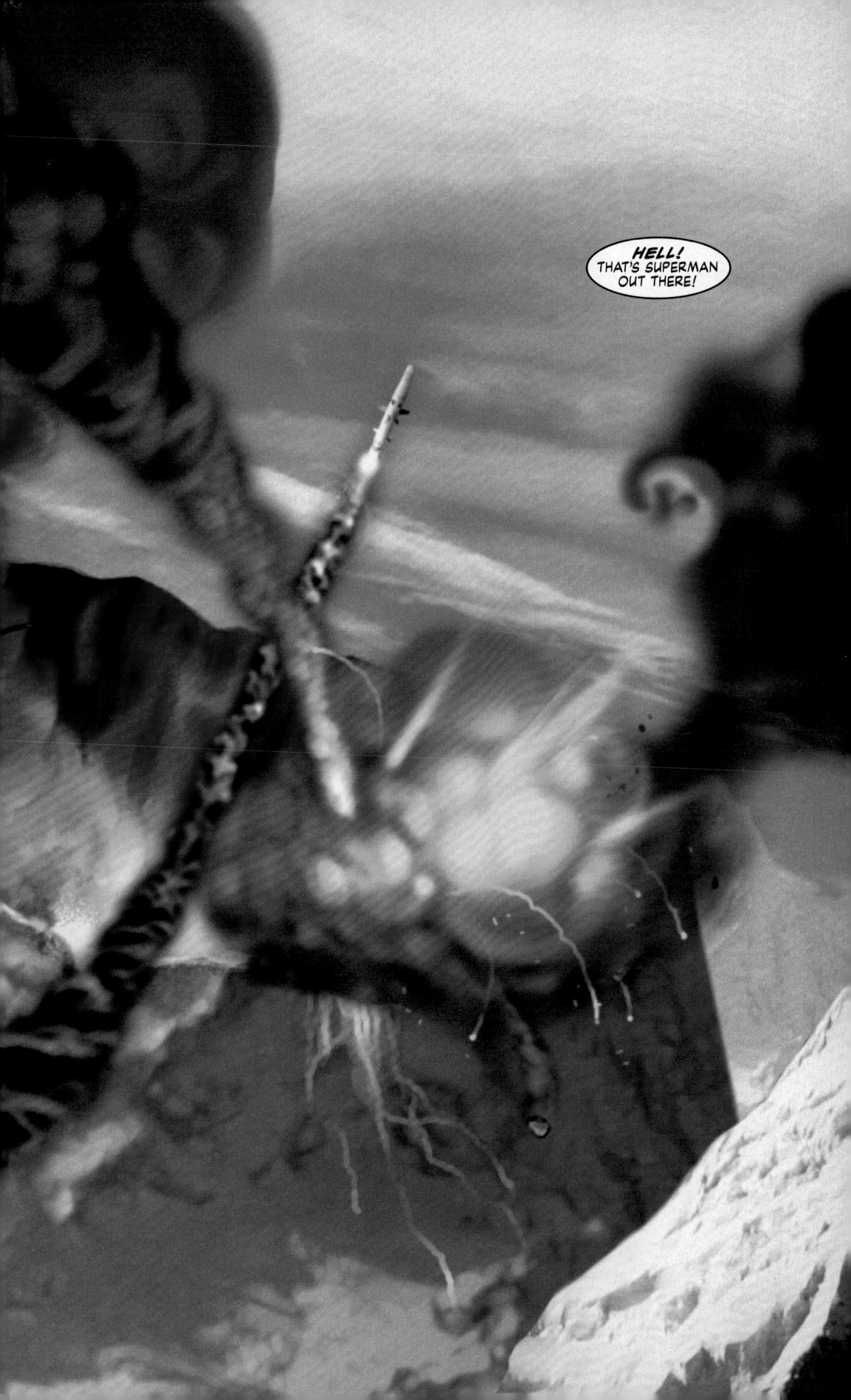
HELL! THAT'S SUPERMAN OUT THERE!

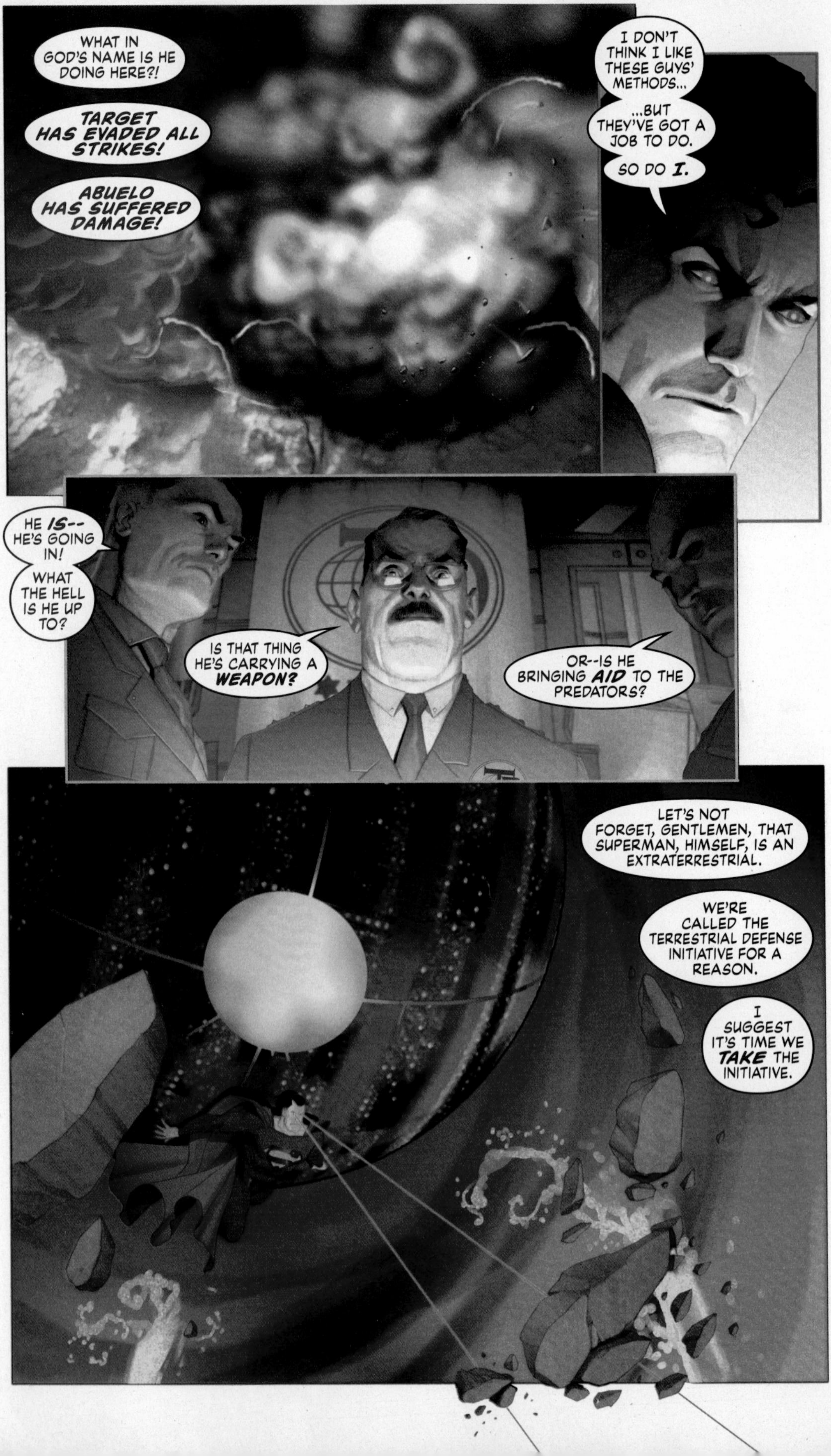
WHAT IN GOD'S NAME IS HE DOING HERE?!
TARGET HAS EVADED ALL STRIKES!
ABUELO HAS SUFFERED DAMAGE!
I DON'T THINK I LIKE THESE GUYS' METHODS...
...BUT THEY'VE GOT A JOB TO DO.
SO DO I.
HE IS-- HE'S GOING IN!
WHAT THE HELL IS HE UP TO?
IS THAT THING HE'S CARRYING A WEAPON?
OR--IS HE BRINGING AID TO THE PREDATORS?
LET'S NOT FORGET, GENTLEMEN, THAT SUPERMAN, HIMSELF, IS AN EXTRATERRESTRIAL.
WE'RE CALLED THE TERRESTRIAL DEFENSE INITIATIVE FOR A REASON.
I SUGGEST IT'S TIME WE TAKE THE INITIATIVE.

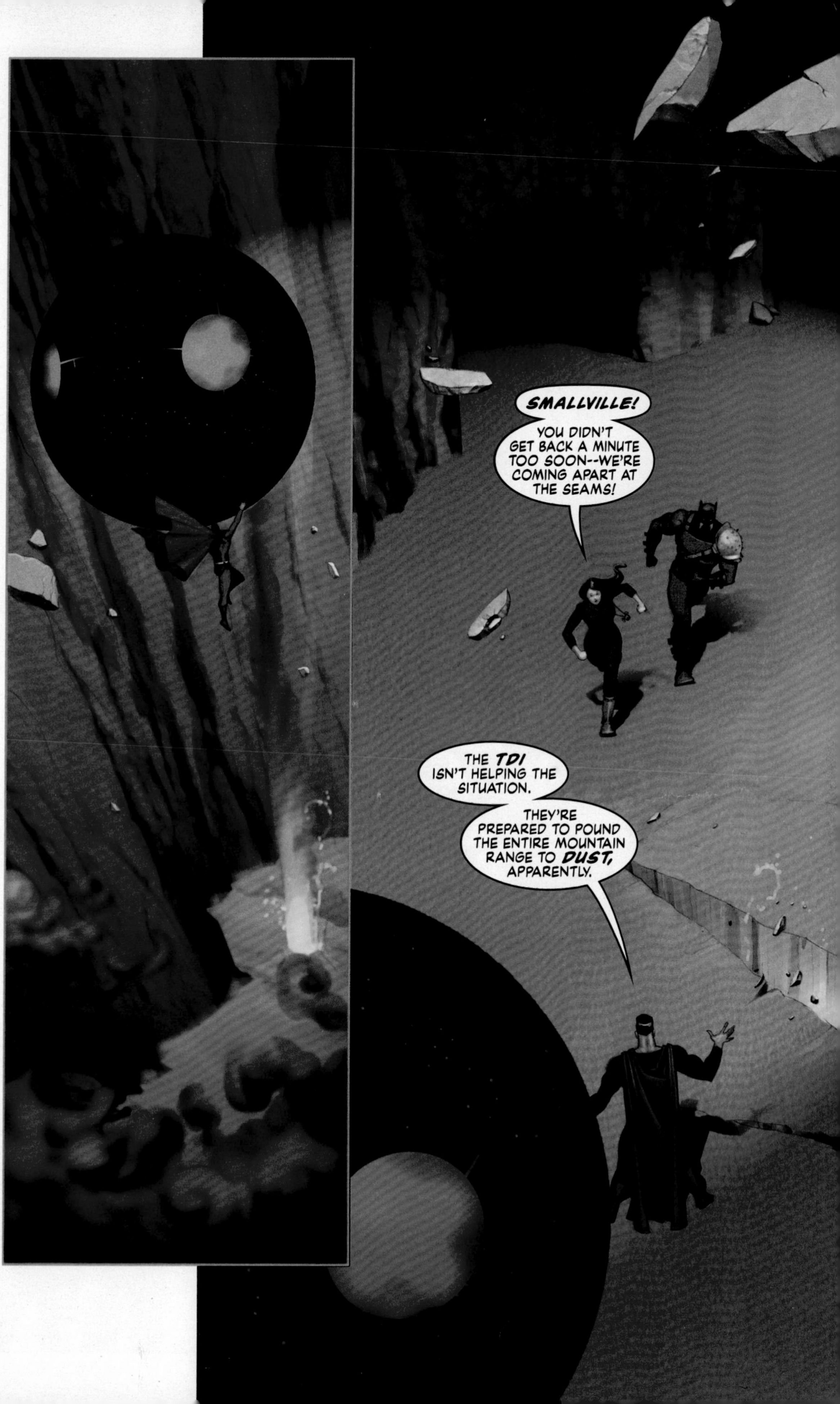
SMALLVILLE!
YOU DIDN'T GET BACK A MINUTE TOO SOON--WE'RE COMING APART AT THE SEAMS!
THE TDI ISN'T HELPING THE SITUATION.
THEY'RE PREPARED TO POUND THE ENTIRE MOUNTAIN RANGE TO DUST, APPARENTLY.

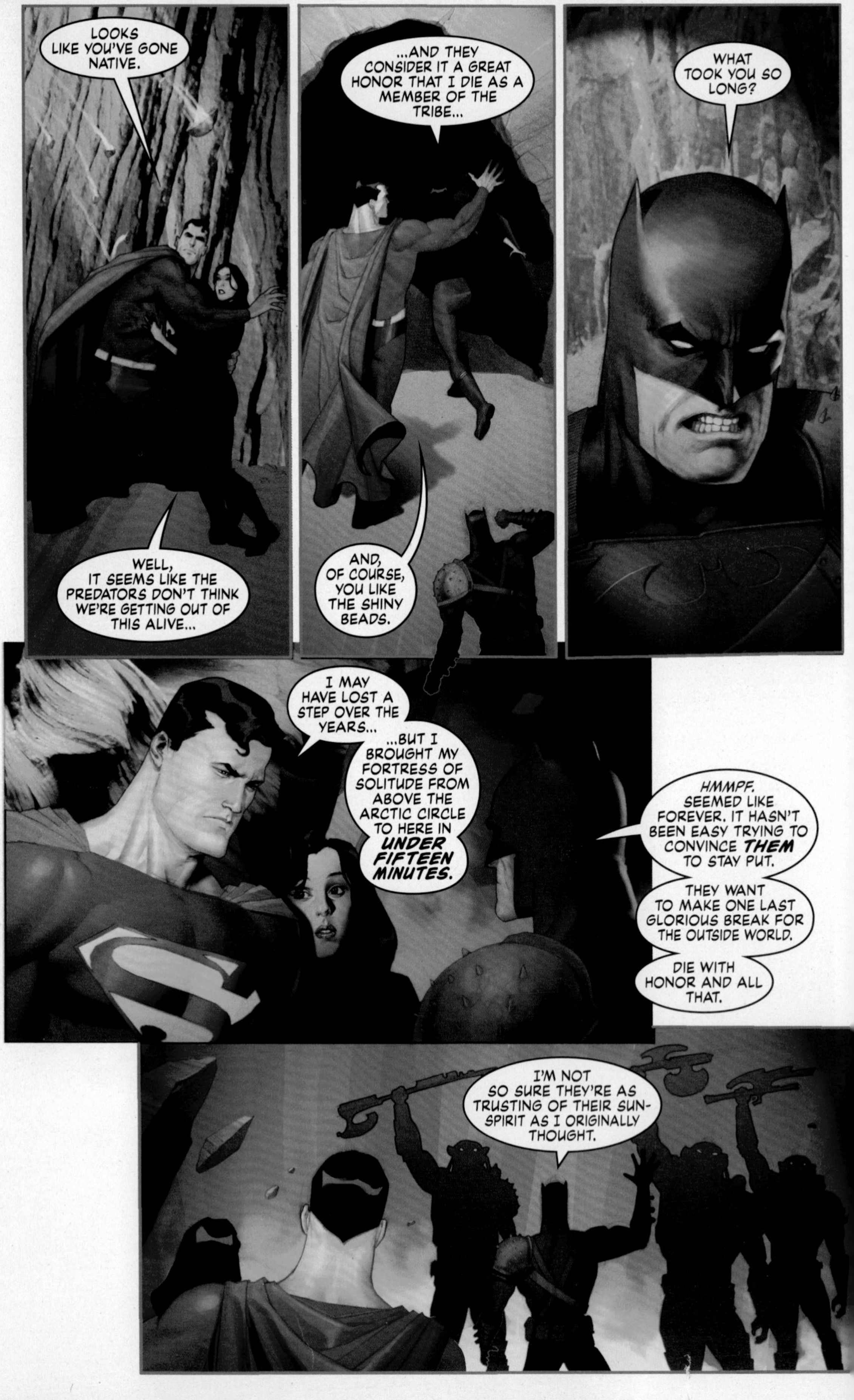
LOOKS LIKE YOU'VE GONE NATIVE.
WELL, IT SEEMS LIKE THE PREDATORS DON'T THINK WE'RE GETTING OUT OF THIS ALIVE...
...AND THEY CONSIDER IT A GREAT HONOR THAT I DIE AS A MEMBER OF THE TRIBE...
AND, OF COURSE, YOU LIKE THE SHINY BEADS.
WHAT TOOK YOU SO LONG?
I MAY HAVE LOST A STEP OVER THE YEARS...
...BUT I BROUGHT MY FORTRESS OF SOLITUDE FROM ABOVE THE ARCTIC CIRCLE TO HERE IN UNDER FIFTEEN MINUTES.
HMMPF. SEEMED LIKE FOREVER. IT HASN'T BEEN EASY TRYING TO CONVINCE THEM TO STAY PUT.
THEY WANT TO MAKE ONE LAST GLORIOUS BREAK FOR THE OUTSIDE WORLD.
DIE WITH HONOR AND ALL THAT.
I'M NOT SO SURE THEY'RE AS TRUSTING OF THEIR SUN-SPIRIT AS I ORIGINALLY THOUGHT.

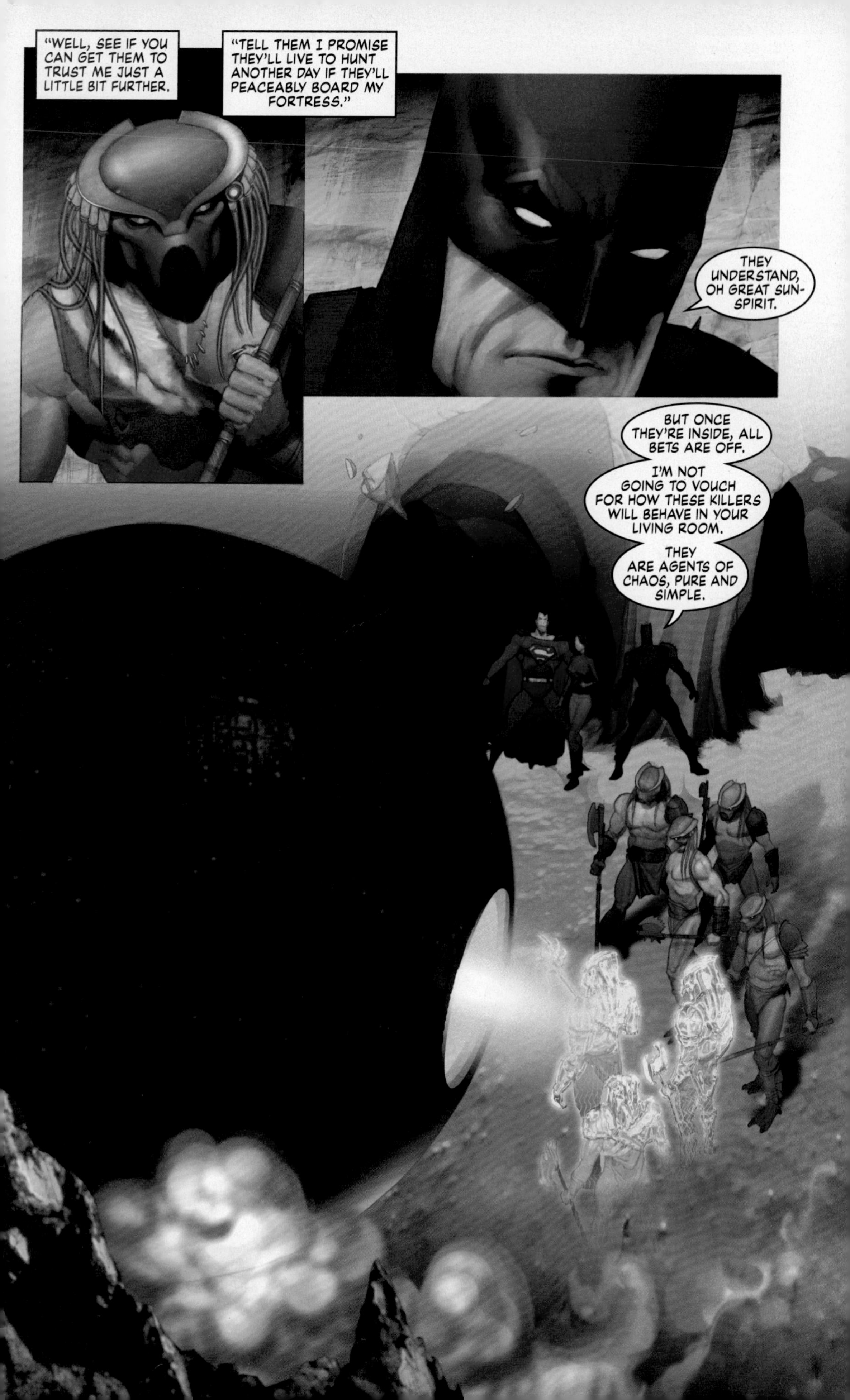
"WELL, SEE IF YOU CAN GET THEM TO TRUST ME JUST A LITTLE BIT FURTHER.
"TELL THEM I PROMISE THEY'LL LIVE TO HUNT ANOTHER DAY IF THEY'LL PEACEABLY BOARD MY FORTRESS."
THEY UNDERSTAND, OH GREAT SUN-SPIRIT.
BUT ONCE THEY'RE INSIDE, ALL BETS ARE OFF.
I'M NOT GOING TO VOUCH FOR HOW THESE KILLERS WILL BEHAVE IN YOUR LIVING ROOM.
THEY ARE AGENTS OF CHAOS, PURE AND SIMPLE.

"IT'LL BE OKAY.

"AS GROUPS ARE TRANSFERRED BY PARTICLE BEAM INTO THE FORTRESS, MY STAFF OF ROBOTS WILL GREET THEM.

"UNIVERSAL DIALECTICS WILL QUICKLY DECIPHER AND MASTER THE PREDATOR LANGUAGE...

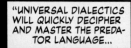

"...AND KELEX WILL EXPLAIN WHAT IS EXPECTED OF THEM."

SHHRRRILLL

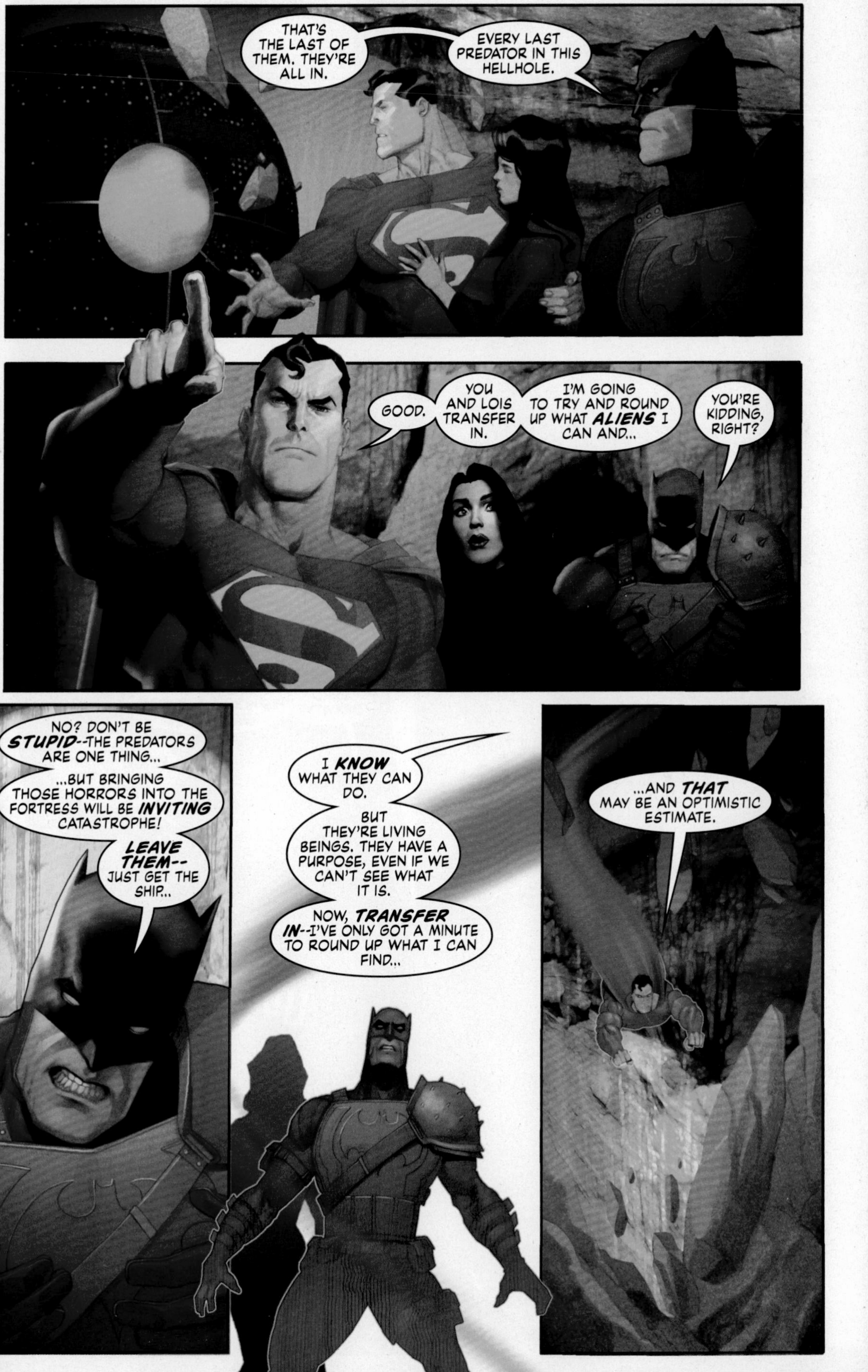
THAT'S THE LAST OF THEM. THEY'RE ALL IN.
EVERY LAST PREDATOR IN THIS HELLHOLE.
GOOD.
YOU AND LOIS TRANSFER IN.
I'M GOING TO TRY AND ROUND UP WHAT ALIENS I CAN AND...
YOU'RE KIDDING, RIGHT?
NO? DON'T BE STUPID--THE PREDATORS ARE ONE THING...
...BUT BRINGING THOSE HORRORS INTO THE FORTRESS WILL BE INVITING CATASTROPHE!
LEAVE THEM--JUST GET THE SHIP...
I KNOW WHAT THEY CAN DO.
BUT THEY'RE LIVING BEINGS. THEY HAVE A PURPOSE, EVEN IF WE CAN'T SEE WHAT IT IS.
NOW, TRANSFER IN--I'VE ONLY GOT A MINUTE TO ROUND UP WHAT I CAN FIND...
...AND THAT MAY BE AN OPTIMISTIC ESTIMATE.

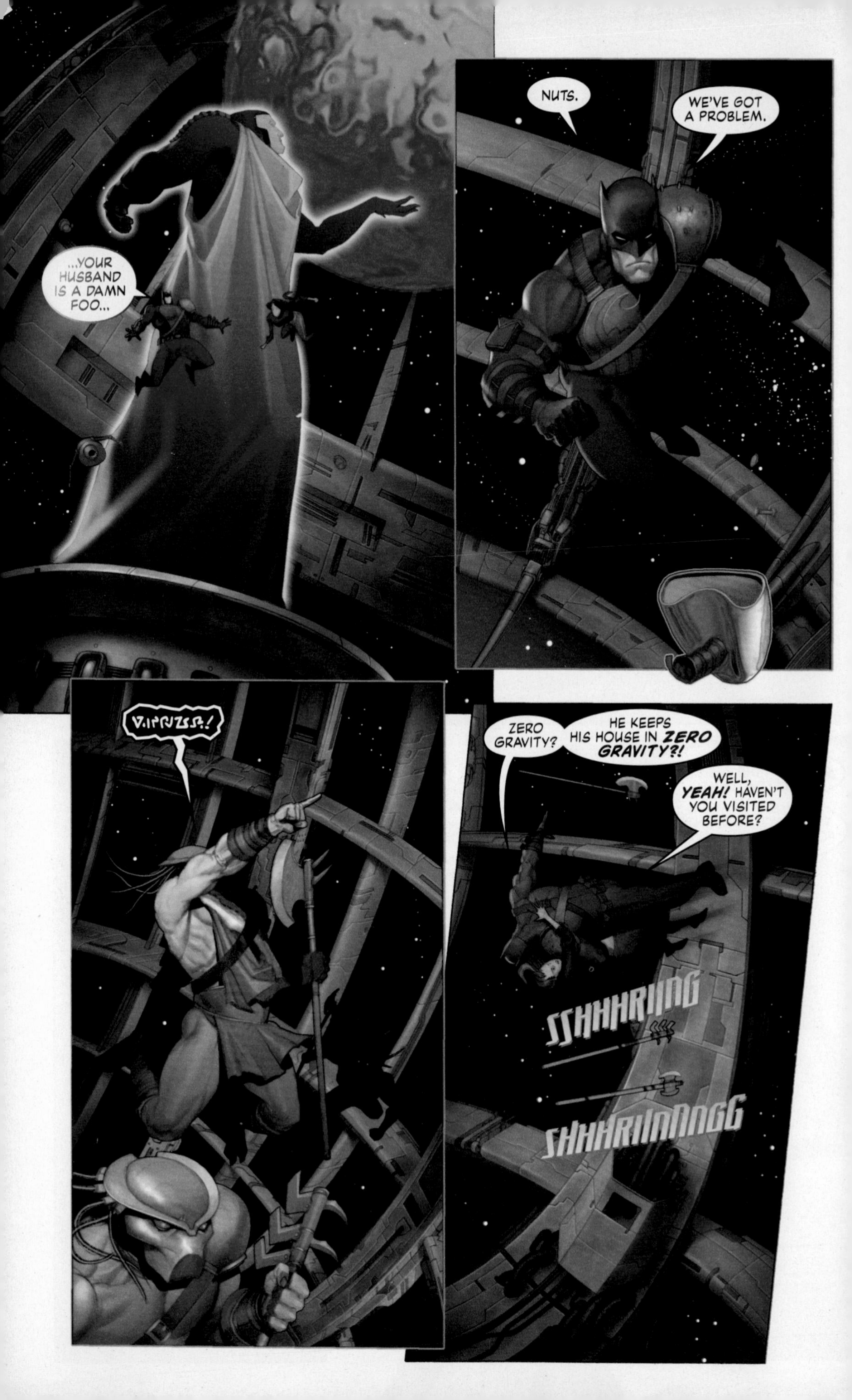
...YOUR HUSBAND IS A DAMN FOO...
NUTS.
WE'VE GOT A PROBLEM.
ZERO GRAVITY?
HE KEEPS HIS HOUSE IN ZERO GRAVITY?!
WELL, YEAH! HAVEN'T YOU VISITED BEFORE?
SSHHHRIIING
SHHHRIIINNNGG

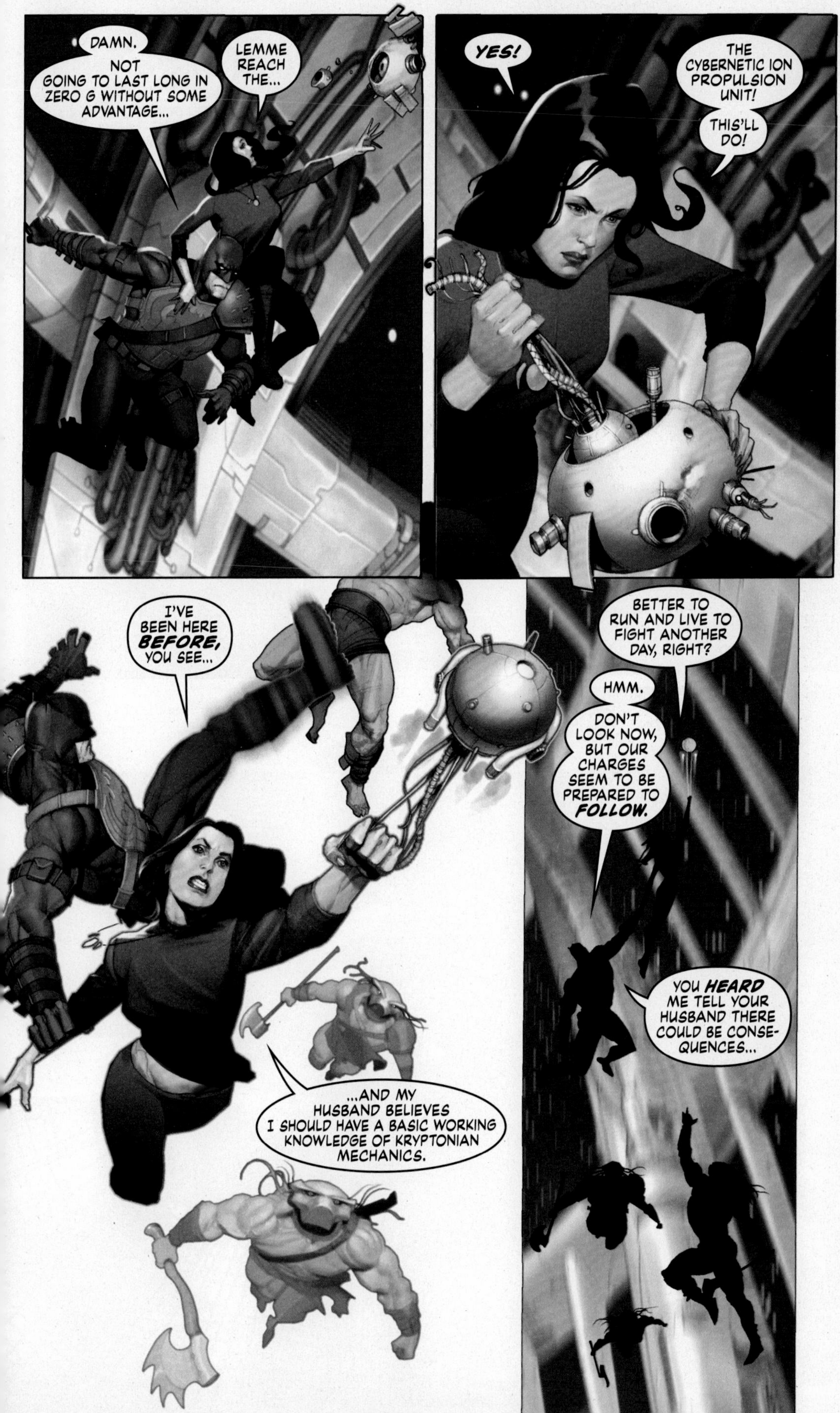
DAMN.
NOT GOING TO LAST LONG IN ZERO G WITHOUT SOME ADVANTAGE...
LEMME REACH THE...
YES!
THE CYBERNETIC ION PROPULSION UNIT!
THIS'LL DO!
I'VE BEEN HERE *BEFORE,* YOU SEE...
...AND MY HUSBAND BELIEVES I SHOULD HAVE A BASIC WORKING KNOWLEDGE OF KRYPTONIAN MECHANICS.
BETTER TO RUN AND LIVE TO FIGHT ANOTHER DAY, RIGHT?
HMM.
DON'T LOOK NOW, BUT OUR CHARGES SEEM TO BE PREPARED TO *FOLLOW.*
YOU *HEARD* ME TELL YOUR HUSBAND THERE COULD BE CONSE-QUENCES...

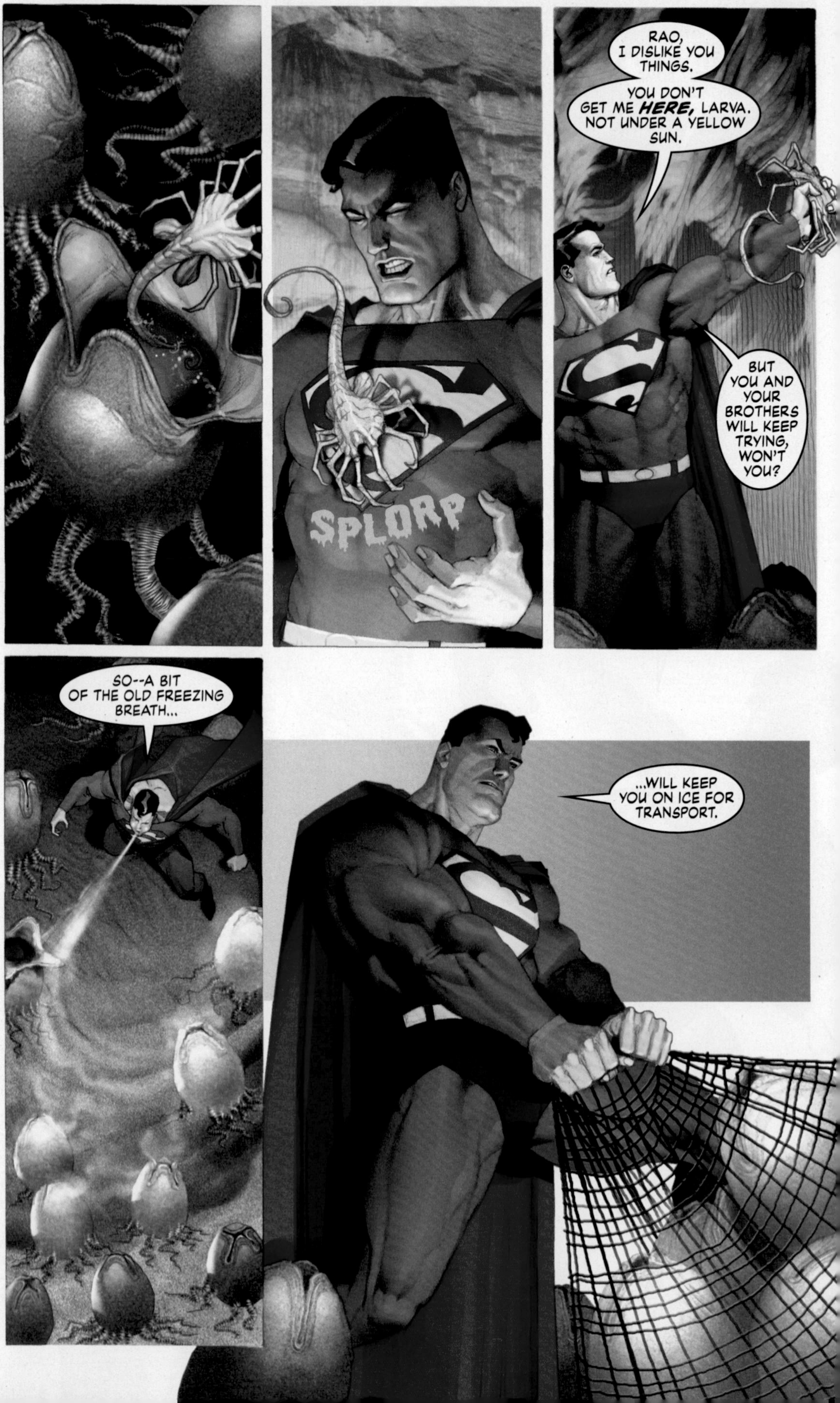
SPLORP
RAO, I DISLIKE YOU THINGS.
YOU DON'T GET ME ***HERE,*** LARVA. NOT UNDER A YELLOW SUN.
BUT YOU AND YOUR BROTHERS WILL KEEP TRYING, WON'T YOU?
SO--A BIT OF THE OLD FREEZING BREATH...
...WILL KEEP YOU ON ICE FOR TRANSPORT.

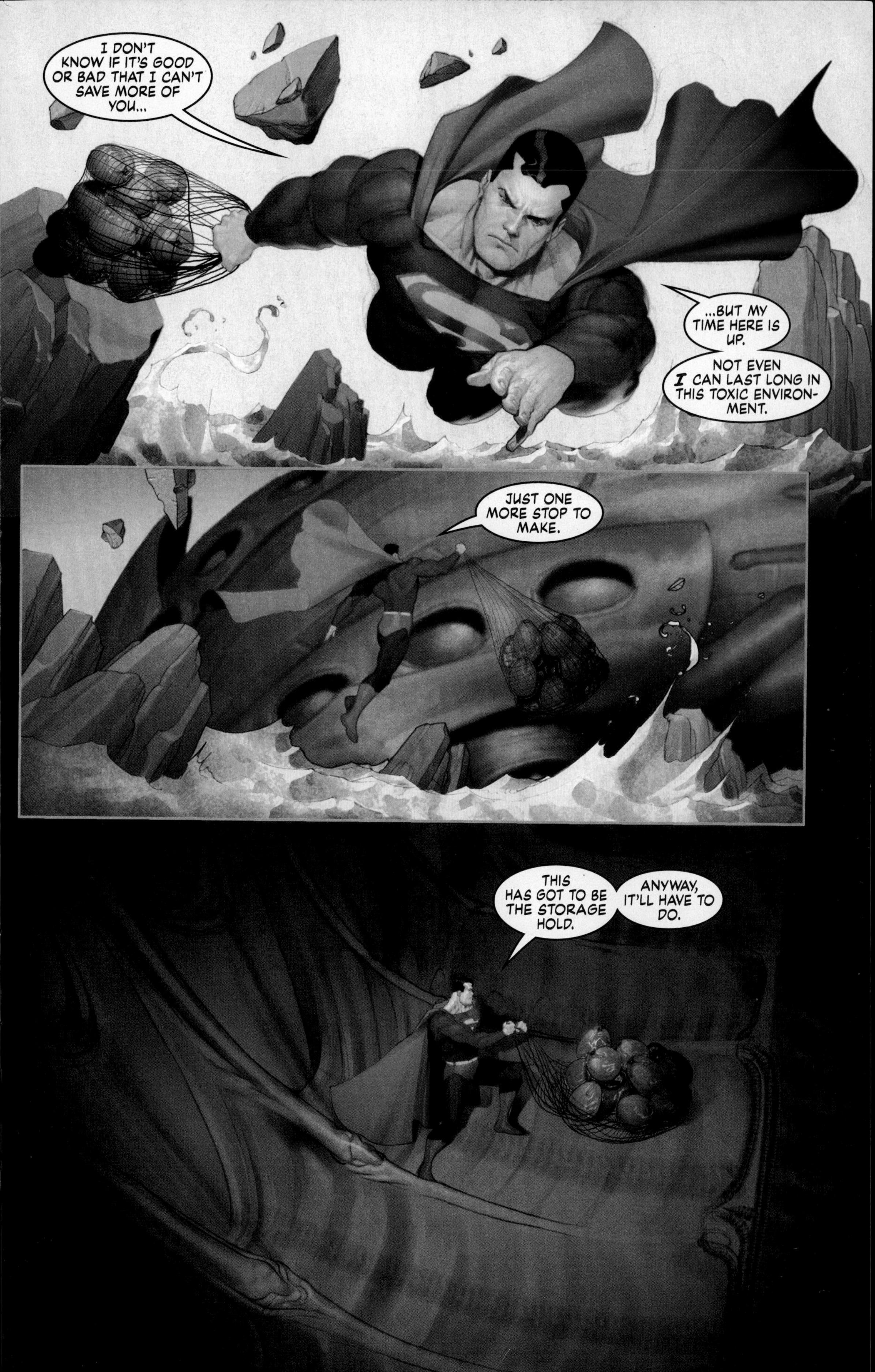
I DON'T KNOW IF IT'S GOOD OR BAD THAT I CAN'T SAVE MORE OF YOU...
...BUT MY TIME HERE IS UP.
NOT EVEN I CAN LAST LONG IN THIS TOXIC ENVIRONMENT.
JUST ONE MORE STOP TO MAKE.
THIS HAS GOT TO BE THE STORAGE HOLD.
ANYWAY, IT'LL HAVE TO DO.

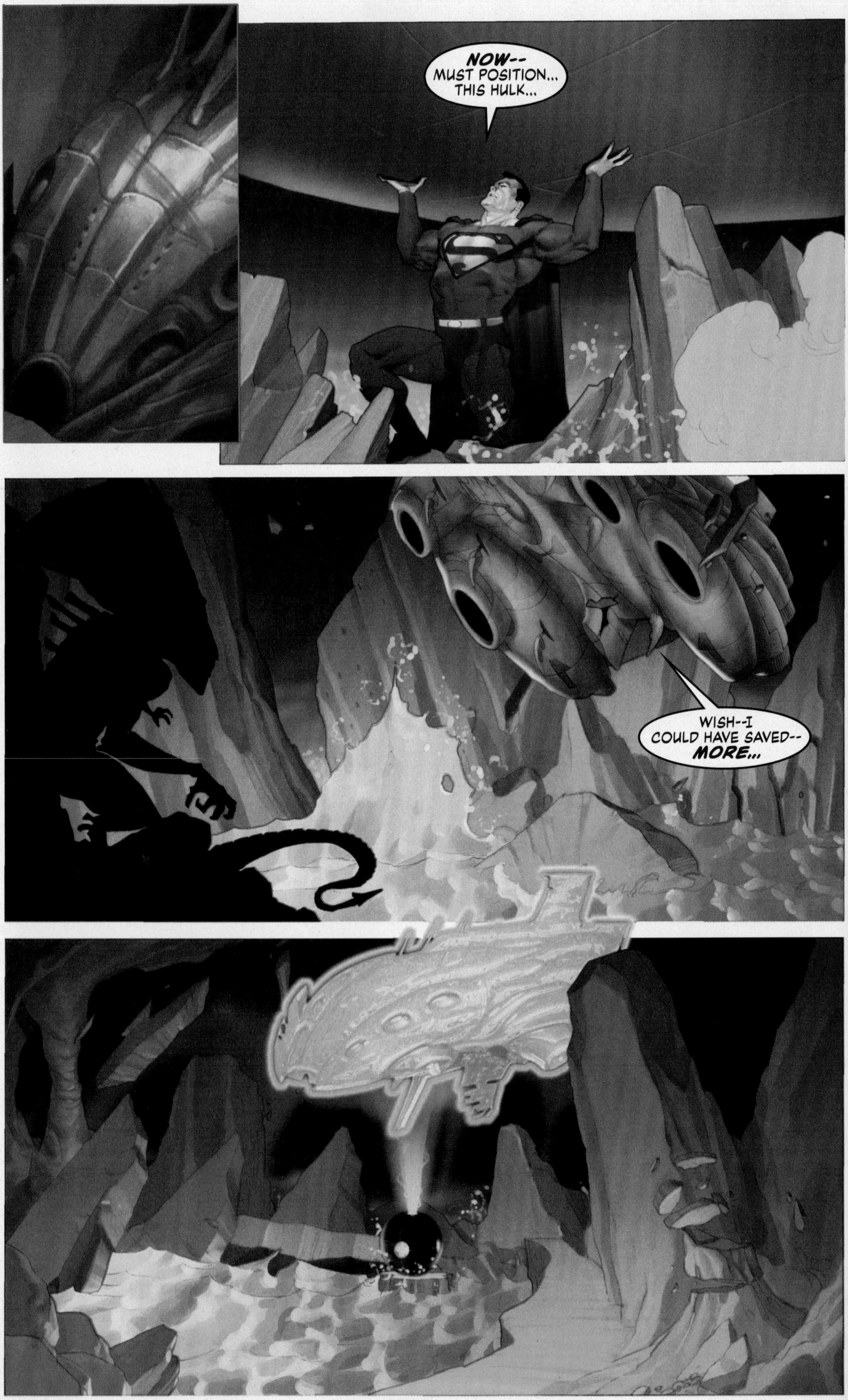
NOW-- MUST POSITION... THIS HULK...
WISH--I COULD HAVE SAVED-- MORE...

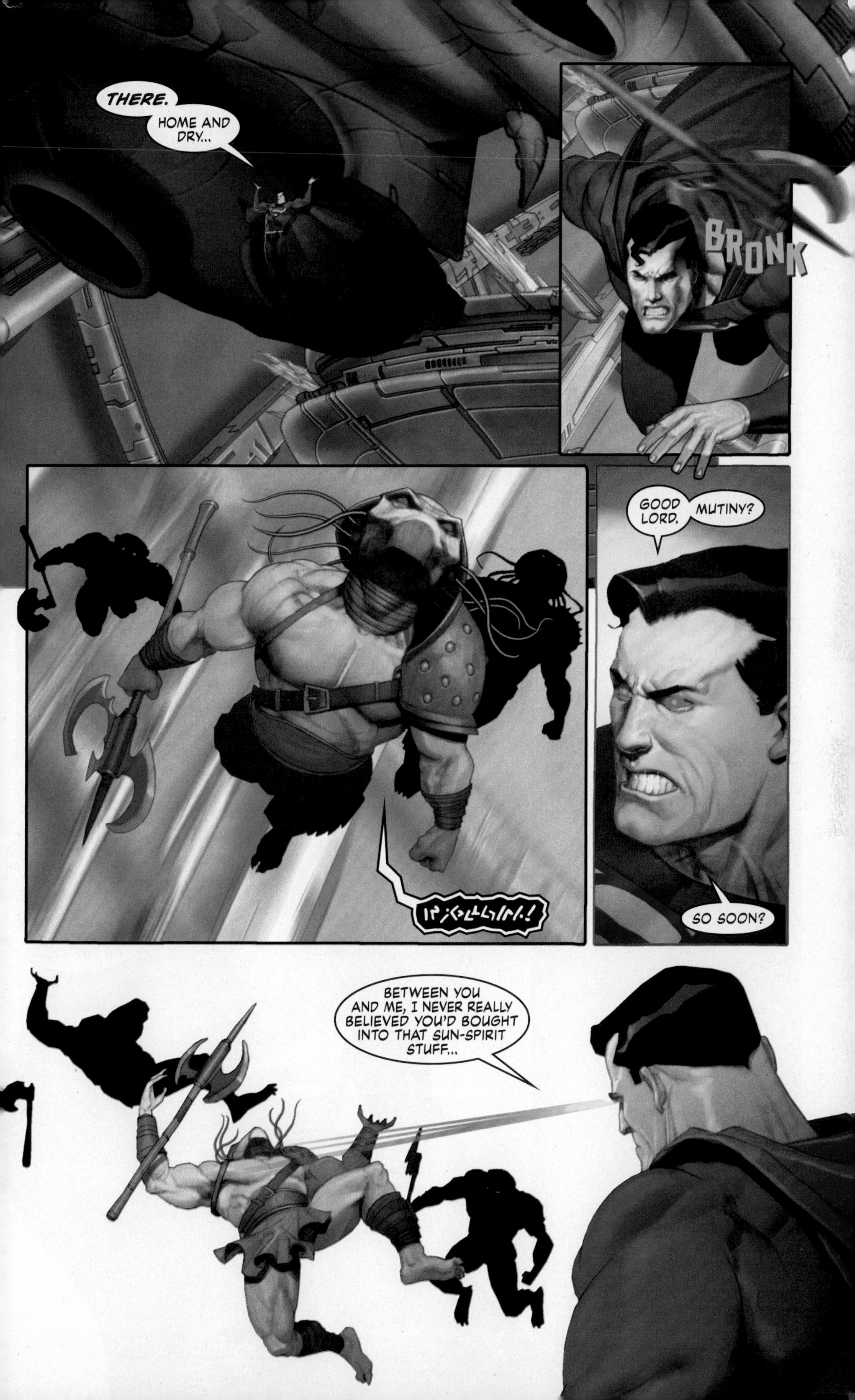
THERE.
HOME AND DRY...
BRONK
GOOD LORD.
MUTINY?
SO SOON?
BETWEEN YOU AND ME, I NEVER REALLY BELIEVED YOU'D BOUGHT INTO THAT SUN-SPIRIT STUFF...

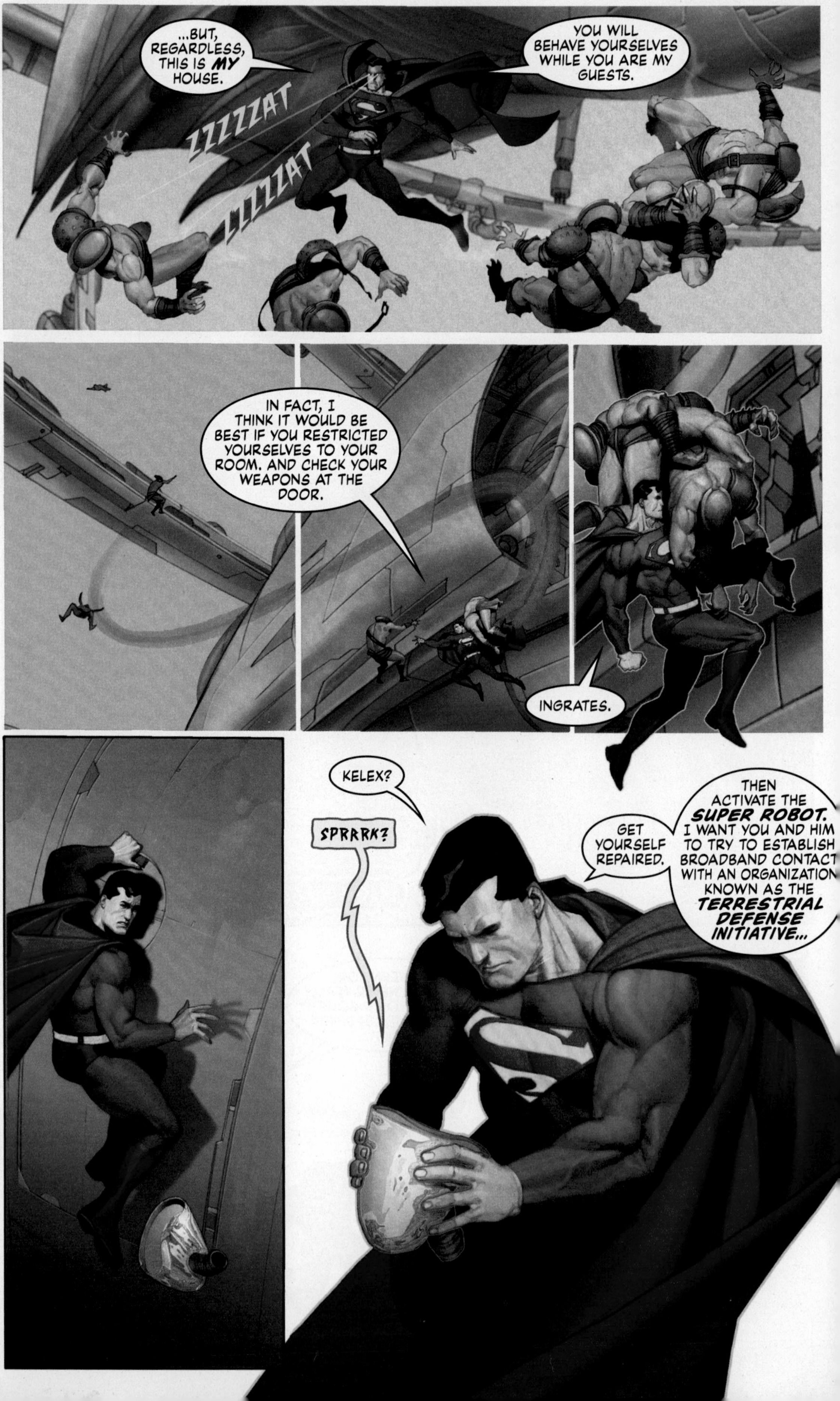
...BUT, REGARDLESS, THIS IS *MY* HOUSE.
YOU WILL BEHAVE YOURSELVES WHILE YOU ARE MY GUESTS.
ZZZZZAT
ZZZZZAT
IN FACT, I THINK IT WOULD BE BEST IF YOU RESTRICTED YOURSELVES TO YOUR ROOM. AND CHECK YOUR WEAPONS AT THE DOOR.
INGRATES.
KELEX?
SPRRRK?
GET YOURSELF REPAIRED.
THEN ACTIVATE THE ***SUPER ROBOT.*** I WANT YOU AND HIM TO TRY TO ESTABLISH BROADBAND CONTACT WITH AN ORGANIZATION KNOWN AS THE ***TERRESTRIAL DEFENSE INITIATIVE...***

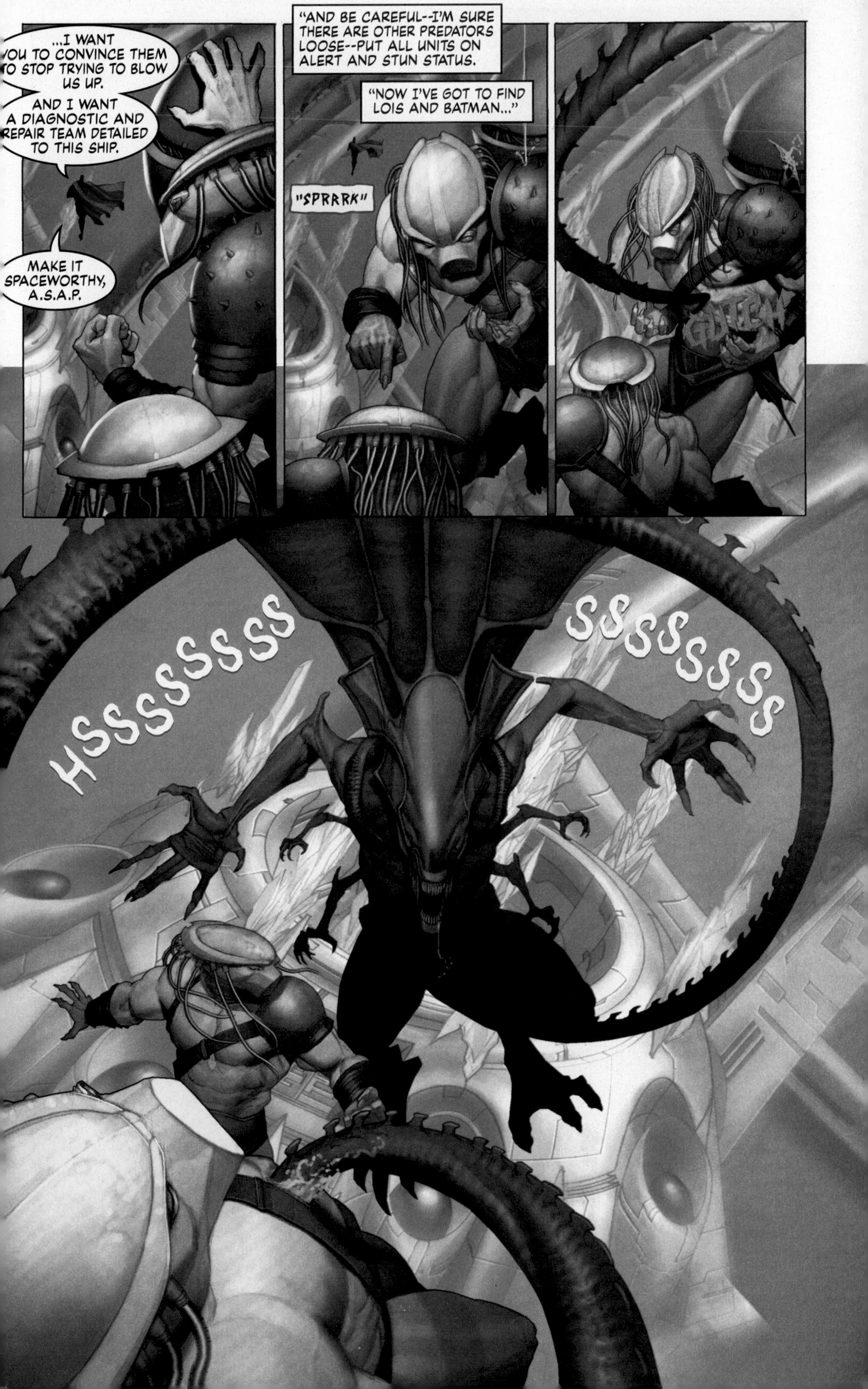
...I WANT YOU TO CONVINCE THEM TO STOP TRYING TO BLOW US UP.
AND I WANT A DIAGNOSTIC AND REPAIR TEAM DETAILED TO THIS SHIP.
MAKE IT SPACEWORTHY, A.S.A.P.
"AND BE CAREFUL--I'M SURE THERE ARE OTHER PREDATORS LOOSE--PUT ALL UNITS ON ALERT AND STUN STATUS.
"NOW I'VE GOT TO FIND LOIS AND BATMAN..."
"SPRRRK"
HSSSSSSSS
SSSSSSSS

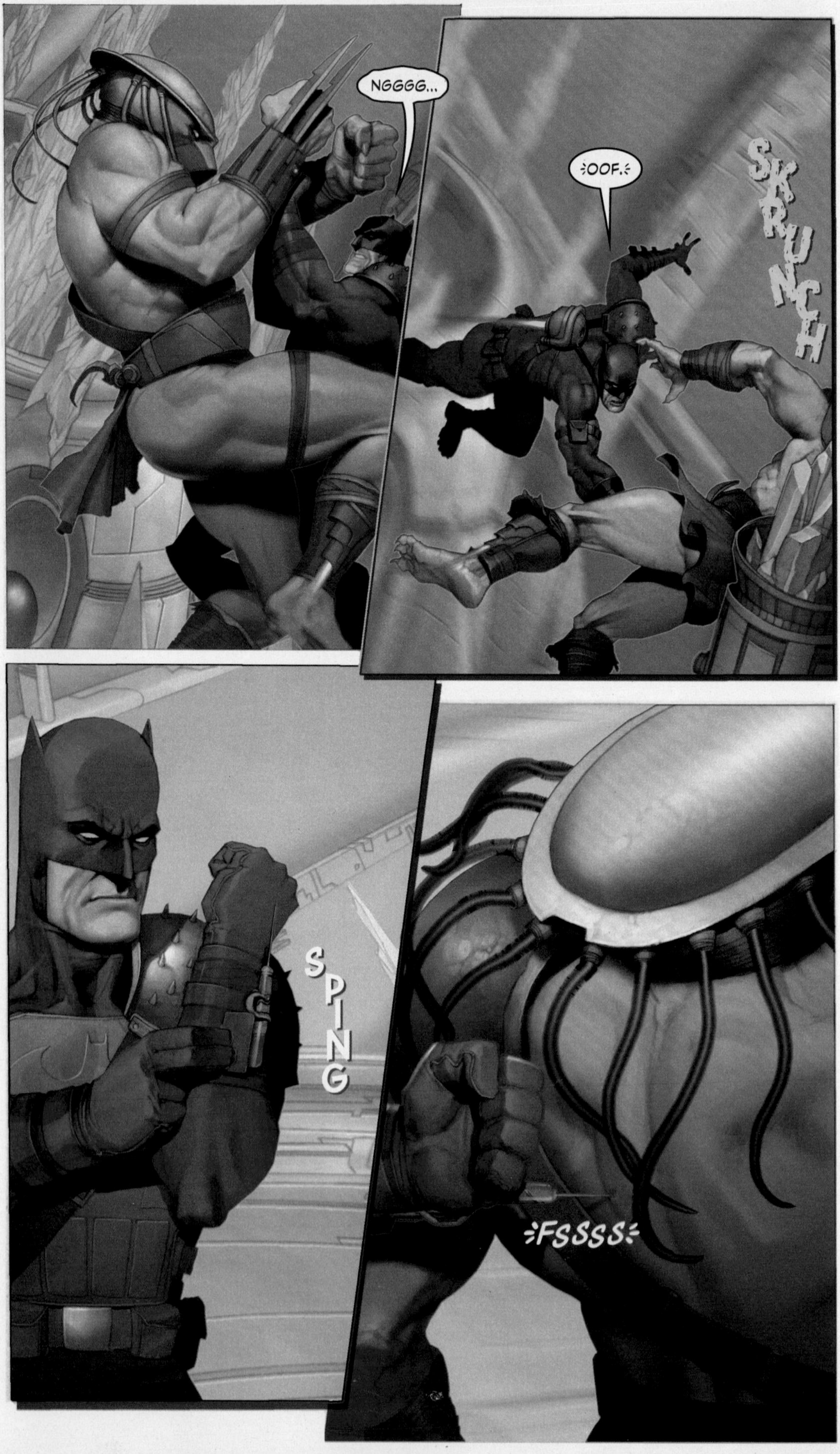
NGGGG...
OOF.
SKRUNCH
SPING
FSSSS

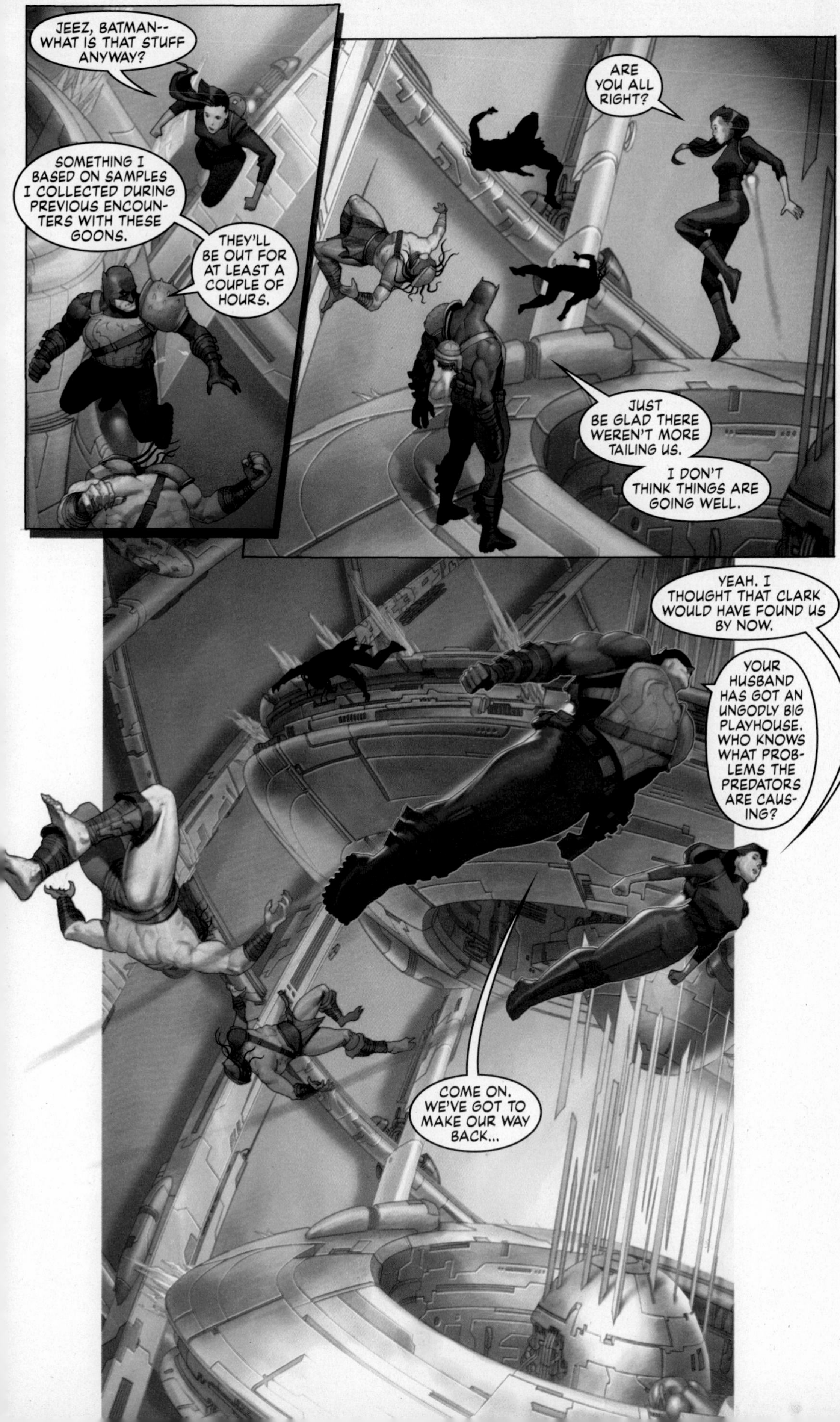
JEEZ, BATMAN-- WHAT IS THAT STUFF ANYWAY?
SOMETHING I BASED ON SAMPLES I COLLECTED DURING PREVIOUS ENCOUNTERS WITH THESE GOONS.
THEY'LL BE OUT FOR AT LEAST A COUPLE OF HOURS.
ARE YOU ALL RIGHT?
JUST BE GLAD THERE WEREN'T MORE TAILING US.
I DON'T THINK THINGS ARE GOING WELL.
YEAH. I THOUGHT THAT CLARK WOULD HAVE FOUND US BY NOW.
YOUR HUSBAND HAS GOT AN UNGODLY BIG PLAYHOUSE. WHO KNOWS WHAT PROBLEMS THE PREDATORS ARE CAUSING?
COME ON. WE'VE GOT TO MAKE OUR WAY BACK...

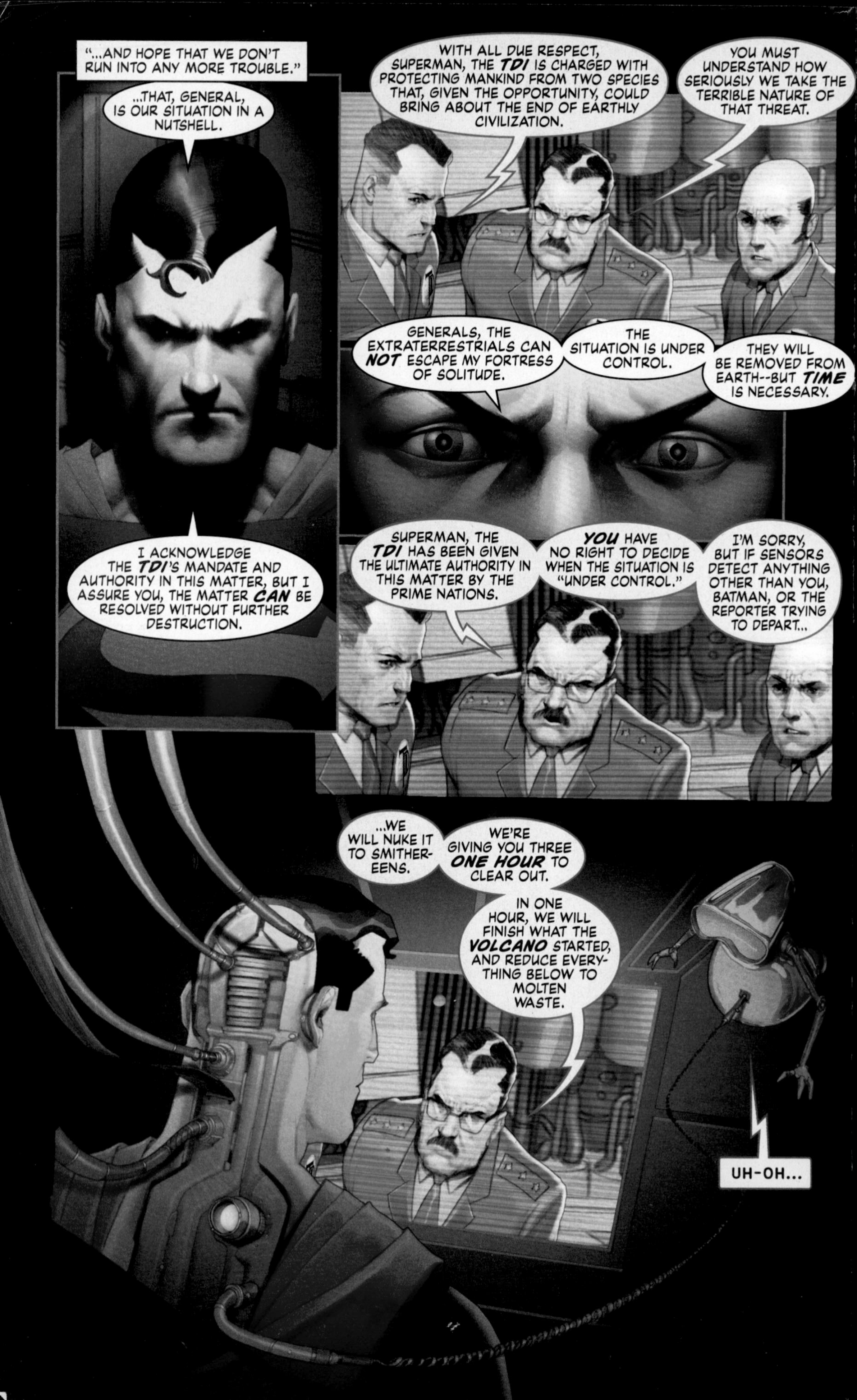
"...AND HOPE THAT WE DON'T RUN INTO ANY MORE TROUBLE."
...THAT, GENERAL, IS OUR SITUATION IN A NUTSHELL.
WITH ALL DUE RESPECT, SUPERMAN, THE TDI IS CHARGED WITH PROTECTING MANKIND FROM TWO SPECIES THAT, GIVEN THE OPPORTUNITY, COULD BRING ABOUT THE END OF EARTHLY CIVILIZATION.
YOU MUST UNDERSTAND HOW SERIOUSLY WE TAKE THE TERRIBLE NATURE OF THAT THREAT.
GENERALS, THE EXTRATERRESTRIALS CAN NOT ESCAPE MY FORTRESS OF SOLITUDE.
THE SITUATION IS UNDER CONTROL.
THEY WILL BE REMOVED FROM EARTH--BUT TIME IS NECESSARY.
I ACKNOWLEDGE THE TDI'S MANDATE AND AUTHORITY IN THIS MATTER, BUT I ASSURE YOU, THE MATTER CAN BE RESOLVED WITHOUT FURTHER DESTRUCTION.
SUPERMAN, THE TDI HAS BEEN GIVEN THE ULTIMATE AUTHORITY IN THIS MATTER BY THE PRIME NATIONS.
YOU HAVE NO RIGHT TO DECIDE WHEN THE SITUATION IS "UNDER CONTROL."
I'M SORRY, BUT IF SENSORS DETECT ANYTHING OTHER THAN YOU, BATMAN, OR THE REPORTER TRYING TO DEPART...
...WE WILL NUKE IT TO SMITHER-EENS.
WE'RE GIVING YOU THREE ONE HOUR TO CLEAR OUT.
IN ONE HOUR, WE WILL FINISH WHAT THE VOLCANO STARTED, AND REDUCE EVERY-THING BELOW TO MOLTEN WASTE.
UH-OH...

"...WILL NUKE IT TO SMITHEREENS-- IN ONE HOUR."

I AM SORRY I CAN NOT IDENTIFY TO WHAT *SMITHEREENS* REFERS...

IT REFERS TO ME HAVING MISCALCULATED, KELEX. WE DON'T HAVE THE TIME I'D HOPED.

BATMAN WAS RIGHT. THINGS DO TEND TO FALL APART WHEN THESE CREATURES ARE INVOLVED.

I'M NARROWING MY SEARCH--LOIS IS NEARBY. LET ME KNOW IF YOU GET ANY SIGN OF BATMAN...

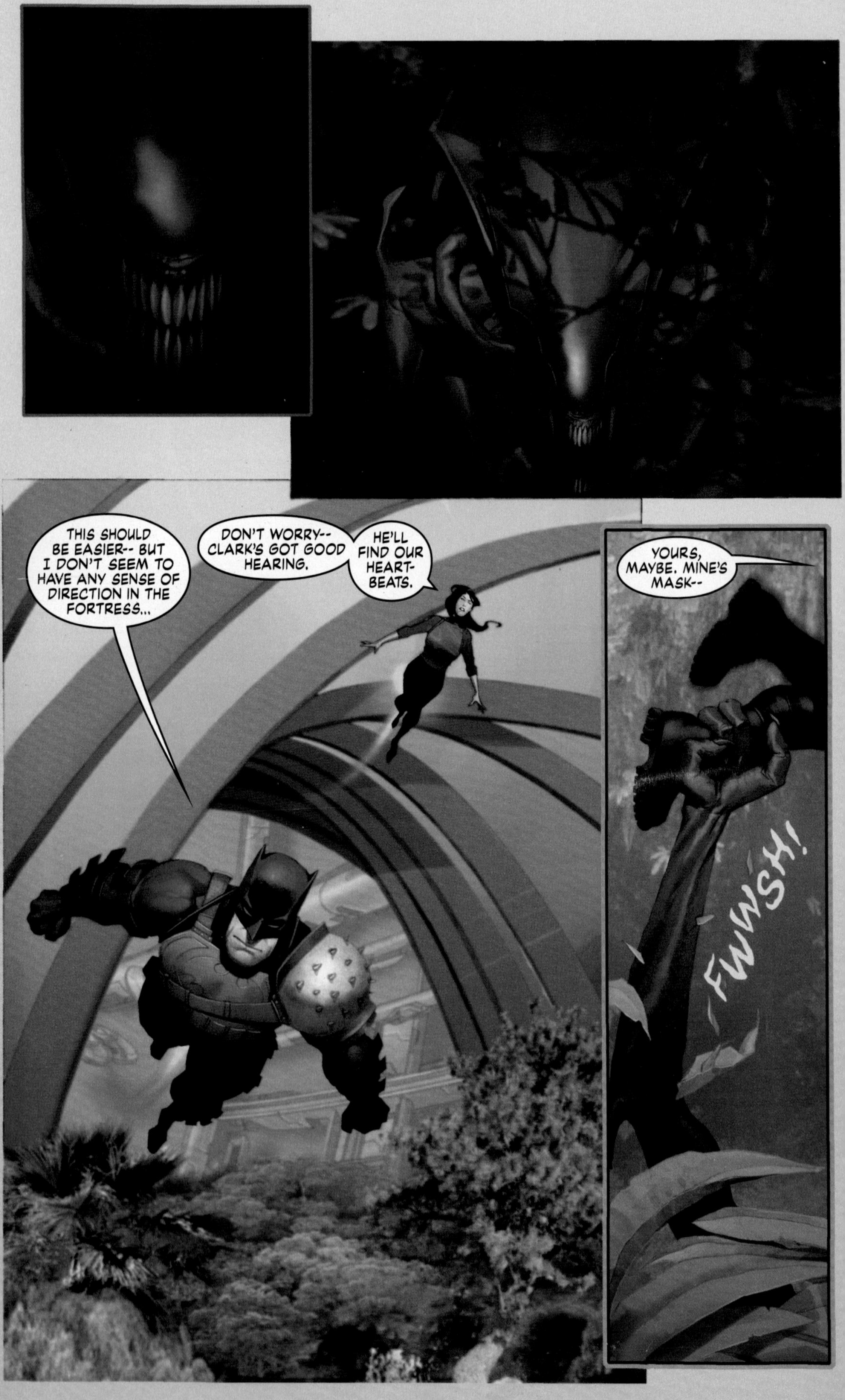
THIS SHOULD BE EASIER-- BUT I DON'T SEEM TO HAVE ANY SENSE OF DIRECTION IN THE FORTRESS...
DON'T WORRY-- CLARK'S GOT GOOD HEARING.
HE'LL FIND OUR HEART-BEATS.
YOURS, MAYBE. MINE'S MASK--
FWWSH!

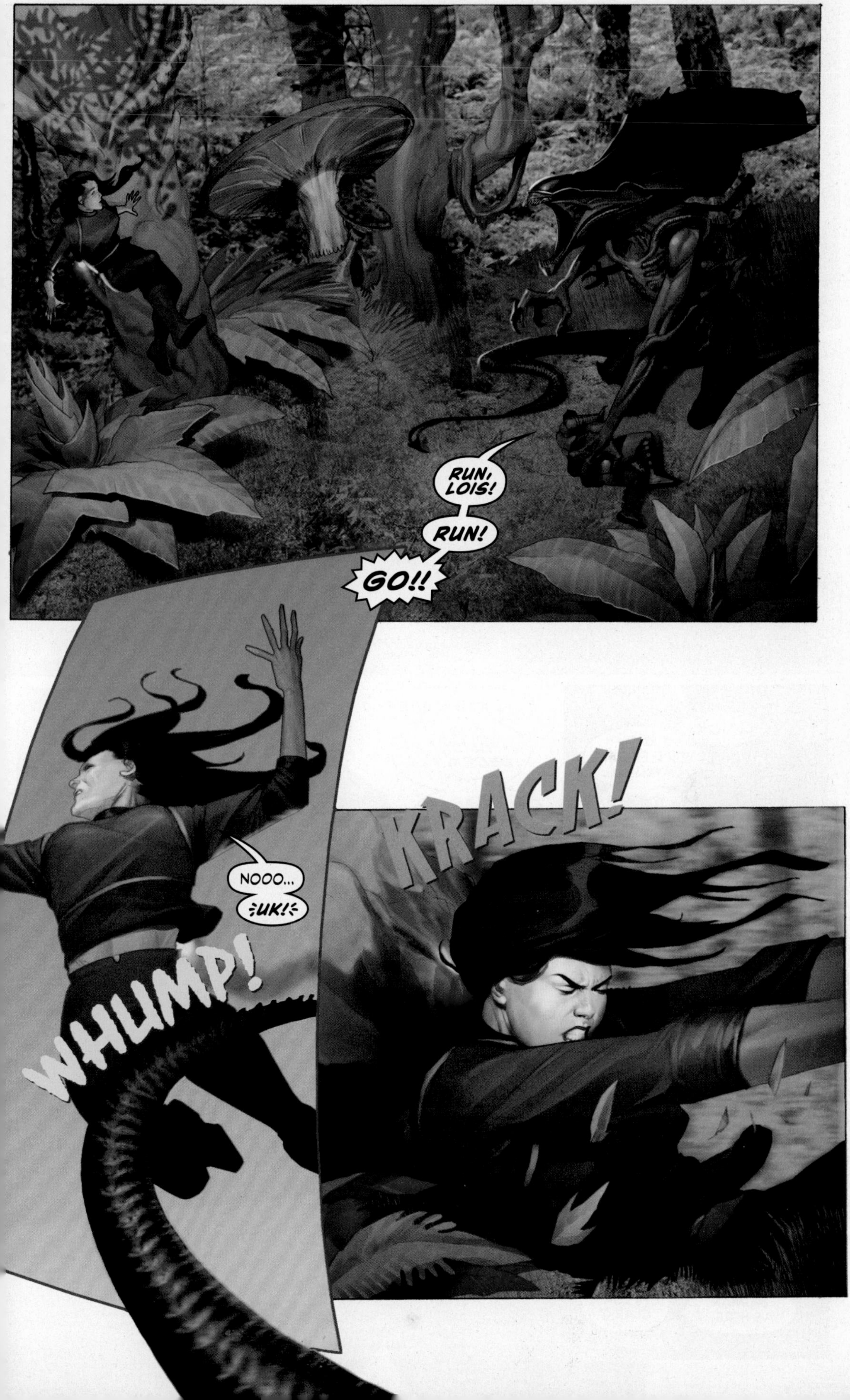
RUN, LOIS!
RUN!
GO!!
NOOO...
UK!
WHUMP!
KRACK!

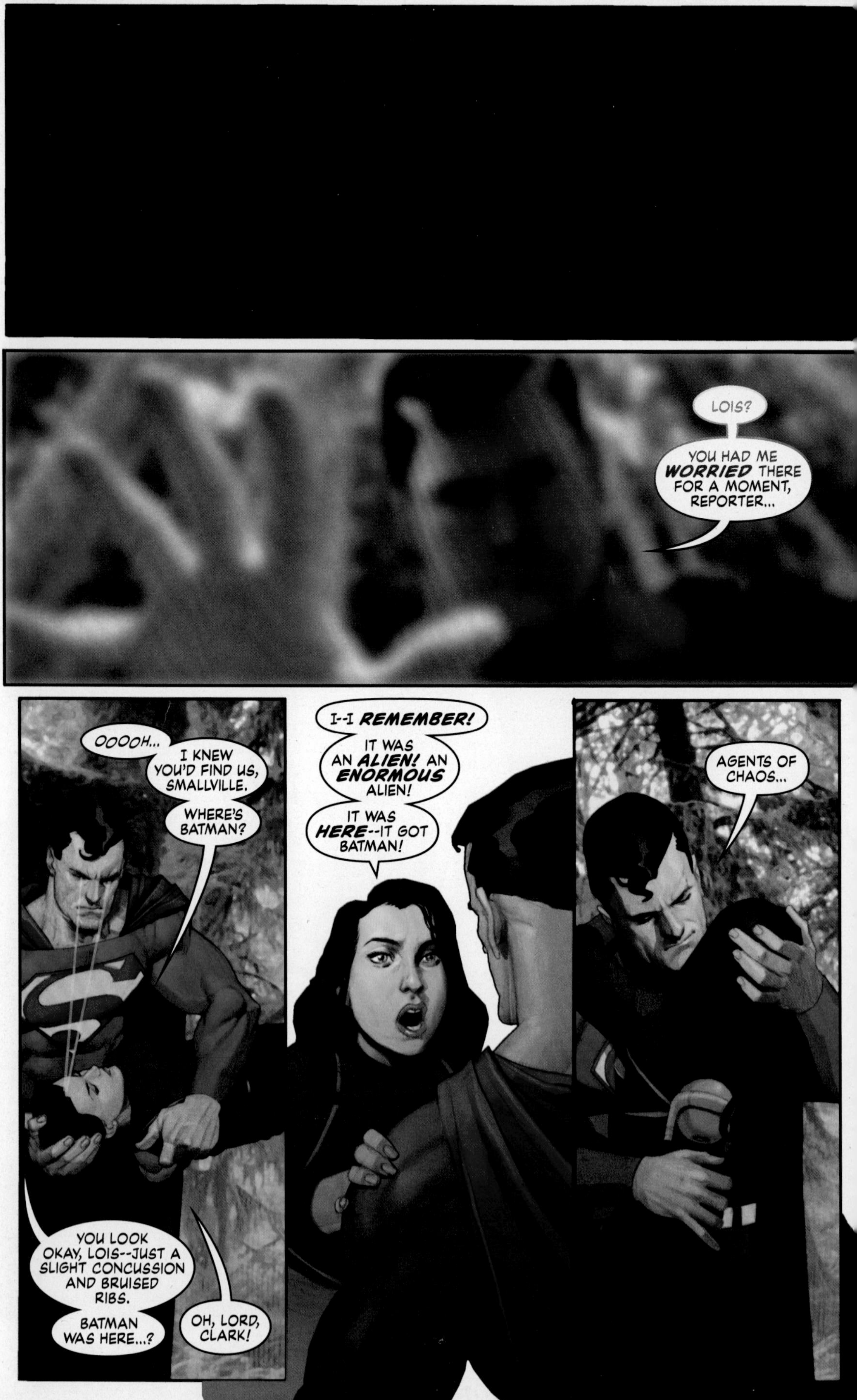
LOIS?
YOU HAD ME WORRIED THERE FOR A MOMENT, REPORTER...
OOOOH...
I KNEW YOU'D FIND US, SMALLVILLE.
WHERE'S BATMAN?
YOU LOOK OKAY, LOIS--JUST A SLIGHT CONCUSSION AND BRUISED RIBS.
BATMAN WAS HERE...?
OH, LORD, CLARK!
I--I REMEMBER!
IT WAS AN ALIEN! AN ENORMOUS ALIEN!
IT WAS HERE--IT GOT BATMAN!
AGENTS OF CHAOS...

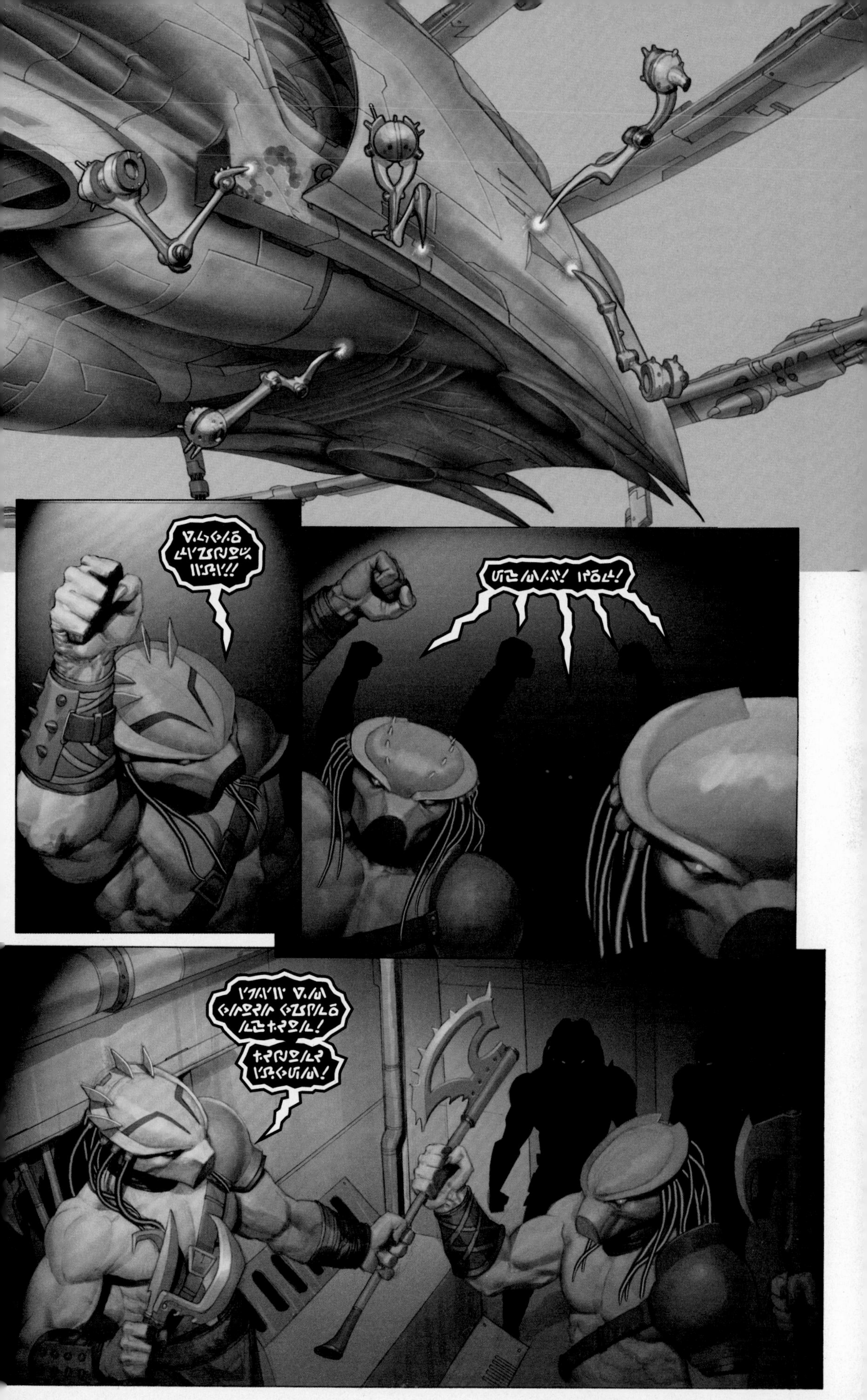

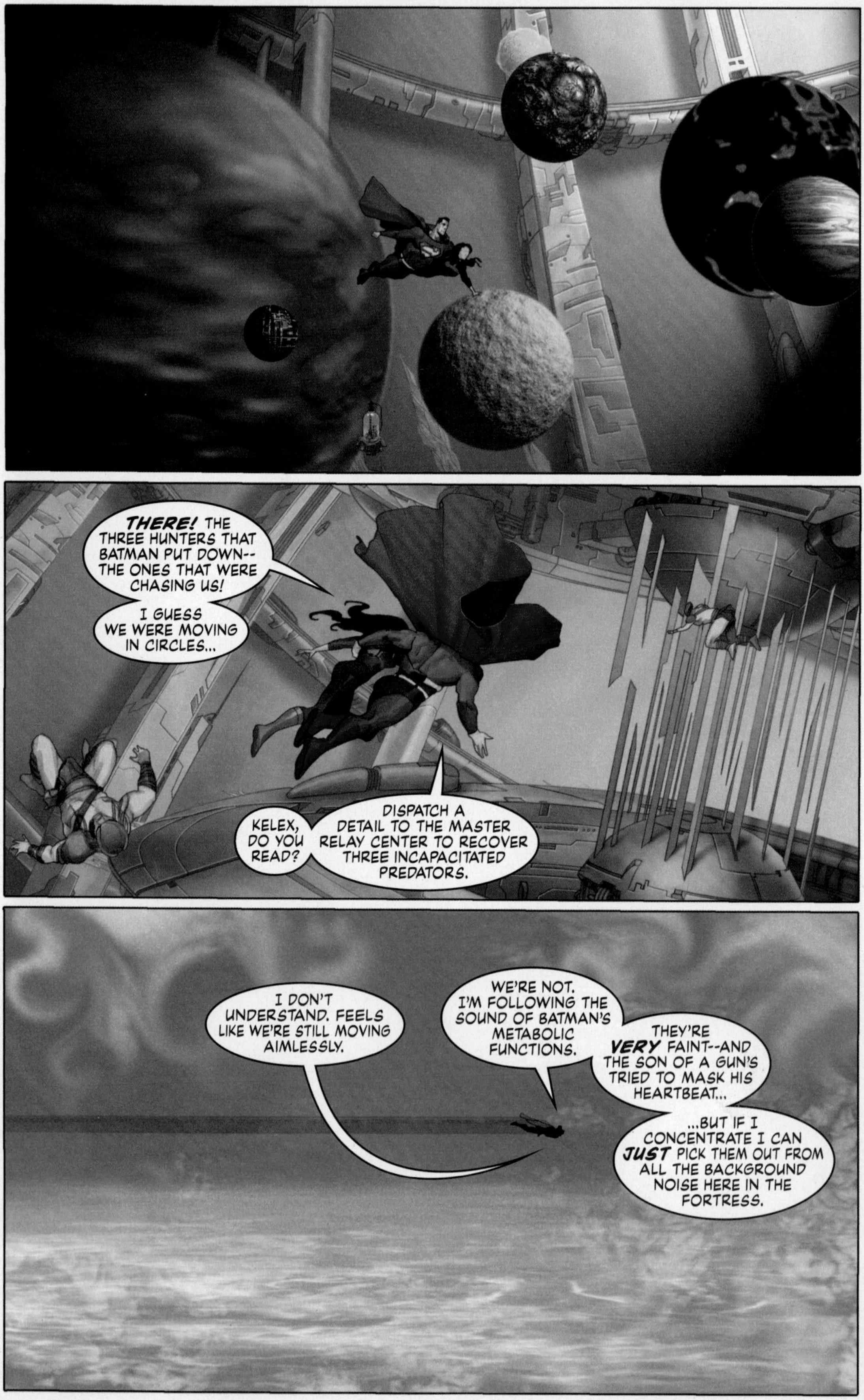
THERE! THE THREE HUNTERS THAT BATMAN PUT DOWN-- THE ONES THAT WERE CHASING US!
I GUESS WE WERE MOVING IN CIRCLES...
KELEX, DO YOU READ?
DISPATCH A DETAIL TO THE MASTER RELAY CENTER TO RECOVER THREE INCAPACITATED PREDATORS.
I DON'T UNDERSTAND. FEELS LIKE WE'RE STILL MOVING AIMLESSLY.
WE'RE NOT. I'M FOLLOWING THE SOUND OF BATMAN'S METABOLIC FUNCTIONS.
THEY'RE VERY FAINT--AND THE SON OF A GUN'S TRIED TO MASK HIS HEARTBEAT...
...BUT IF I CONCENTRATE I CAN JUST PICK THEM OUT FROM ALL THE BACKGROUND NOISE HERE IN THE FORTRESS.

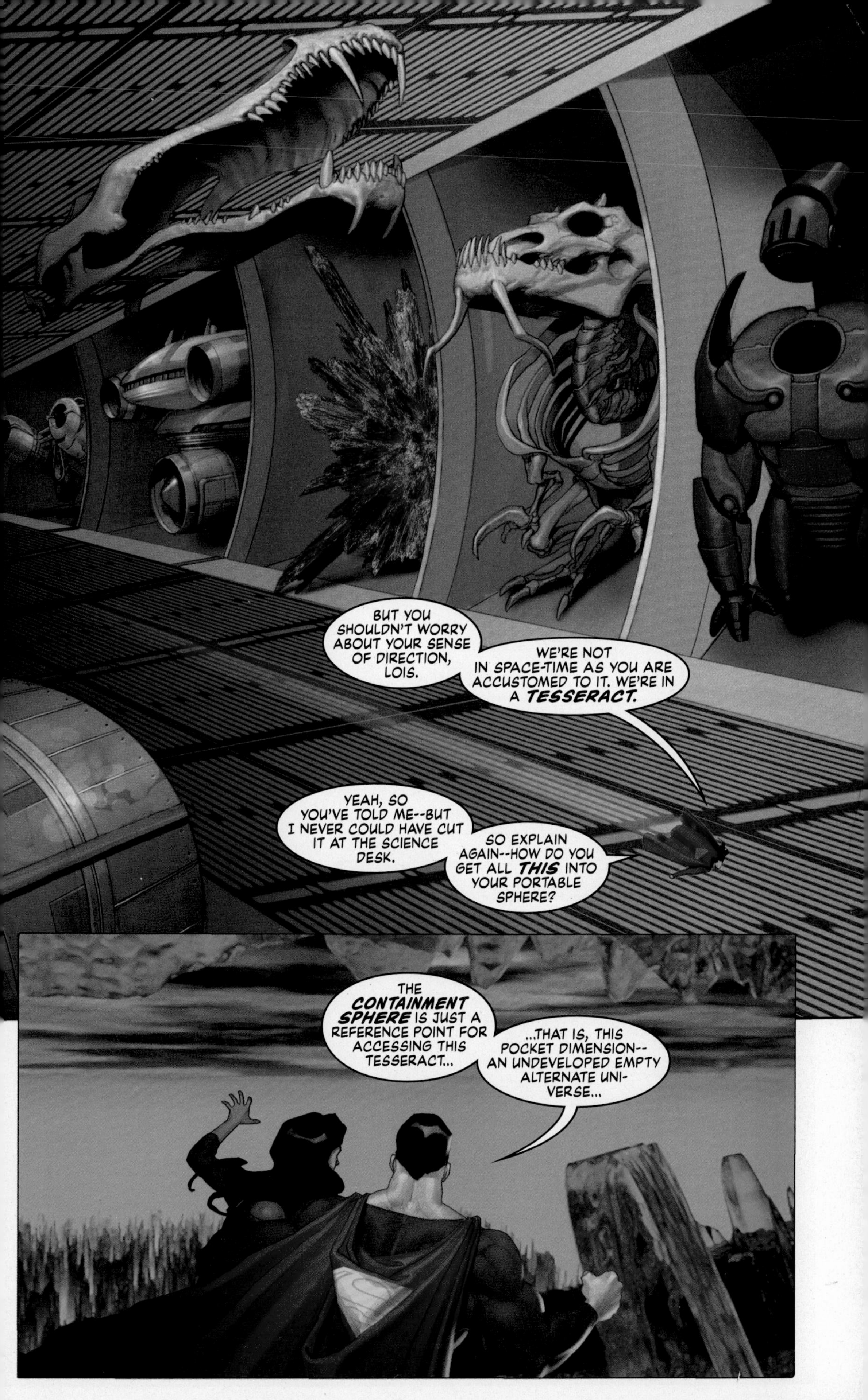
BUT YOU SHOULDN'T WORRY ABOUT YOUR SENSE OF DIRECTION, LOIS.
WE'RE NOT IN SPACE-TIME AS YOU ARE ACCUSTOMED TO IT. WE'RE IN A ***TESSERACT.***
YEAH, SO YOU'VE TOLD ME--BUT I NEVER COULD HAVE CUT IT AT THE SCIENCE DESK.
SO EXPLAIN AGAIN--HOW DO YOU GET ALL ***THIS*** INTO YOUR PORTABLE SPHERE?
THE ***CONTAINMENT SPHERE*** IS JUST A REFERENCE POINT FOR ACCESSING THIS TESSERACT...
...THAT IS, THIS POCKET DIMENSION--AN UNDEVELOPED EMPTY ALTERNATE UNI-VERSE...

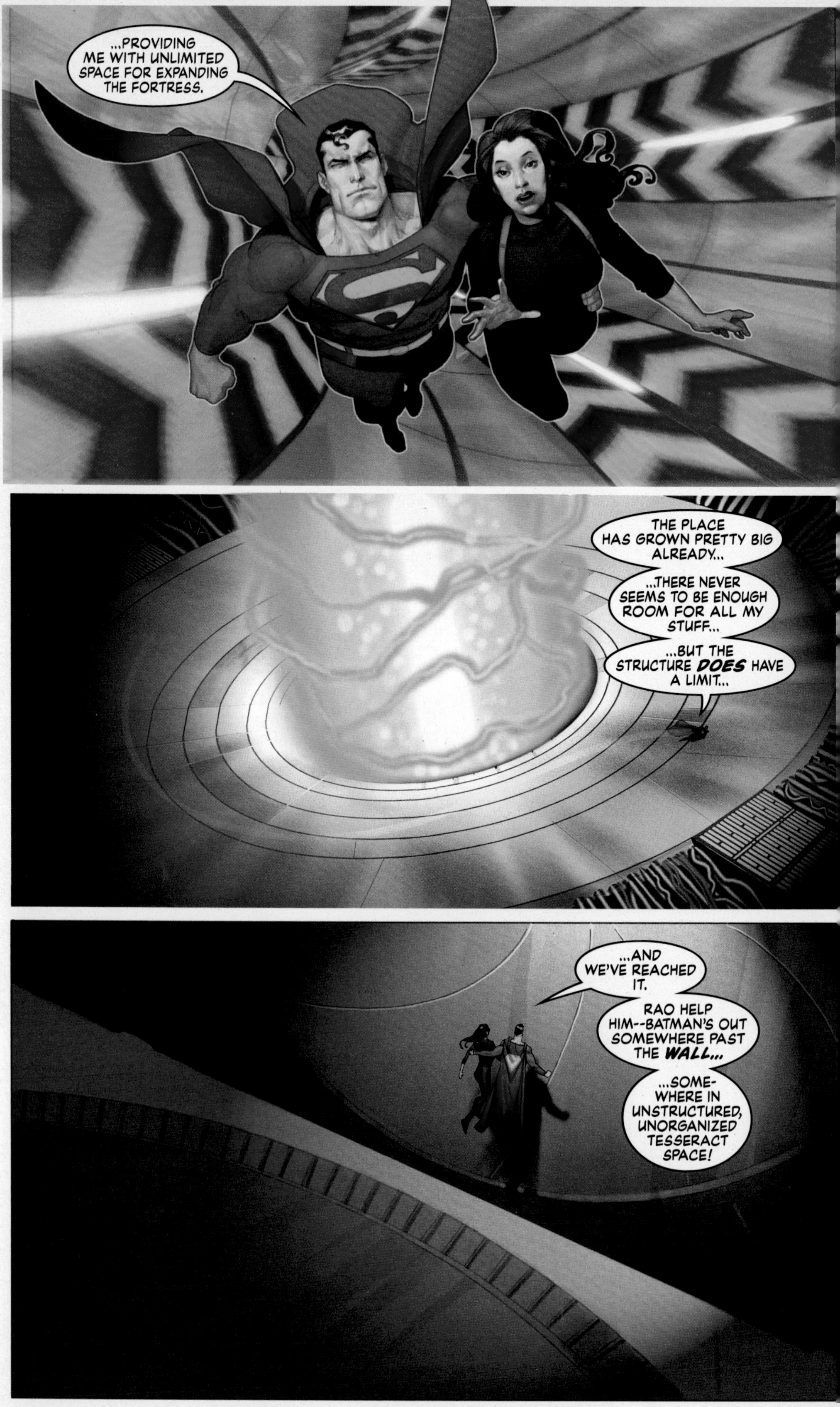
...PROVIDING ME WITH UNLIMITED SPACE FOR EXPANDING THE FORTRESS.
THE PLACE HAS GROWN PRETTY BIG ALREADY...
...THERE NEVER SEEMS TO BE ENOUGH ROOM FOR ALL MY STUFF...
...BUT THE STRUCTURE DOES HAVE A LIMIT...
...AND WE'VE REACHED IT.
RAO HELP HIM--BATMAN'S OUT SOMEWHERE PAST THE WALL...
...SOME-WHERE IN UNSTRUCTURED, UNORGANIZED TESSERACT SPACE!

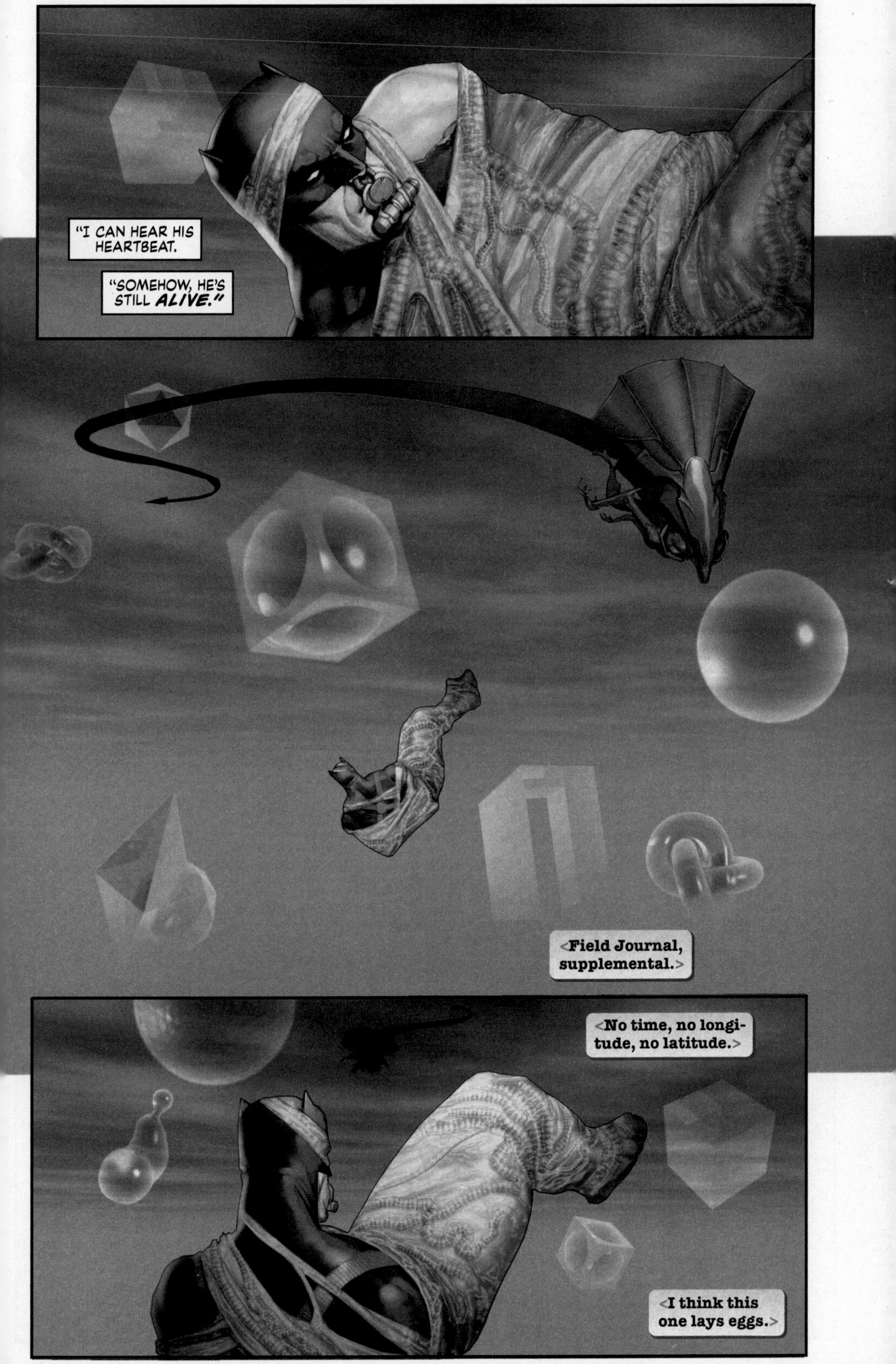
"I CAN HEAR HIS HEARTBEAT.
"SOMEHOW, HE'S STILL ALIVE."
<Field Journal, supplemental.>
<No time, no longitude, no latitude.>
<I think this one lays eggs.>

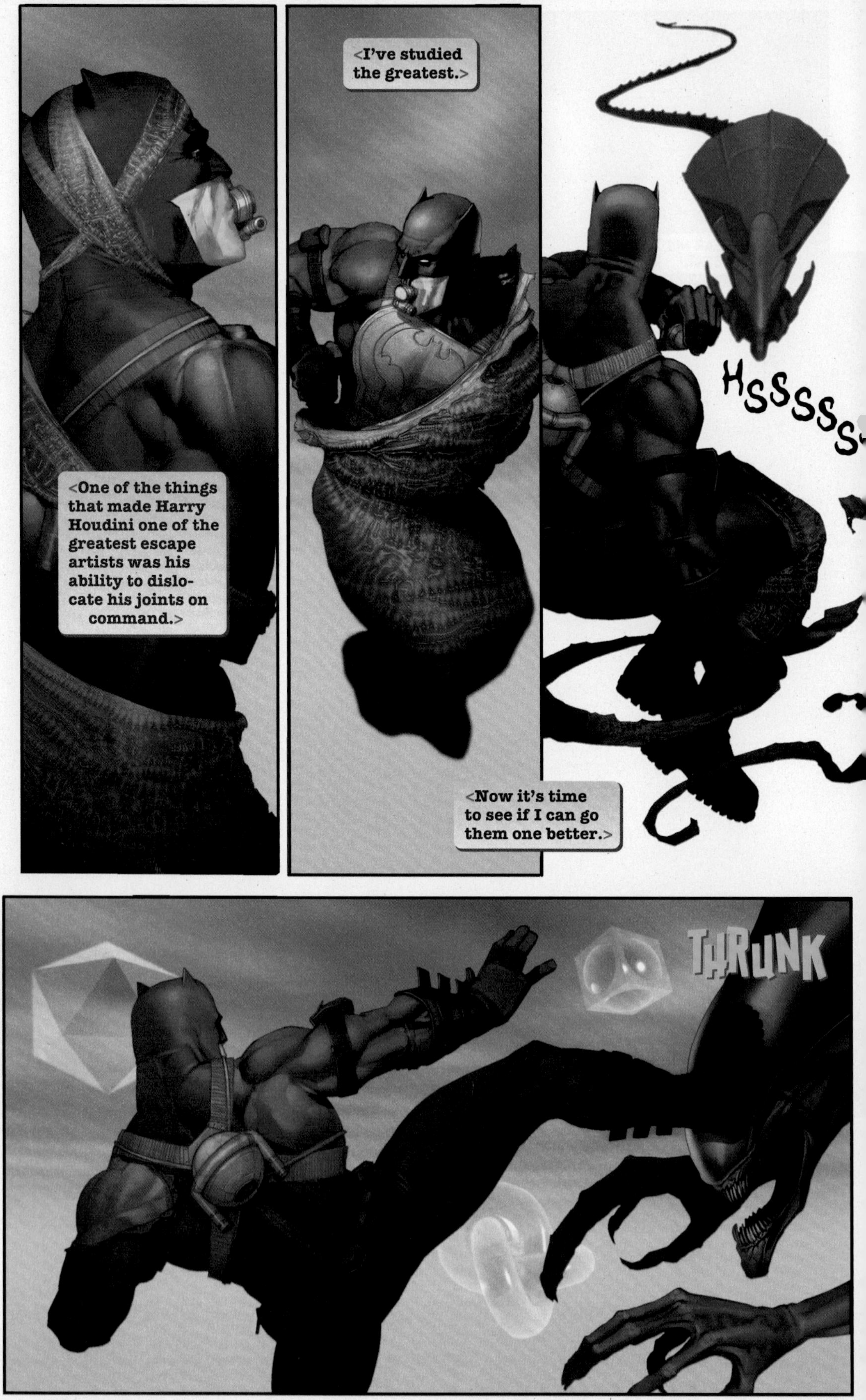
<One of the things that made Harry Houdini one of the greatest escape artists was his ability to dislo-cate his joints on command.>
<I've studied the greatest.>
<Now it's time to see if I can go them one better.>
HSSSSS
THRUNK

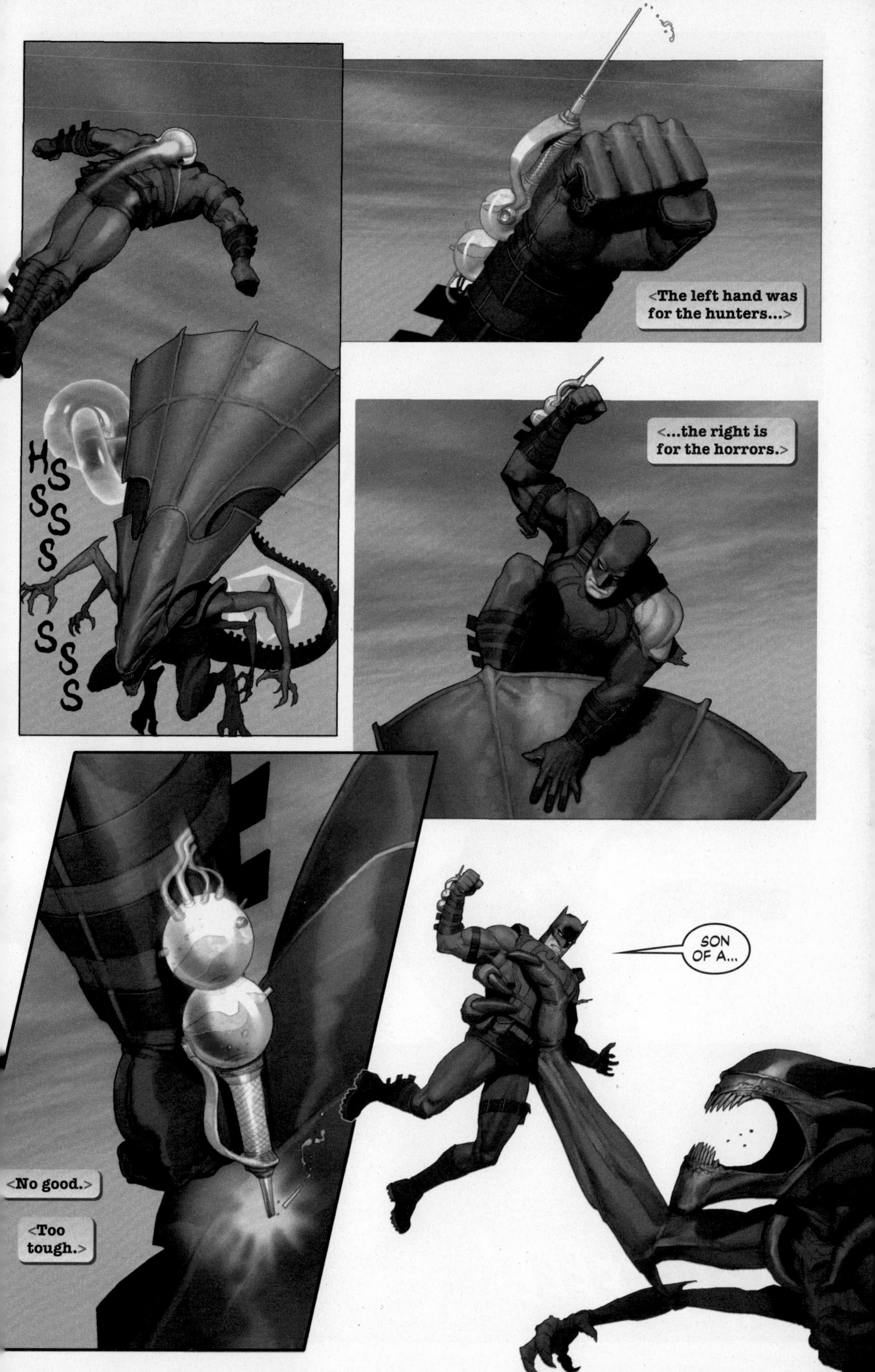
HSSSSSSSSS
<The left hand was for the hunters...>
<...the right is for the horrors.>
<No good.>
<Too tough.>
SON OF A...

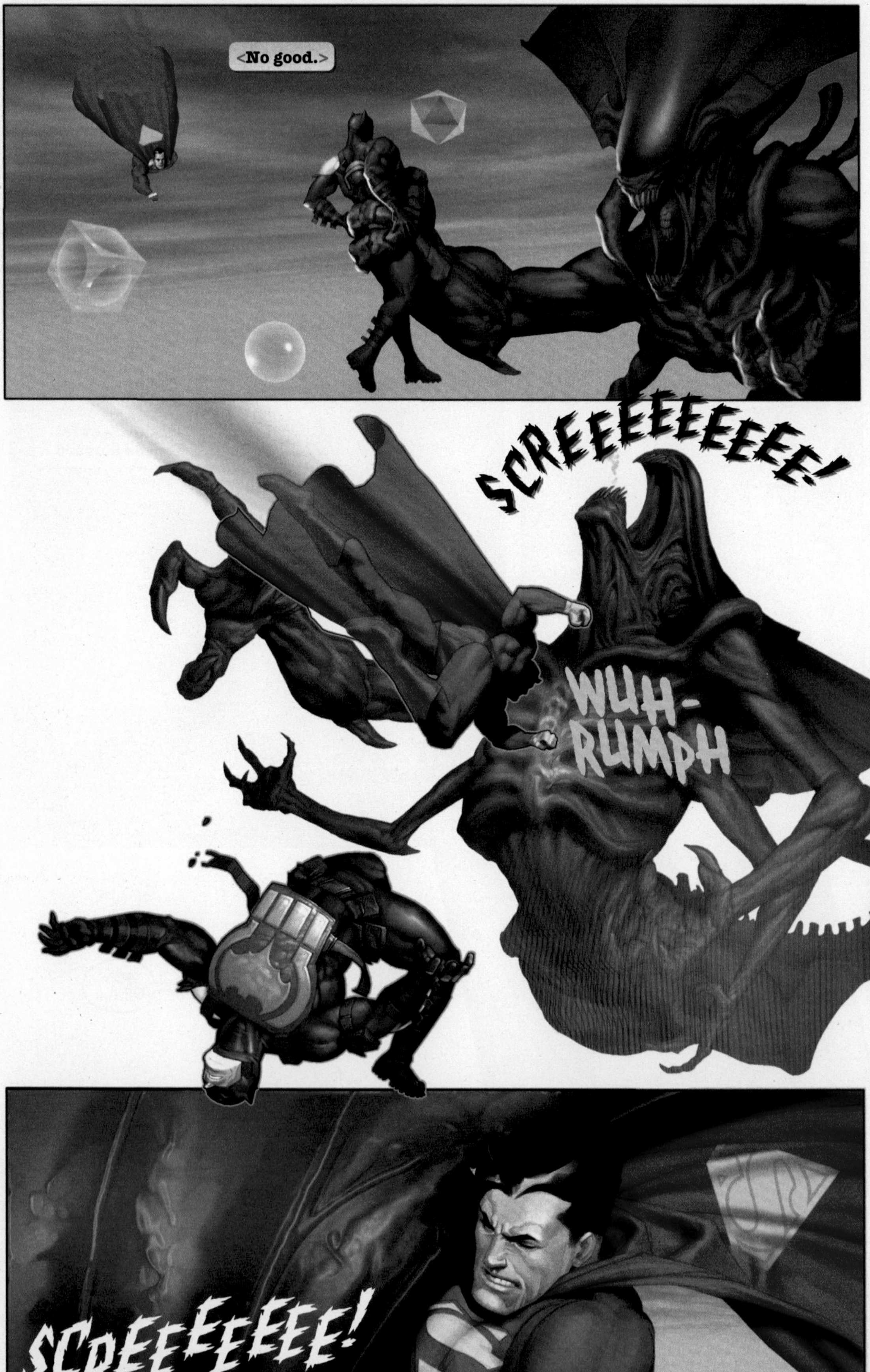
<No good.>
SCREEEEEEEEE!
WUH-RUMPH
SCREEEEEEE!

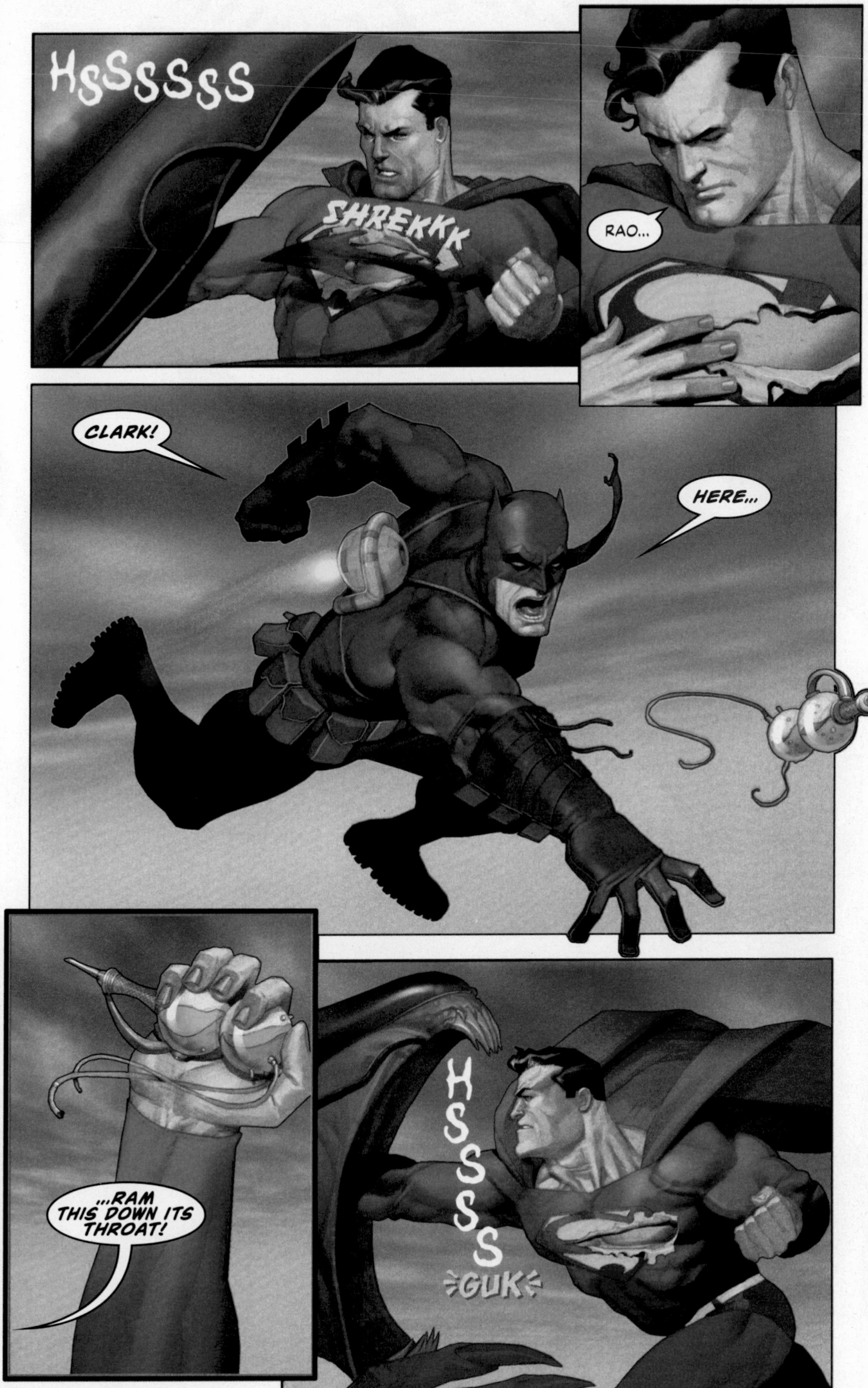
HSSSSSS
SHREKKK
RAO...
CLARK!
HERE...
...RAM THIS DOWN ITS THROAT!
HSSSS
GUK

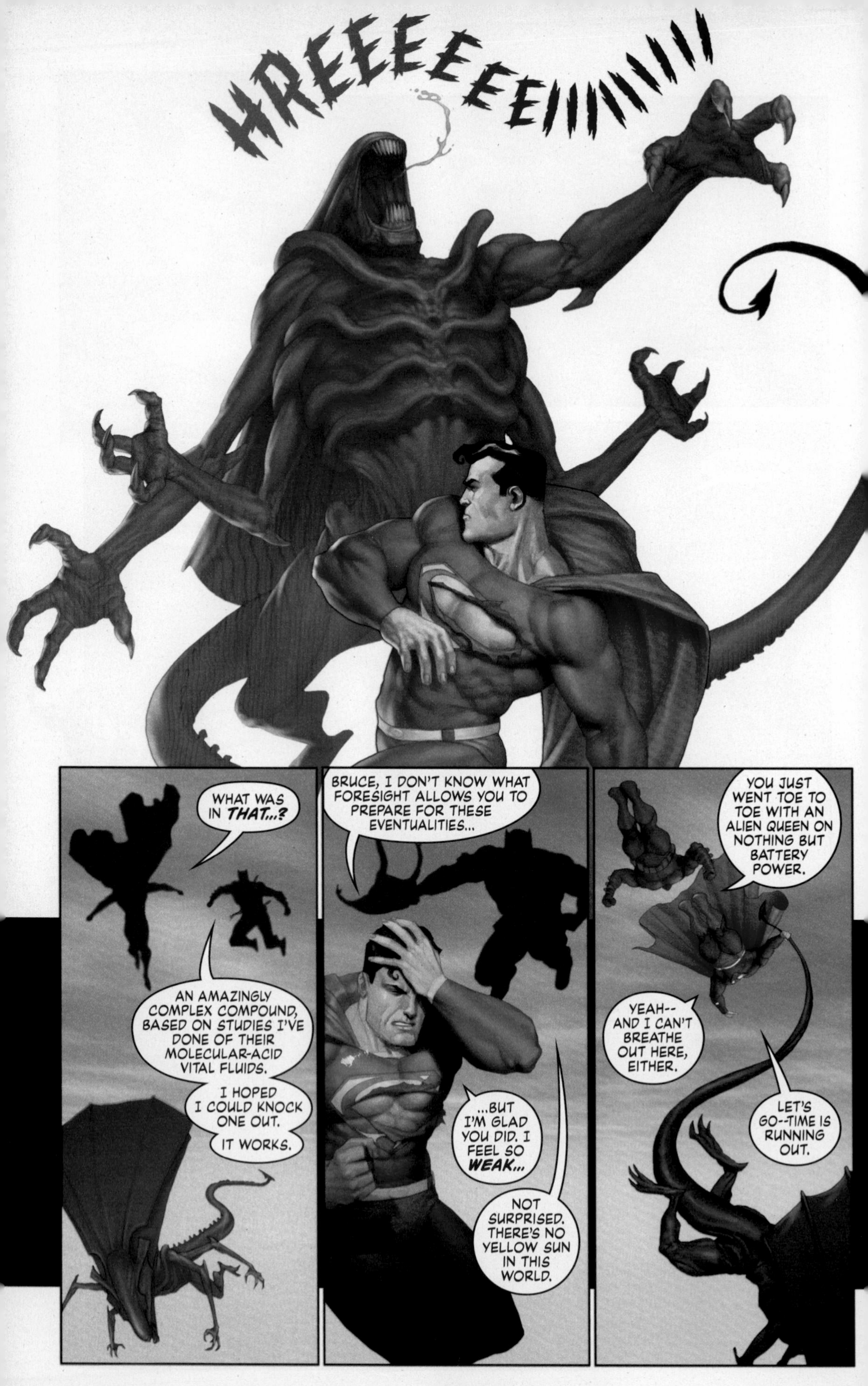
HREEEEEEE!!!!!!!!
WHAT WAS IN THAT...?
AN AMAZINGLY COMPLEX COMPOUND, BASED ON STUDIES I'VE DONE OF THEIR MOLECULAR-ACID VITAL FLUIDS.
I HOPED I COULD KNOCK ONE OUT.
IT WORKS.
BRUCE, I DON'T KNOW WHAT FORESIGHT ALLOWS YOU TO PREPARE FOR THESE EVENTUALITIES...
...BUT I'M GLAD YOU DID. I FEEL SO WEAK...
NOT SURPRISED. THERE'S NO YELLOW SUN IN THIS WORLD.
YOU JUST WENT TOE TO TOE WITH AN ALIEN QUEEN ON NOTHING BUT BATTERY POWER.
YEAH-- AND I CAN'T BREATHE OUT HERE, EITHER.
LET'S GO--TIME IS RUNNING OUT.

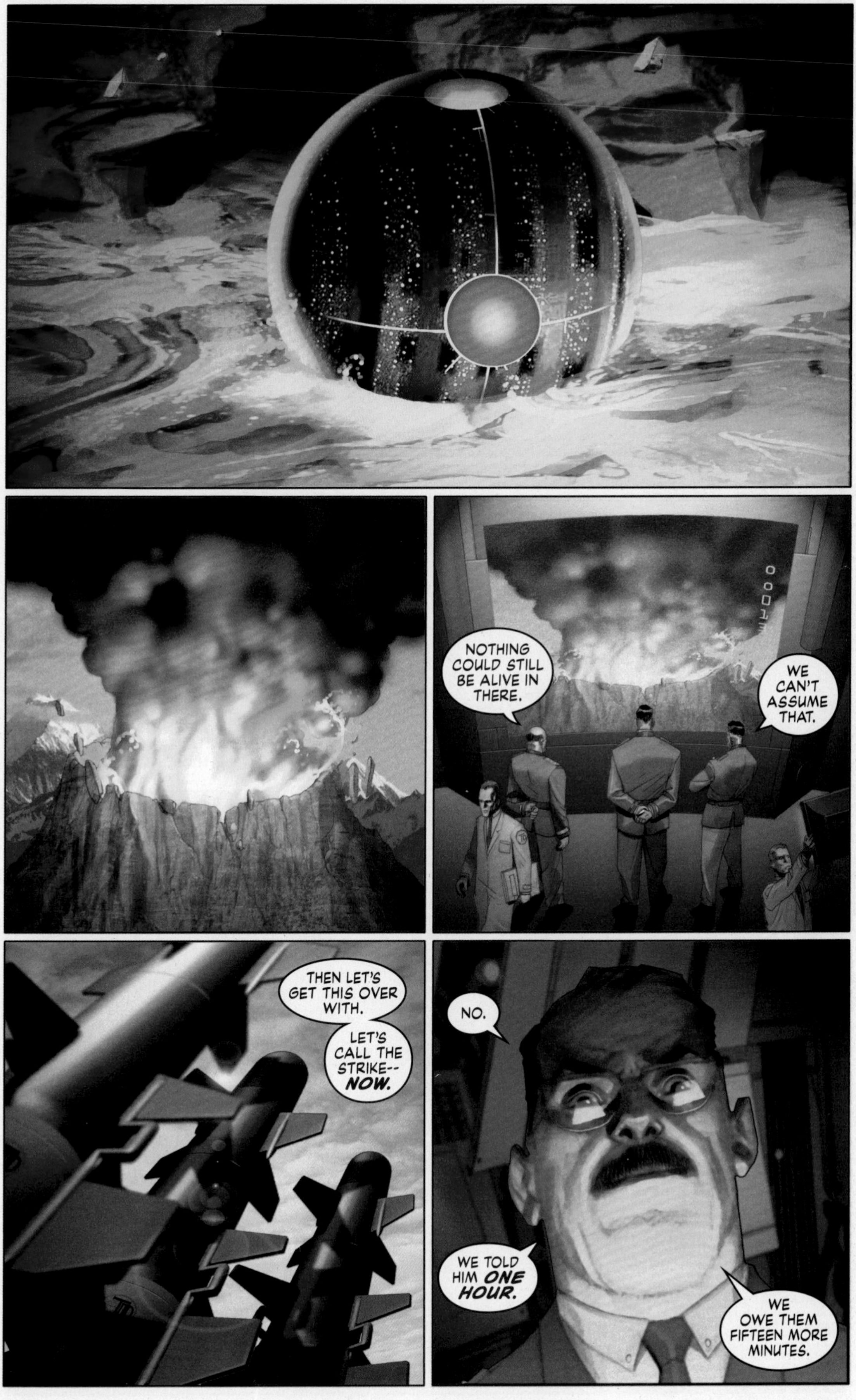
NOTHING COULD STILL BE ALIVE IN THERE.
WE CAN'T ASSUME THAT.
THEN LET'S GET THIS OVER WITH.
LET'S CALL THE STRIKE-- *NOW.*
NO.
WE TOLD HIM *ONE HOUR.*
WE OWE THEM FIFTEEN MORE MINUTES.

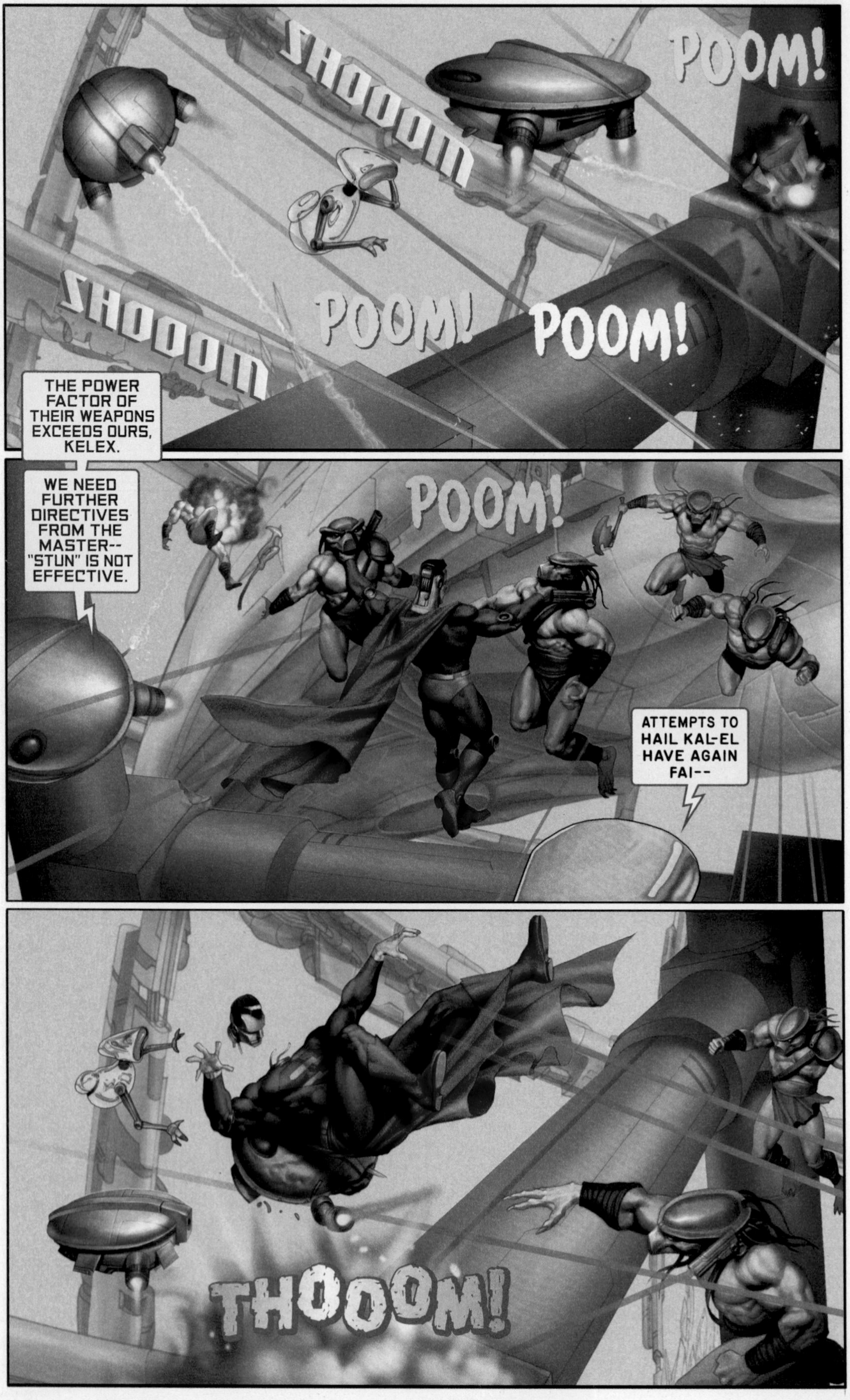
SHOOOM
POOM!
SHOOOM
POOM!
POOM!
THE POWER FACTOR OF THEIR WEAPONS EXCEEDS OURS, KELEX.
WE NEED FURTHER DIRECTIVES FROM THE MASTER-- "STUN" IS NOT EFFECTIVE.
POOM!
ATTEMPTS TO HAIL KAL-EL HAVE AGAIN FAI--
THOOOM!

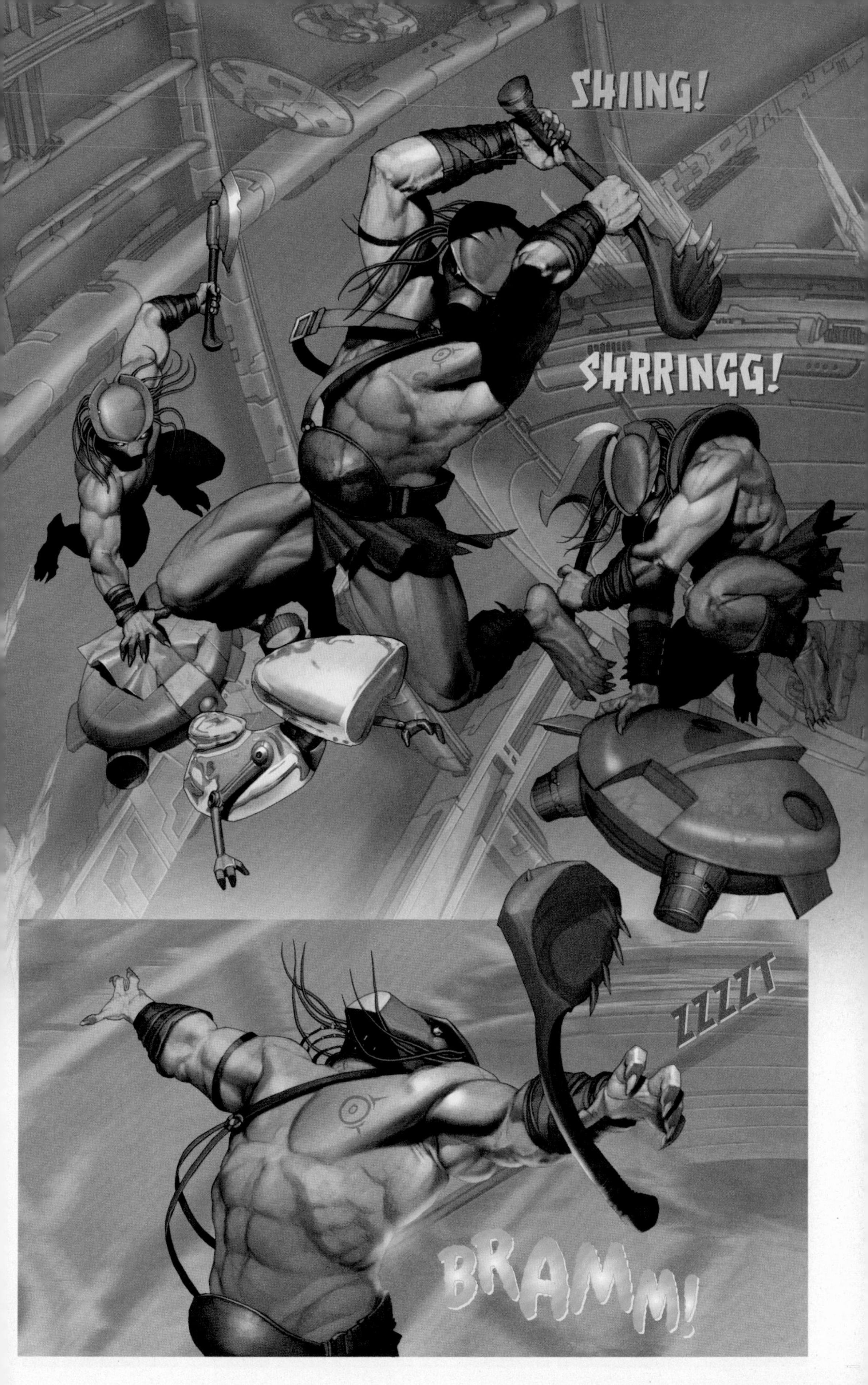
SHIING!
SHRRINGG!
ZZZZT
BRAMM!

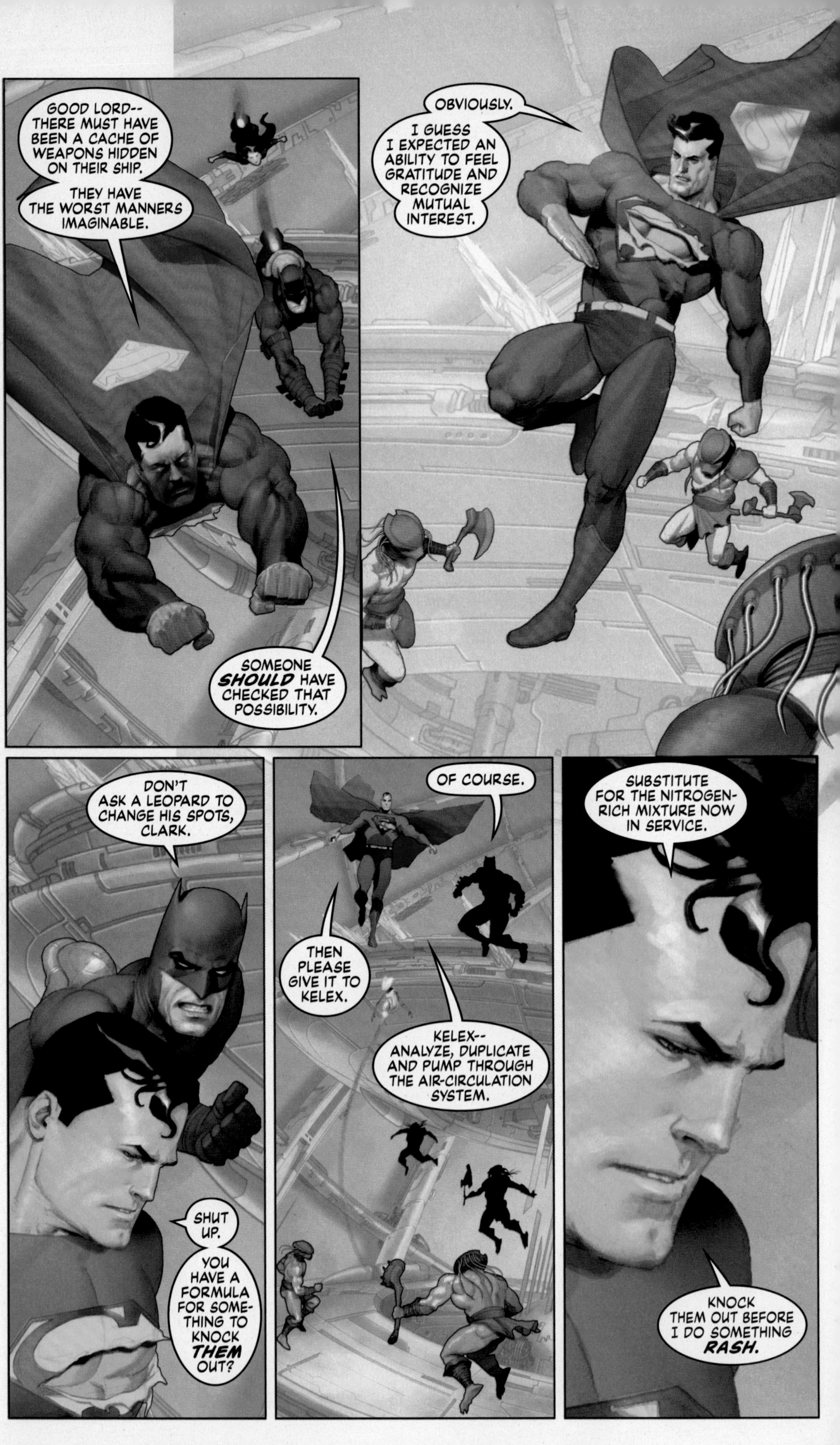
GOOD LORD-- THERE MUST HAVE BEEN A CACHE OF WEAPONS HIDDEN ON THEIR SHIP.
THEY HAVE THE WORST MANNERS IMAGINABLE.
SOMEONE SHOULD HAVE CHECKED THAT POSSIBILITY.
OBVIOUSLY.
I GUESS I EXPECTED AN ABILITY TO FEEL GRATITUDE AND RECOGNIZE MUTUAL INTEREST.
DON'T ASK A LEOPARD TO CHANGE HIS SPOTS, CLARK.
SHUT UP.
YOU HAVE A FORMULA FOR SOMETHING TO KNOCK THEM OUT?
OF COURSE.
THEN PLEASE GIVE IT TO KELEX.
KELEX-- ANALYZE, DUPLICATE AND PUMP THROUGH THE AIR-CIRCULATION SYSTEM.
SUBSTITUTE FOR THE NITROGEN-RICH MIXTURE NOW IN SERVICE.
KNOCK THEM OUT BEFORE I DO SOMETHING RASH.

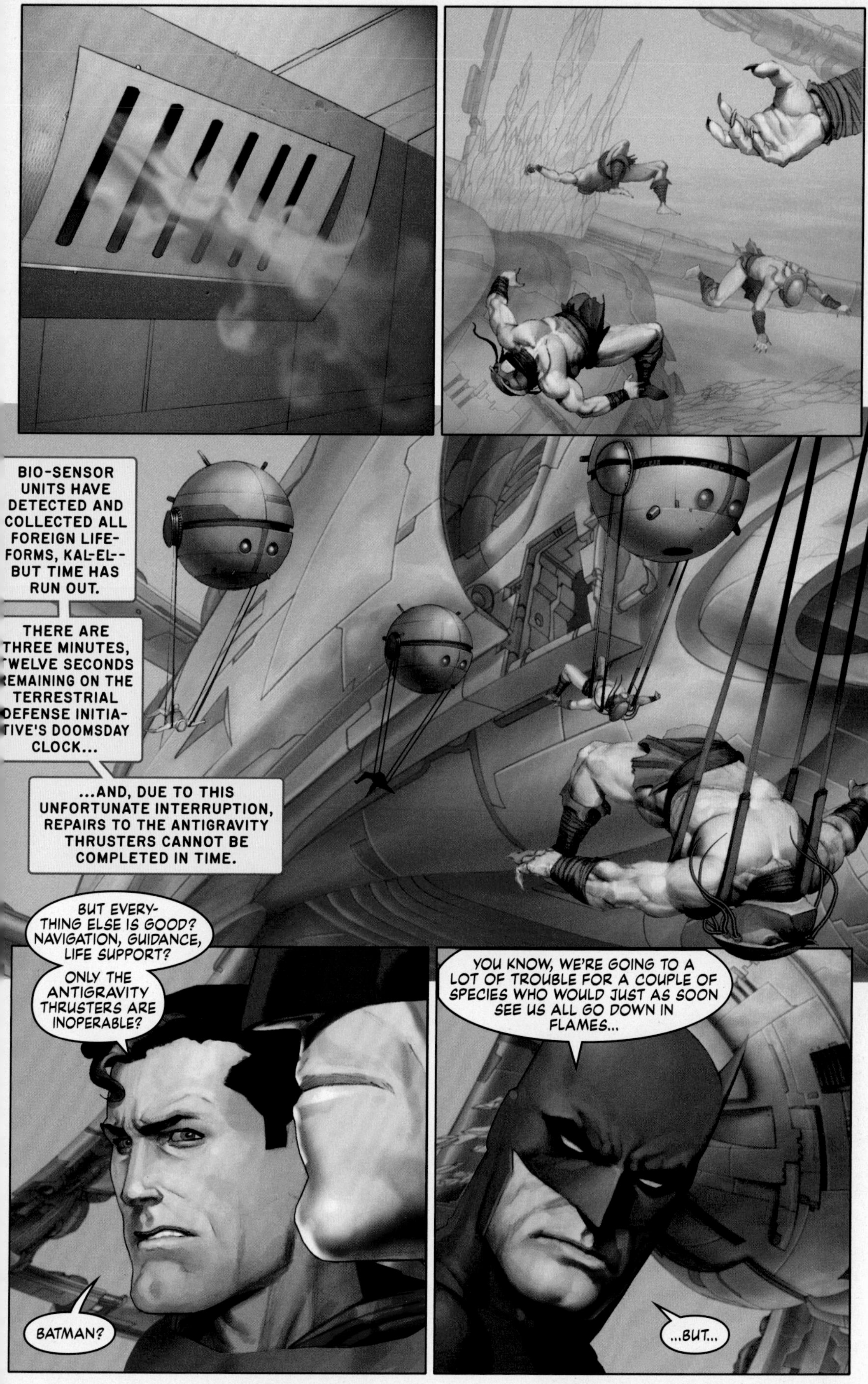
BIO-SENSOR UNITS HAVE DETECTED AND COLLECTED ALL FOREIGN LIFE-FORMS, KAL-EL--BUT TIME HAS RUN OUT.
THERE ARE THREE MINUTES, TWELVE SECONDS REMAINING ON THE TERRESTRIAL DEFENSE INITIATIVE'S DOOMSDAY CLOCK...
...AND, DUE TO THIS UNFORTUNATE INTERRUPTION, REPAIRS TO THE ANTIGRAVITY THRUSTERS CANNOT BE COMPLETED IN TIME.
BUT EVERYTHING ELSE IS GOOD? NAVIGATION, GUIDANCE, LIFE SUPPORT?
ONLY THE ANTIGRAVITY THRUSTERS ARE INOPERABLE?
BATMAN?
YOU KNOW, WE'RE GOING TO A LOT OF TROUBLE FOR A COUPLE OF SPECIES WHO WOULD JUST AS SOON SEE US ALL GO DOWN IN FLAMES...
...BUT...

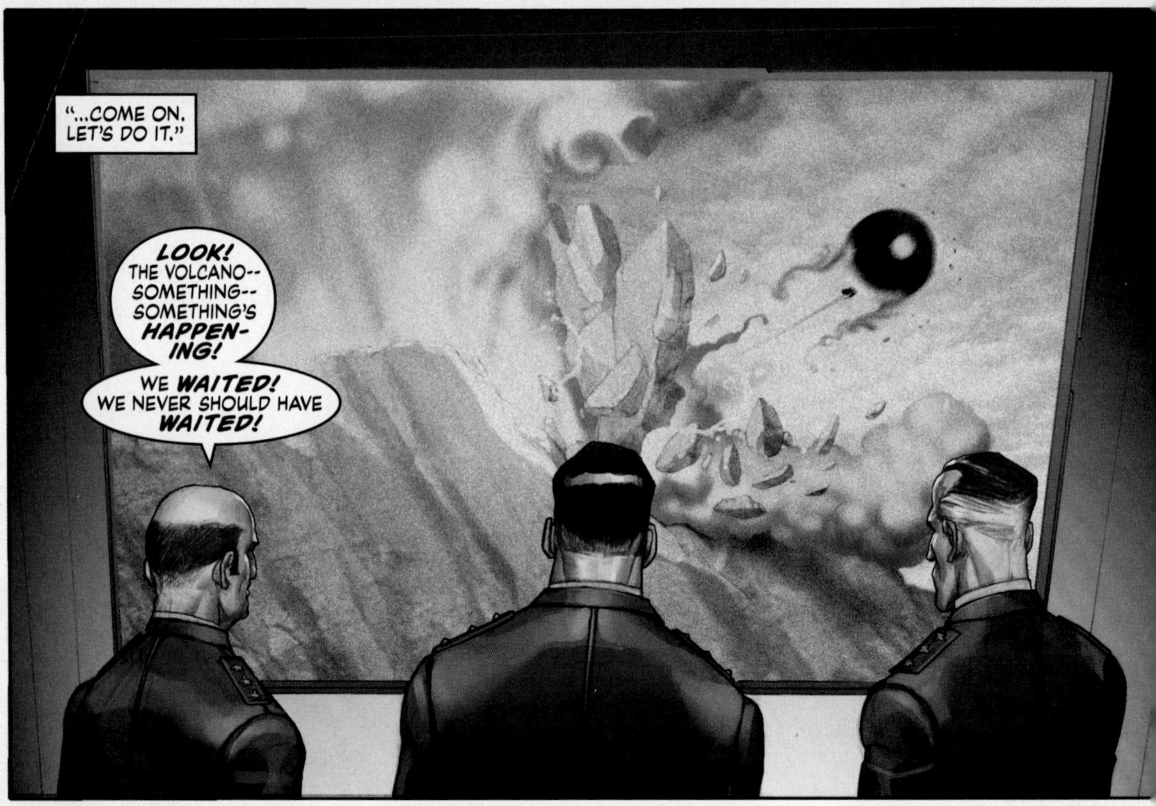
"...COME ON. LET'S DO IT."
LOOK! THE VOLCANO-- SOMETHING-- SOMETHING'S HAPPEN- ING!
WE WAITED! WE NEVER SHOULD HAVE WAITED!

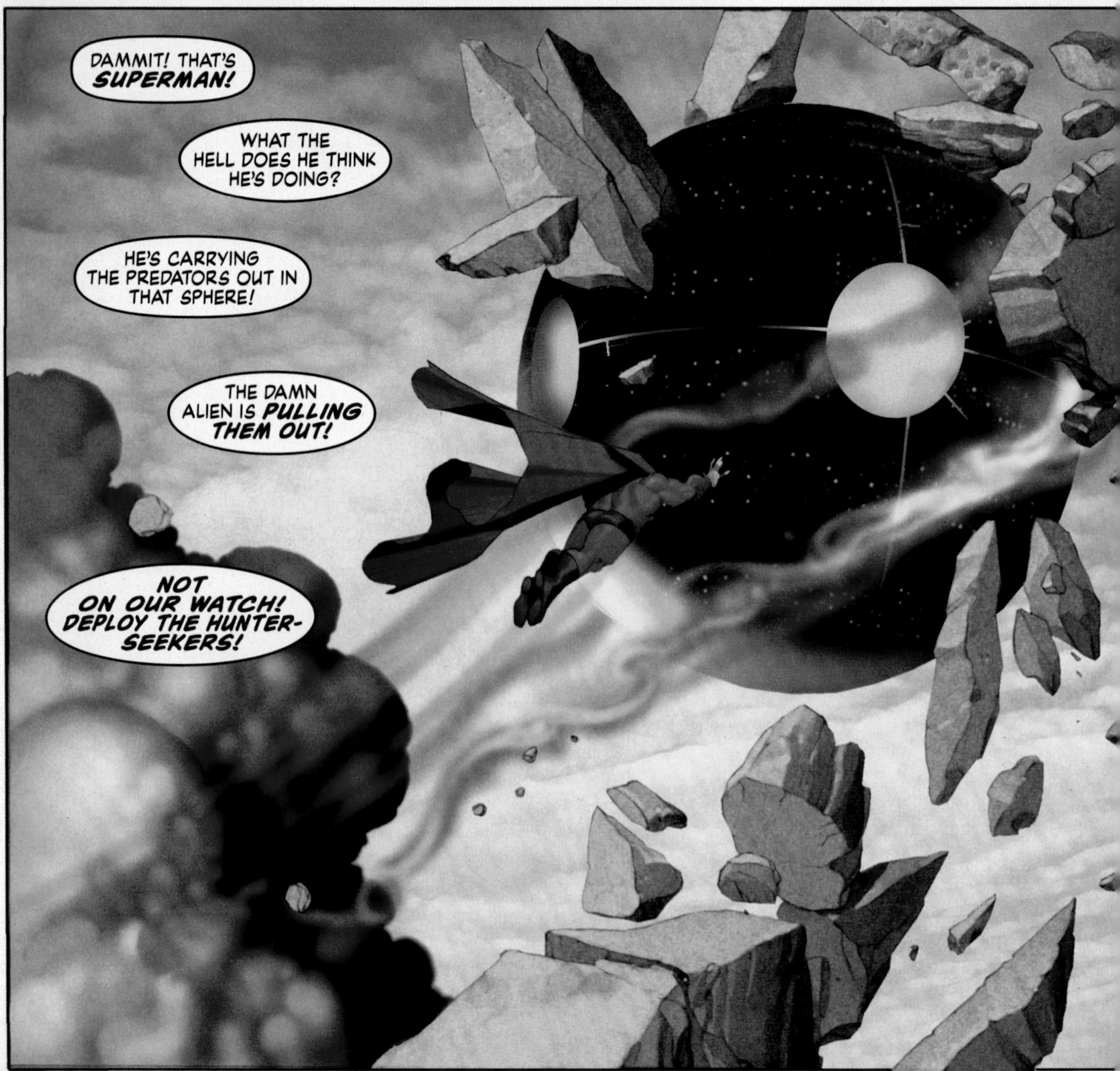
DAMMIT! THAT'S SUPERMAN!
WHAT THE HELL DOES HE THINK HE'S DOING?
HE'S CARRYING THE PREDATORS OUT IN THAT SPHERE!
THE DAMN ALIEN IS PULLING THEM OUT!
NOT ON OUR WATCH! DEPLOY THE HUNTER-SEEKERS!

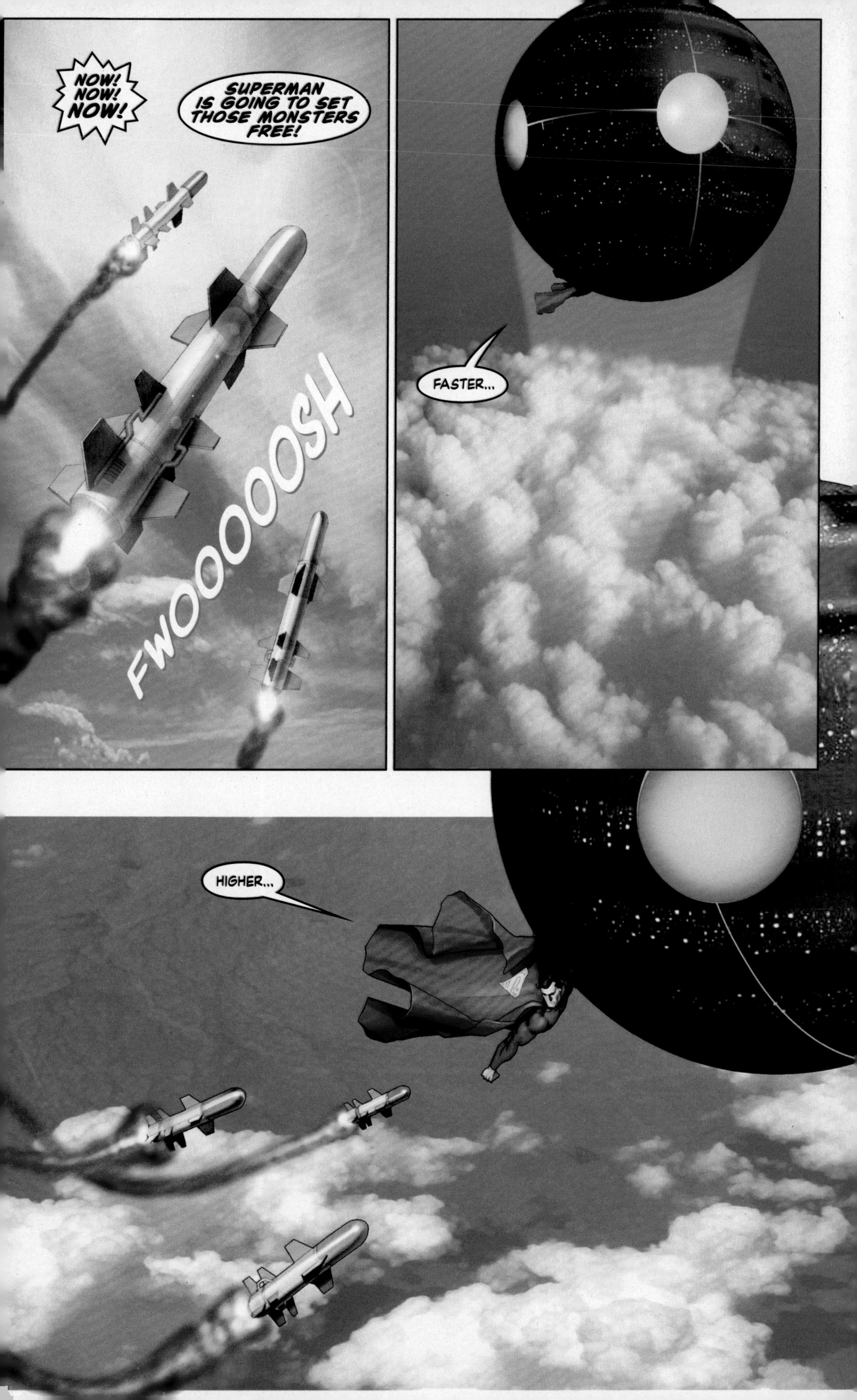
NOW! NOW! NOW!
SUPERMAN IS GOING TO SET THOSE MONSTERS FREE!
FWOOOOOSH
FASTER...
HIGHER...

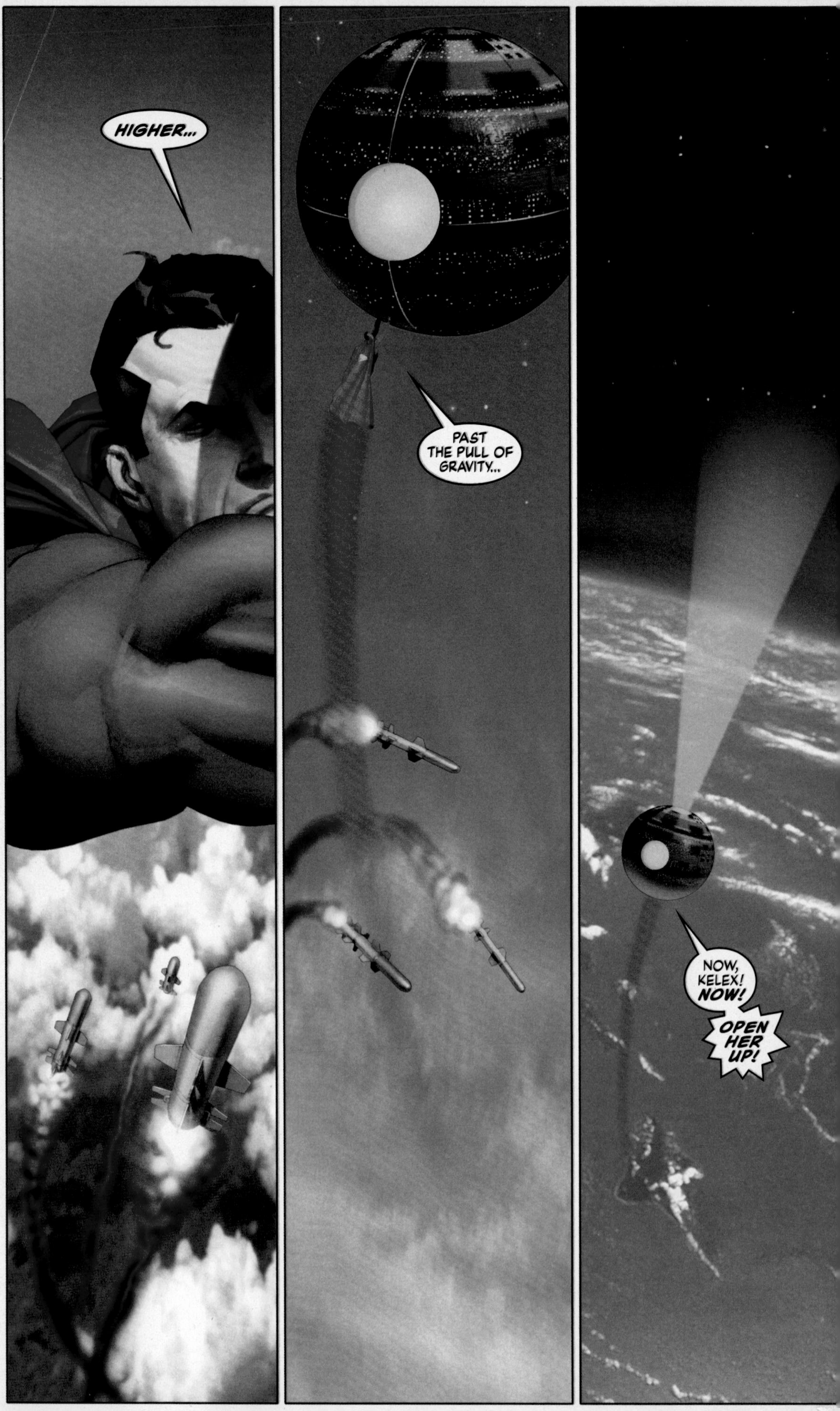
HIGHER...
PAST THE PULL OF GRAVITY...
NOW, KELEX! NOW!
OPEN HER UP!

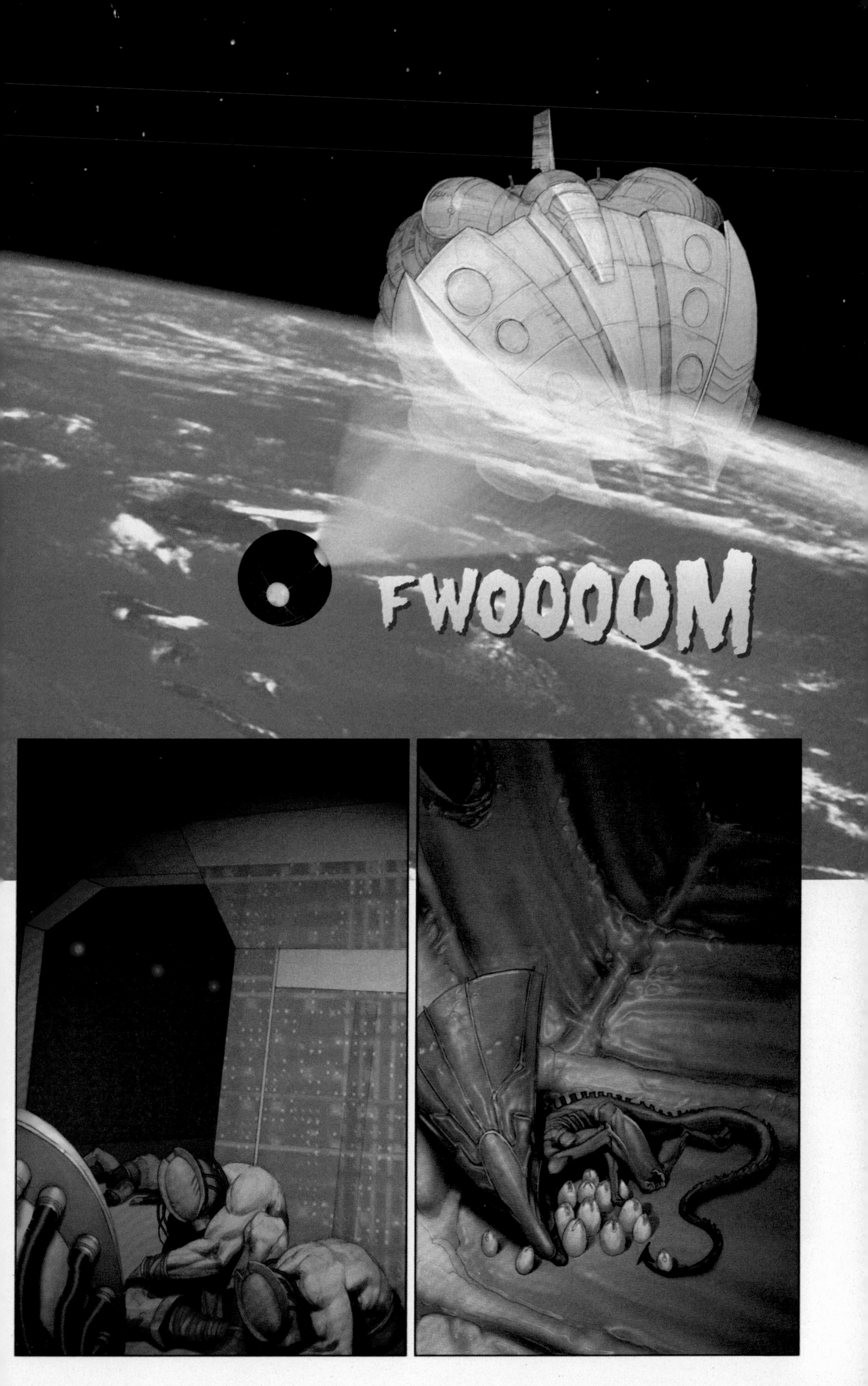
FWOOOOM

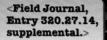

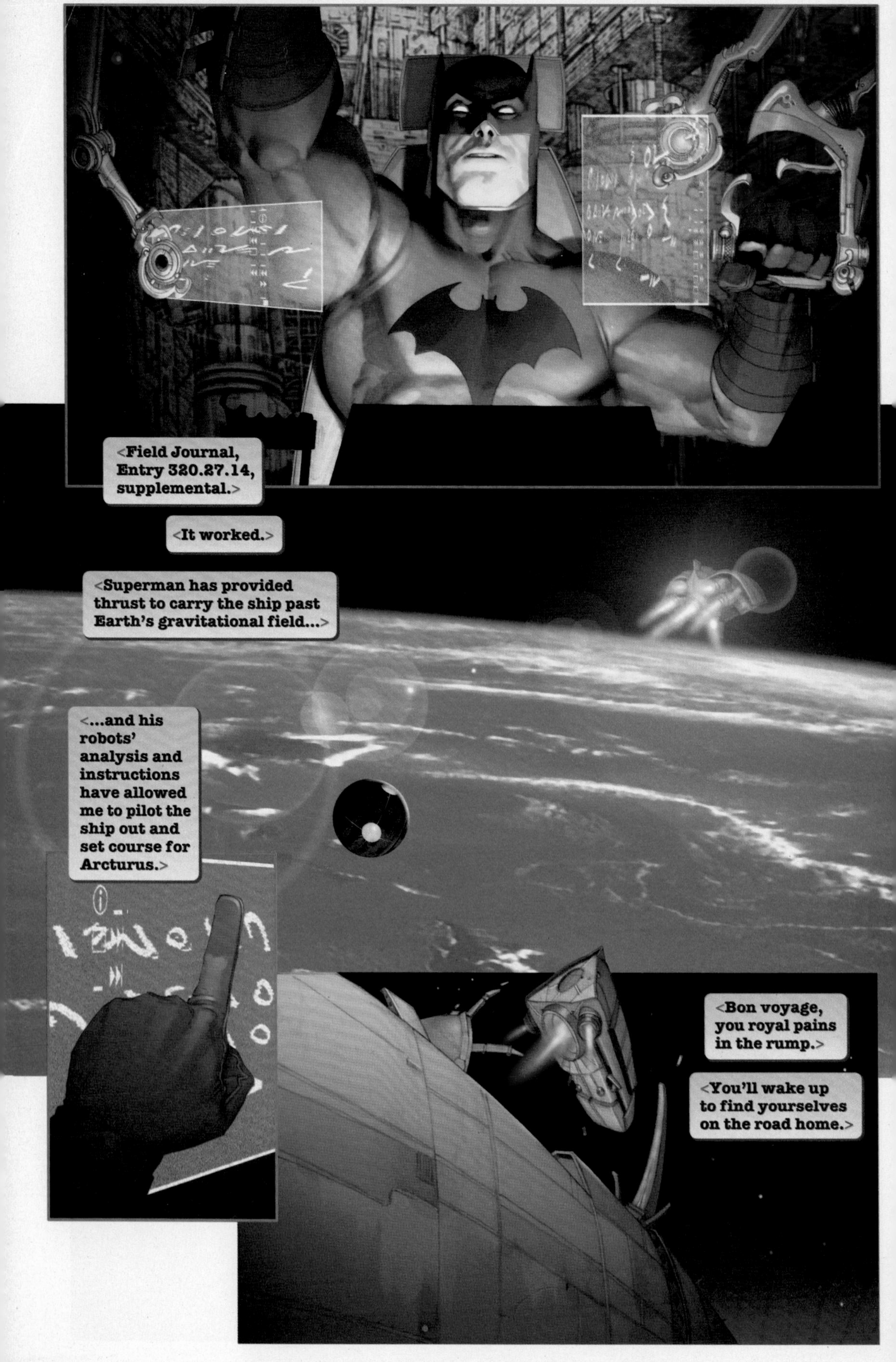

<Field Journal,
Entry 320.27.14,
supplemental.>

<It worked.>

<Superman has provided
thrust to carry the ship past
Earth's gravitational field...>

<...and his
robots'
analysis and
instructions
have allowed
me to pilot the
ship out and
set course for
Arcturus.>

<Bon voyage,
you royal pains
in the rump.>

<You'll wake up
to find yourselves
on the road home.>

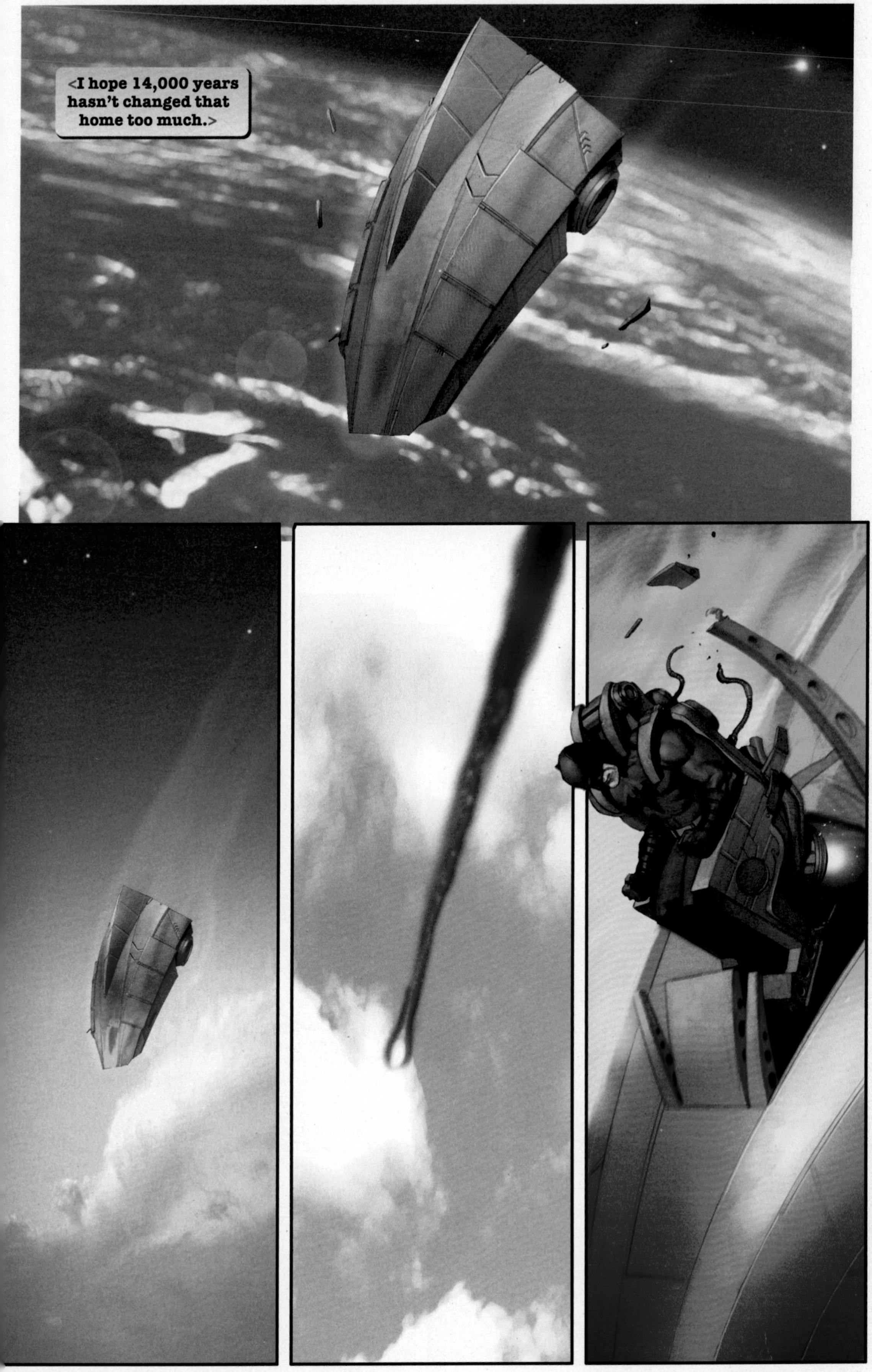
<I hope 14,000 years
hasn't changed that
home too much.>

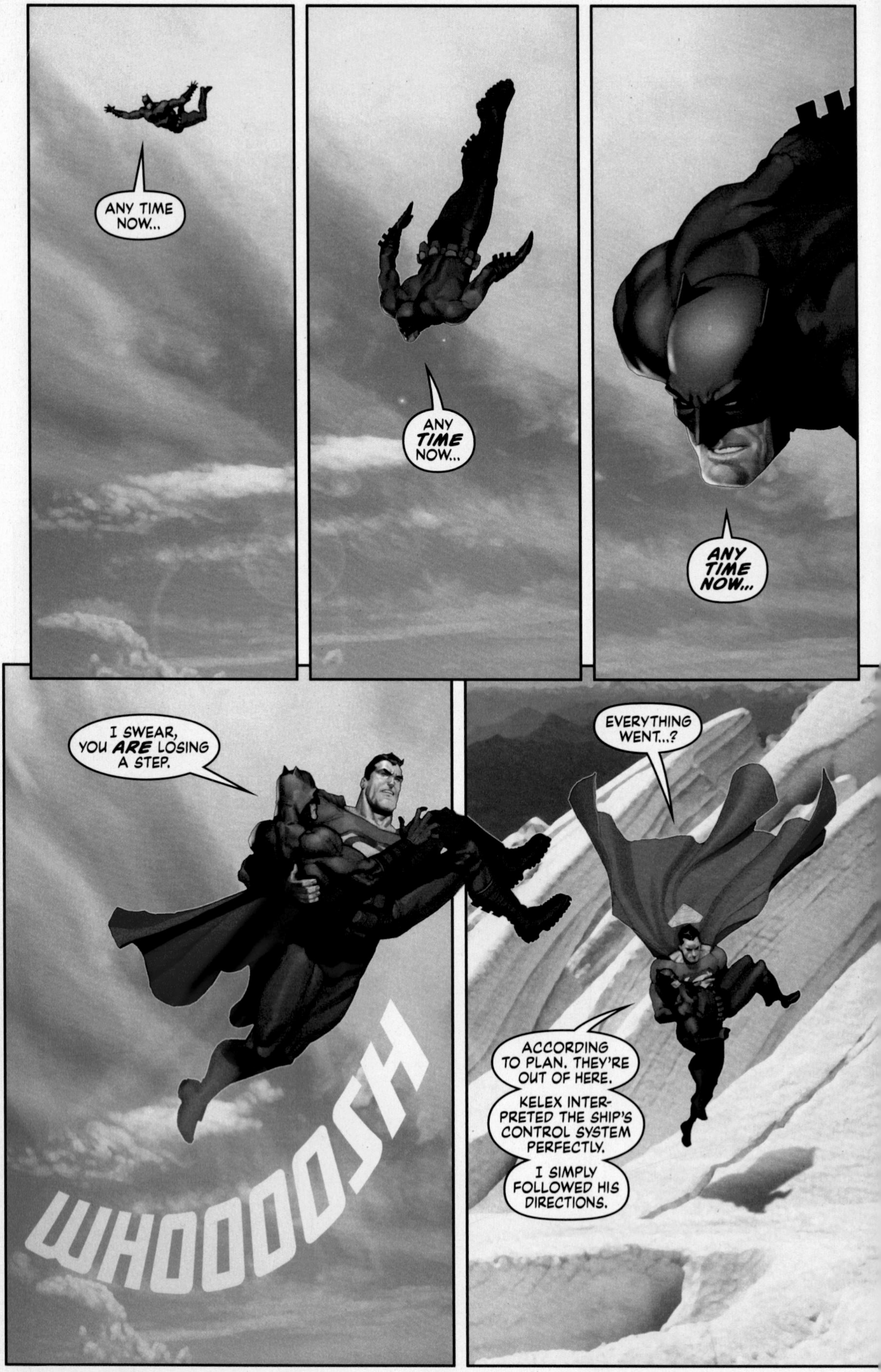
ANY TIME NOW...
ANY TIME NOW...
ANY TIME NOW...
I SWEAR, YOU ARE LOSING A STEP.
WHOOOOSH
EVERYTHING WENT...?
ACCORDING TO PLAN. THEY'RE OUT OF HERE.
KELEX INTERPRETED THE SHIP'S CONTROL SYSTEM PERFECTLY.
I SIMPLY FOLLOWED HIS DIRECTIONS.

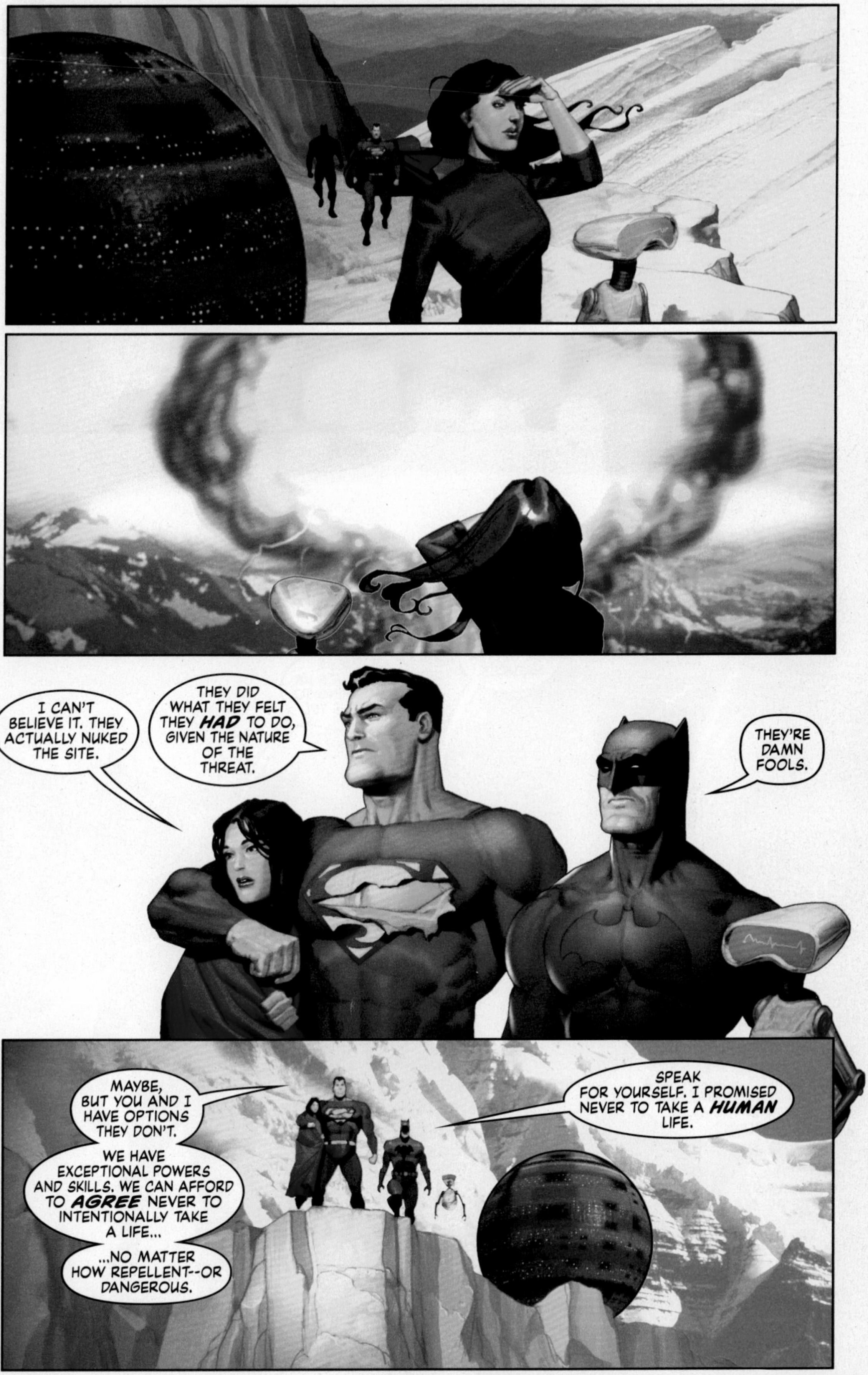
I CAN'T BELIEVE IT. THEY ACTUALLY NUKED THE SITE.
THEY DID WHAT THEY FELT THEY *HAD* TO DO, GIVEN THE NATURE OF THE THREAT.
THEY'RE DAMN FOOLS.
MAYBE, BUT YOU AND I HAVE OPTIONS THEY DON'T.
WE HAVE EXCEPTIONAL POWERS AND SKILLS. WE CAN AFFORD TO *AGREE* NEVER TO INTENTIONALLY TAKE A LIFE...
...NO MATTER HOW REPELLENT--OR DANGEROUS.
SPEAK FOR YOURSELF. I PROMISED NEVER TO TAKE A *HUMAN* LIFE.

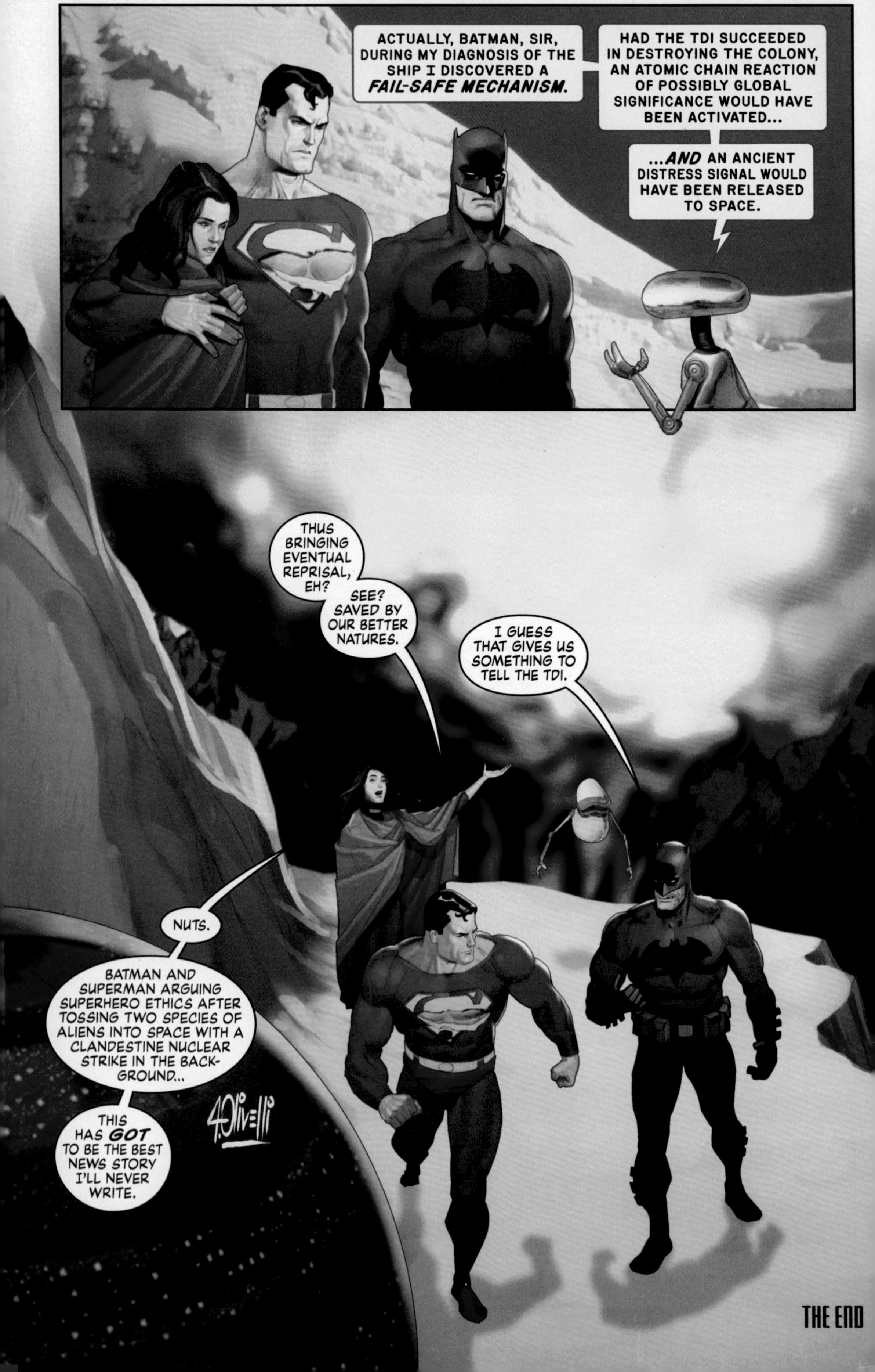
ACTUALLY, BATMAN, SIR, DURING MY DIAGNOSIS OF THE SHIP I DISCOVERED A FAIL-SAFE MECHANISM.
HAD THE TDI SUCCEEDED IN DESTROYING THE COLONY, AN ATOMIC CHAIN REACTION OF POSSIBLY GLOBAL SIGNIFICANCE WOULD HAVE BEEN ACTIVATED...
...AND AN ANCIENT DISTRESS SIGNAL WOULD HAVE BEEN RELEASED TO SPACE.
THUS BRINGING EVENTUAL REPRISAL, EH?
SEE? SAVED BY OUR BETTER NATURES.
I GUESS THAT GIVES US SOMETHING TO TELL THE TDI.
NUTS.
BATMAN AND SUPERMAN ARGUING SUPERHERO ETHICS AFTER TOSSING TWO SPECIES OF ALIENS INTO SPACE WITH A CLANDESTINE NUCLEAR STRIKE IN THE BACK-GROUND...
THIS HAS GOT TO BE THE BEST NEWS STORY I'LL NEVER WRITE.
G.Olivetti
THE END

SUPERMAN AND BATMAN VS. ALIENS AND PREDATOR

SKETCH GALLERY

THE FOLLOWING PAGES ARE SOME OF ARIEL OLIVETTI'S BREAKDOWNS FOR SUPERMAN AND BATMAN VS. ALIENS AND PREDATOR

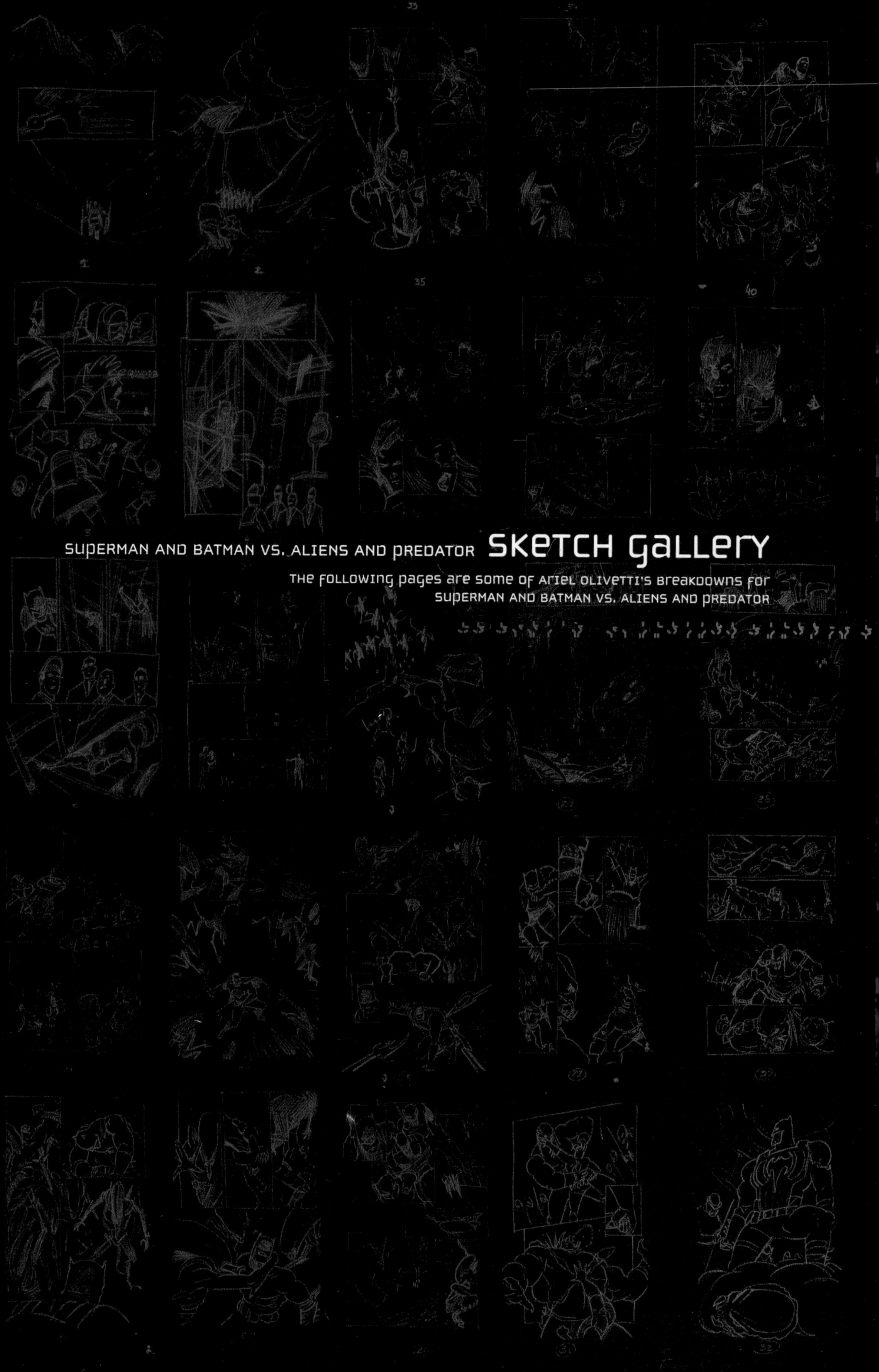

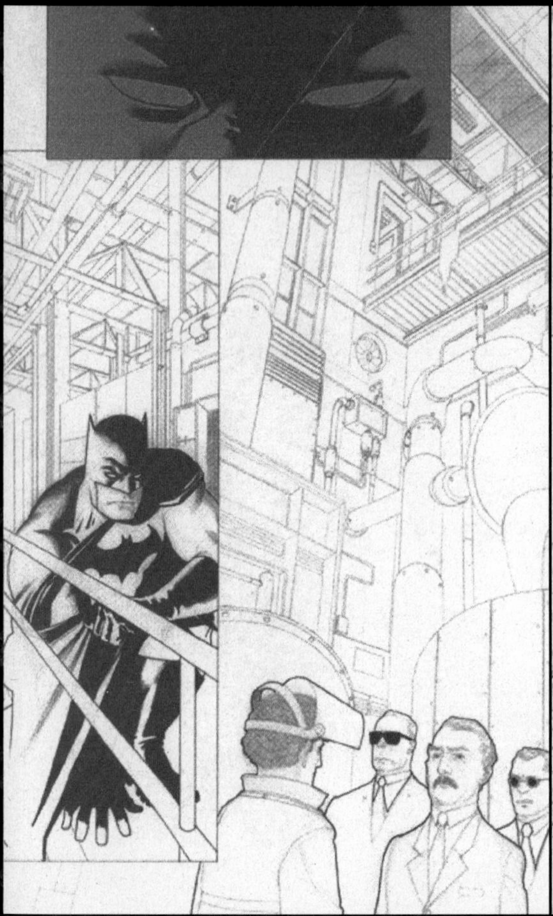

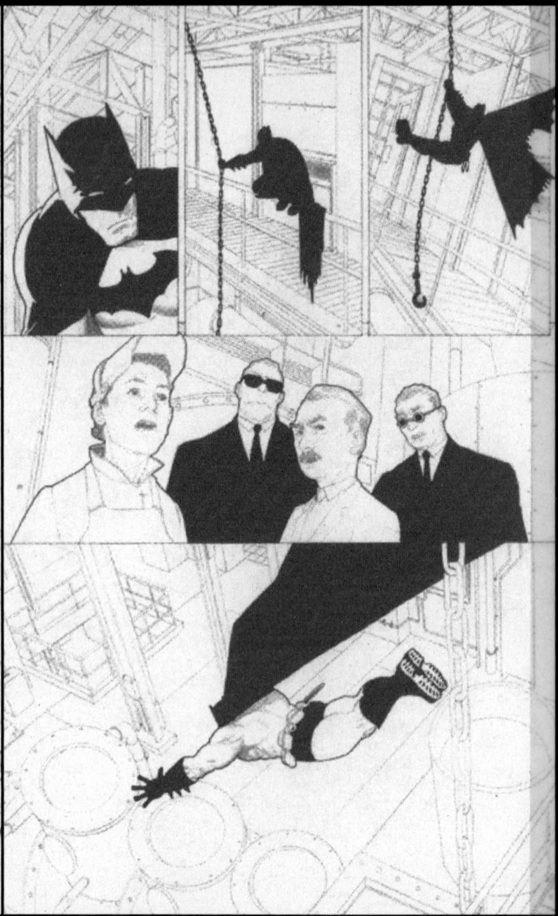

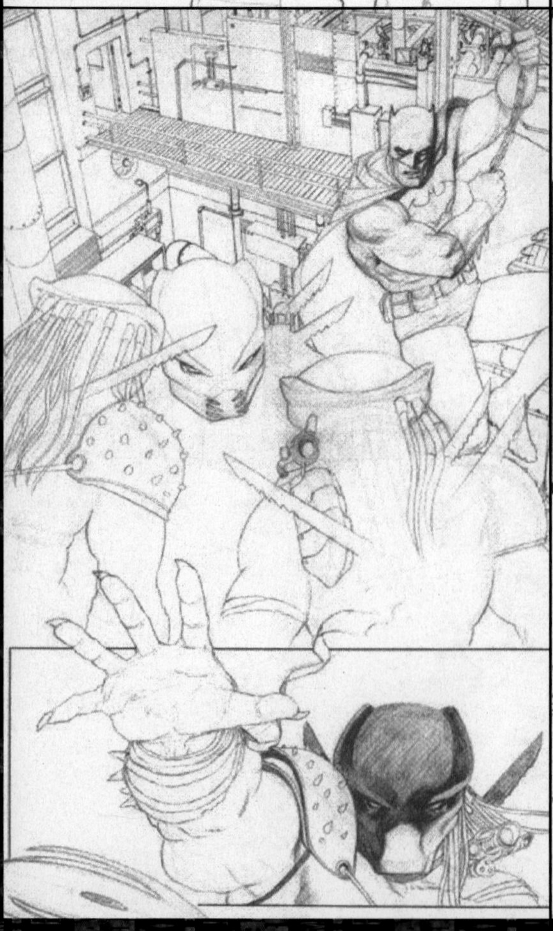

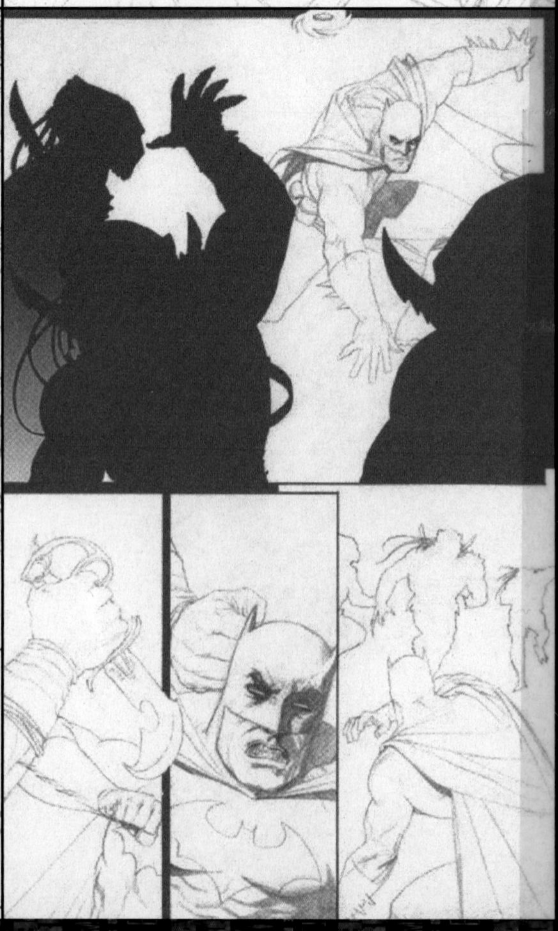

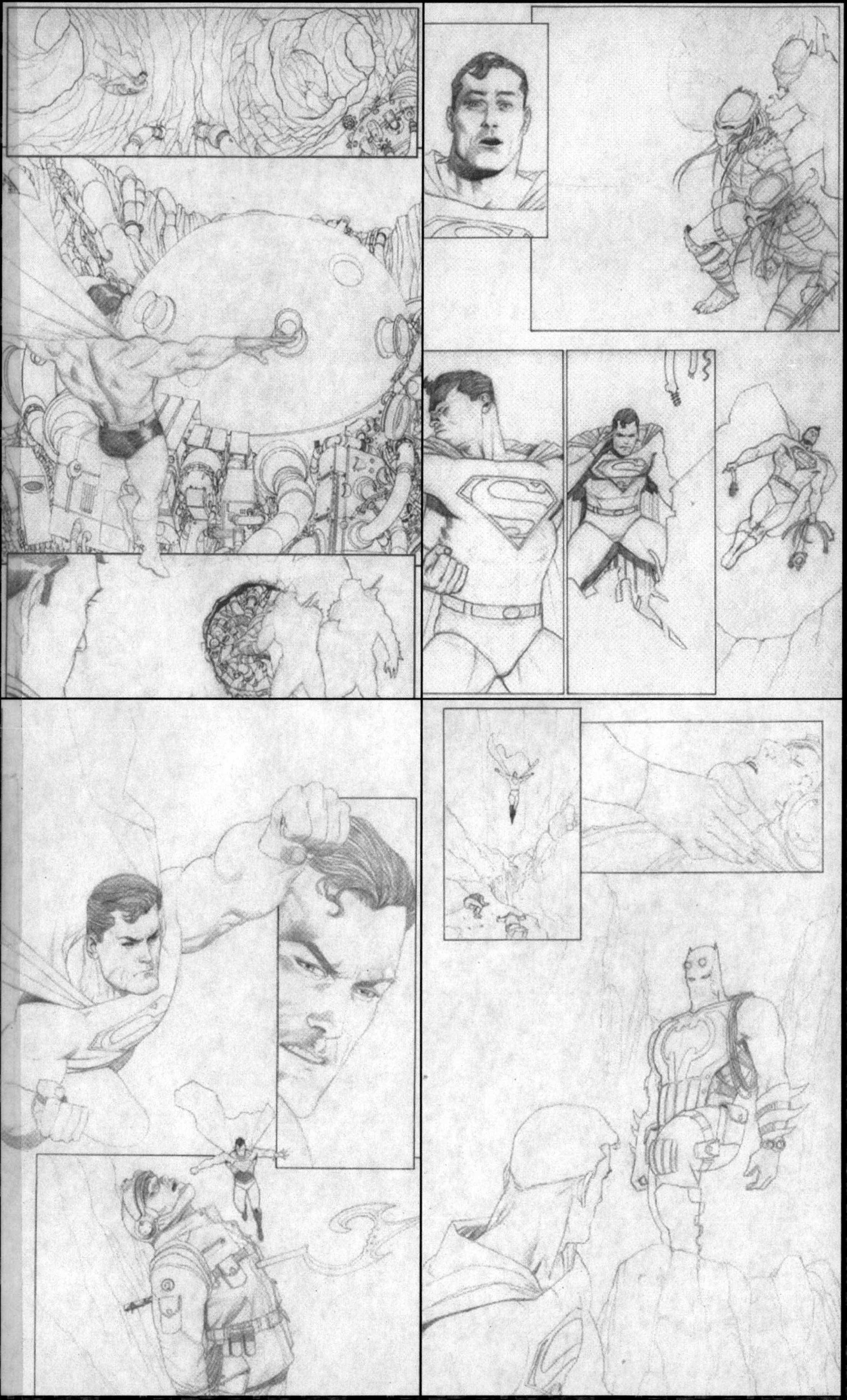

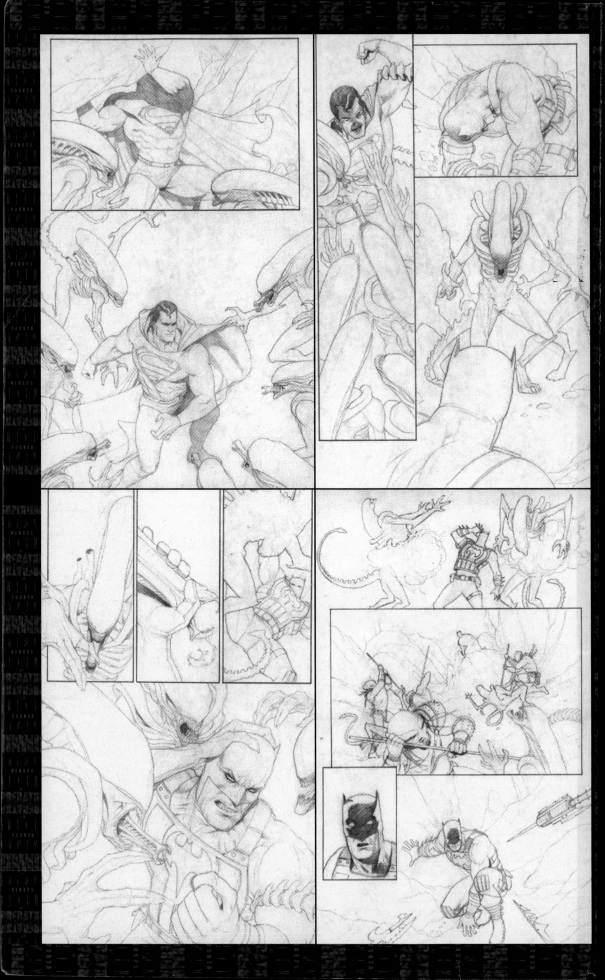

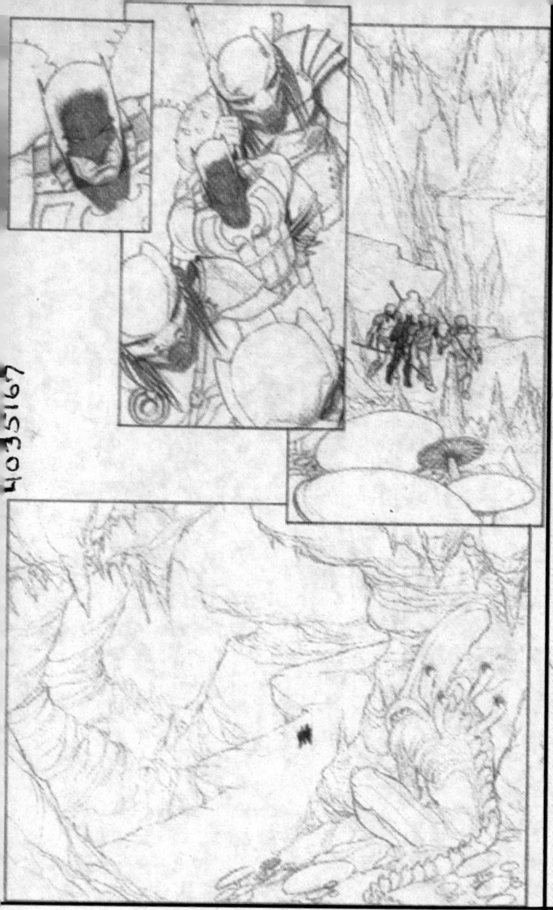

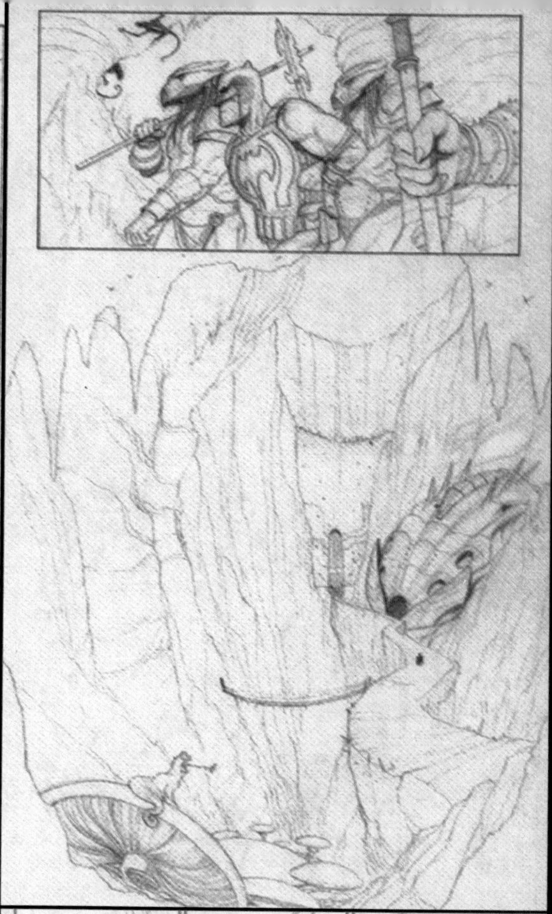

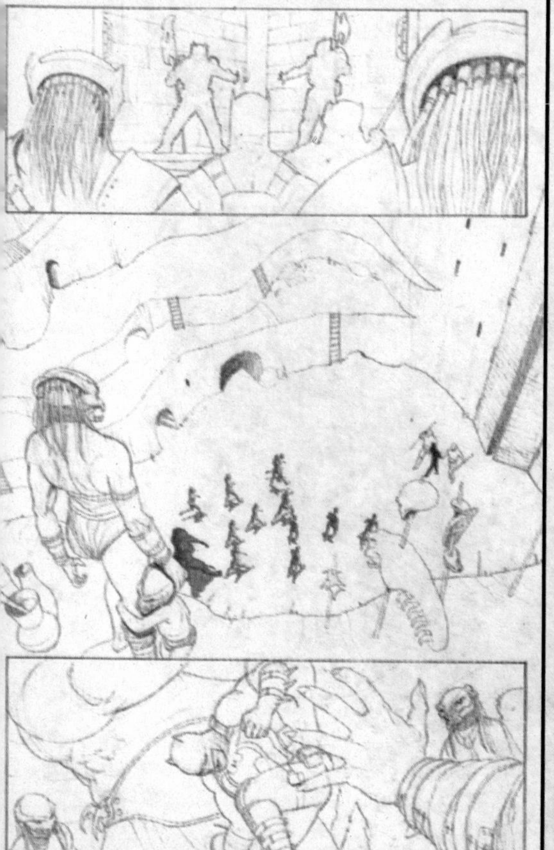

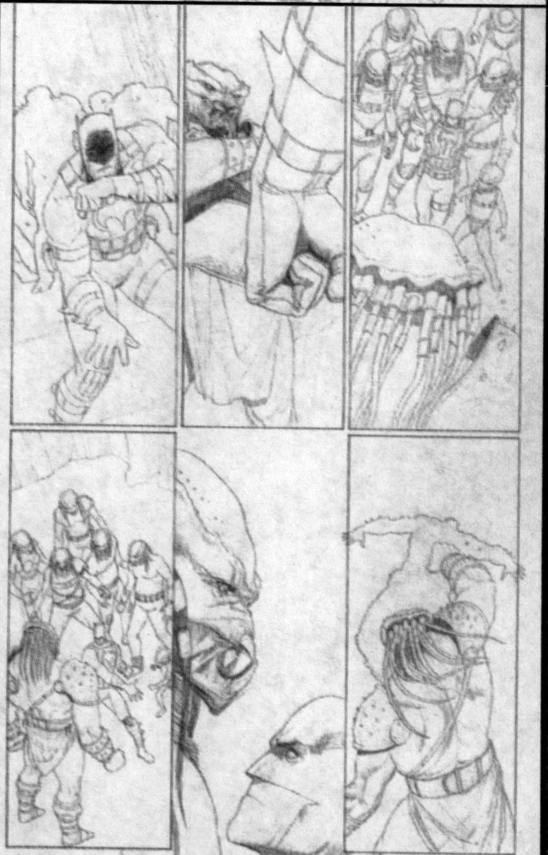

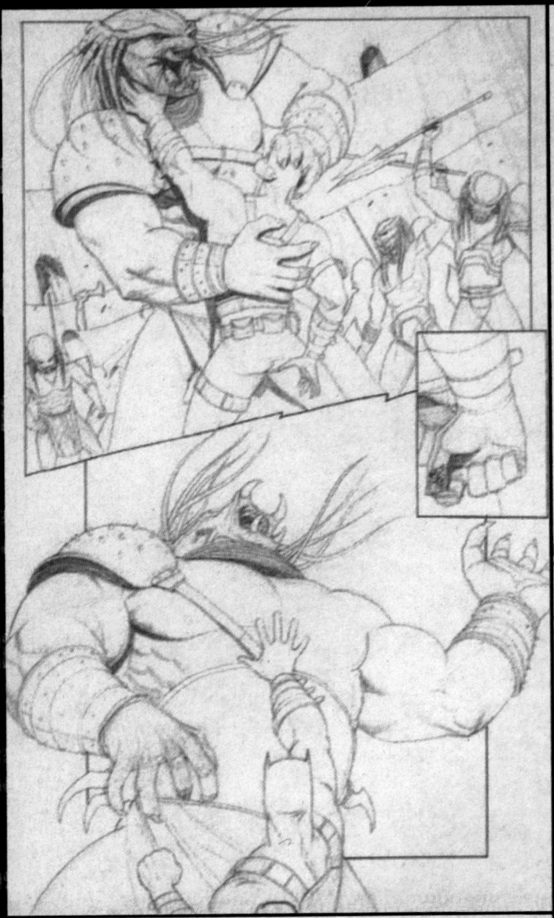

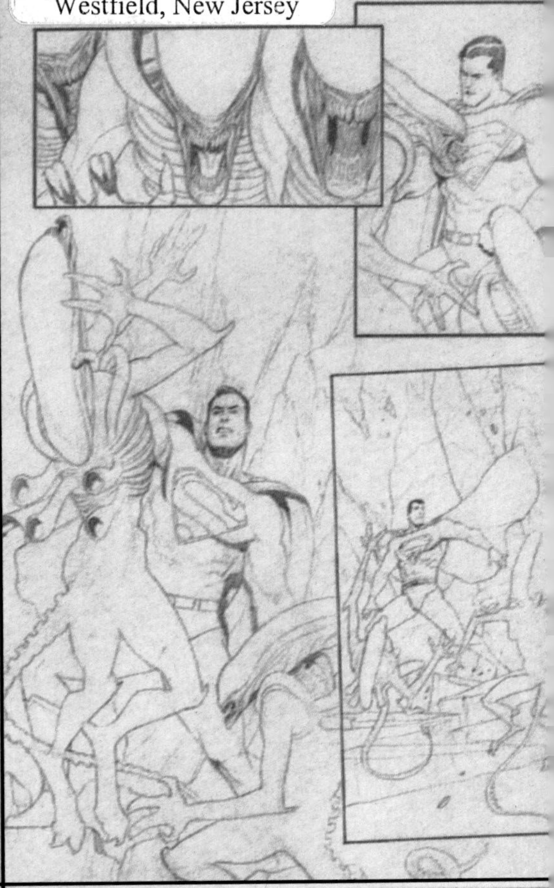

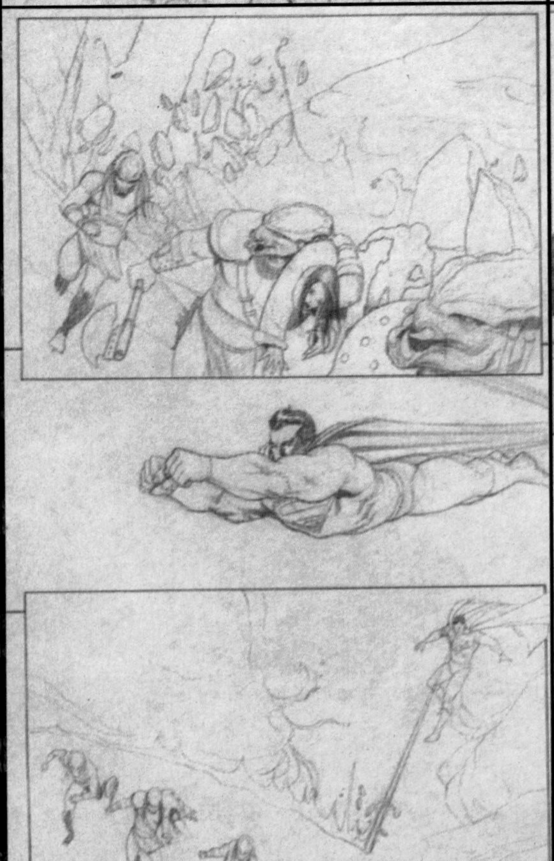

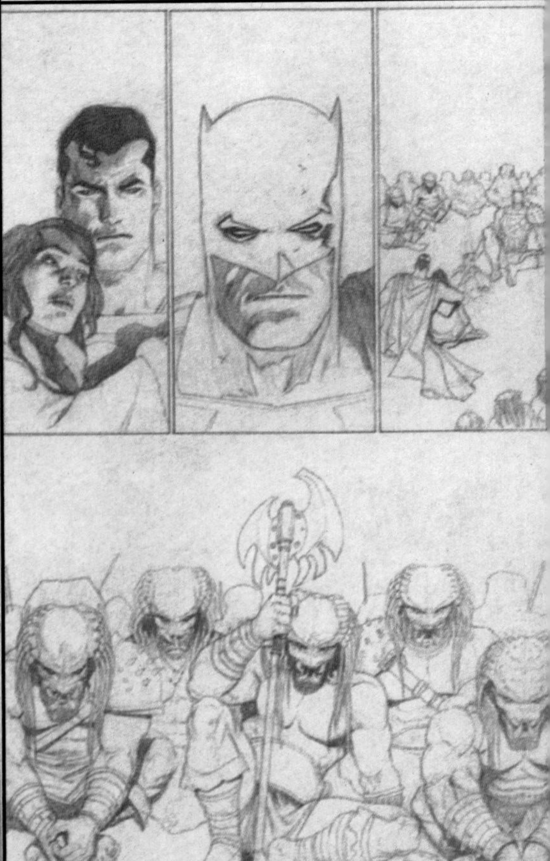

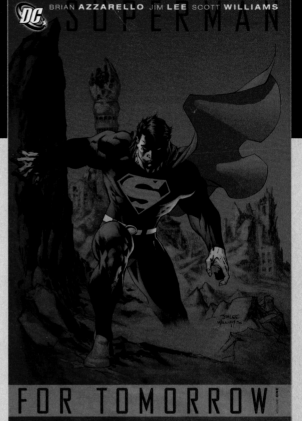

KNIGHT
S
IN THESE COLLECTIONS
FROM DC COMICS:

BATMAN

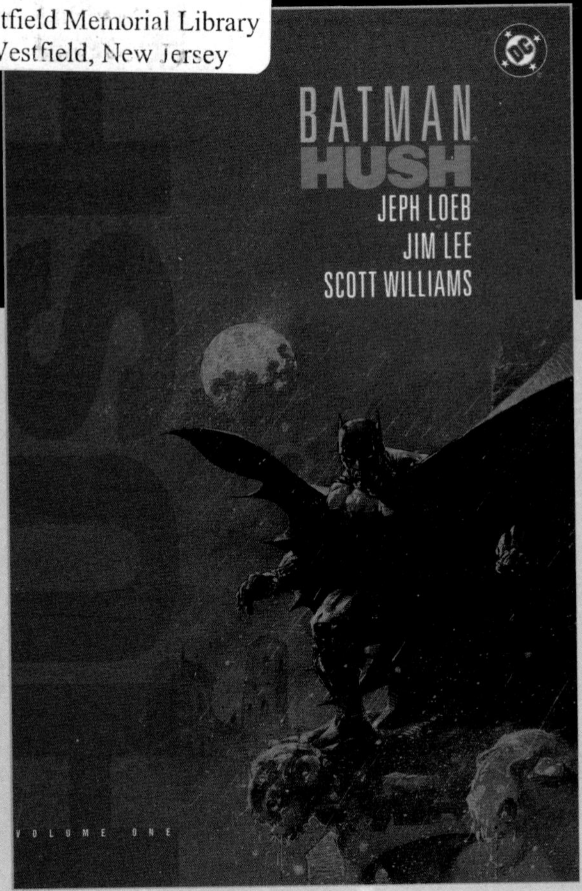
BATMAN
HUSH
JEPH LOEB
JIM LEE
SCOTT WILLIAMS
VOLUME ONE

BATMAN: HUSH VOLUME 1

Jeph Loeb, Jim Lee and **Scott Williams** tell an epic tale of friendship, trust and betrayal, in the first volume of a tale that spans a lifetime of the Dark Knight.

"THE ACTION IS EXCITING AND THE DETAIL IS METICULOUS."
— CRITIQUES ON INFINITE EARTHS

BATMAN:
THE DARK KNIGHT RETURNS

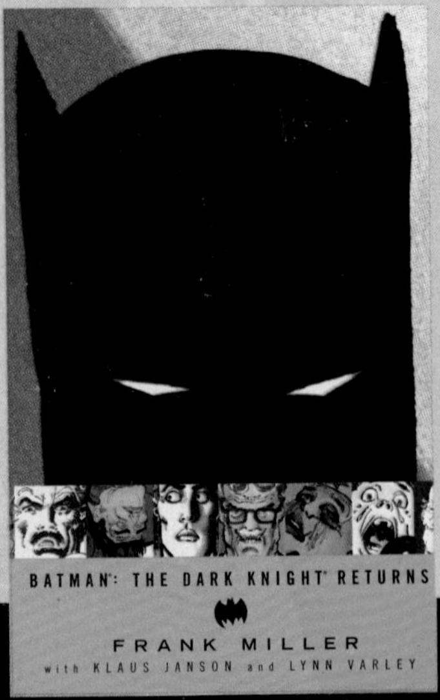
BATMAN: THE DARK KNIGHT RETURNS
FRANK MILLER
with KLAUS JANSON and LYNN VARLEY

FRANK MILLER
KLAUS JANSON
LYNN VARLEY

BATMAN:
THE LONG HALLOWEEN

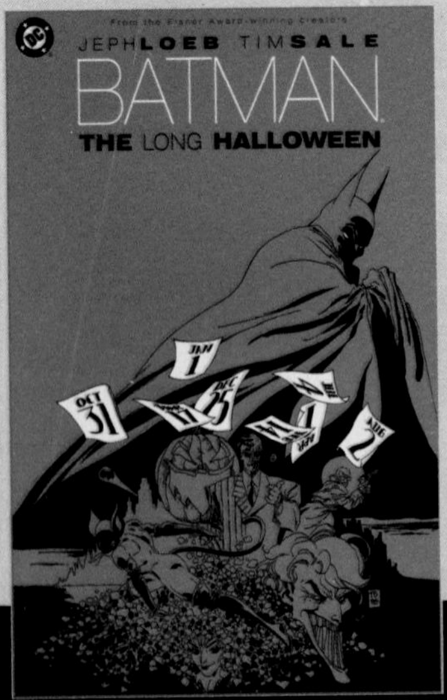
JEPH LOEB TIM SALE
BATMAN
THE LONG HALLOWEEN

JEPH LOEB
TIM SALE

BATMAN:
YEAR ONE

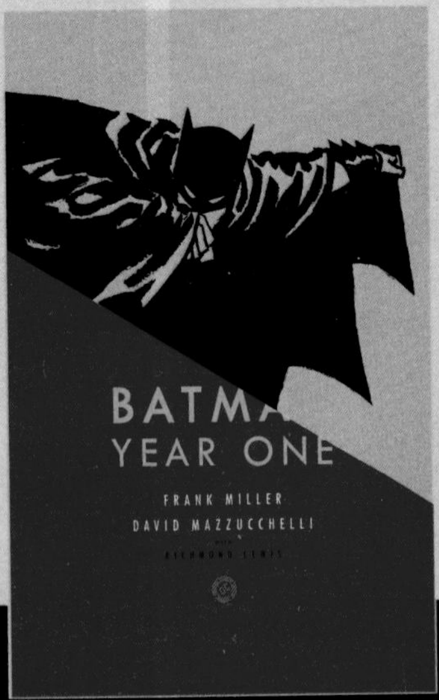
BATMAN
YEAR ONE
FRANK MILLER
DAVID MAZZUCCHELLI

FRANK MILLER
DAVID MAZZUCCHELLI